Teaching Activities Manual for

The **Bible** for **Young Catholics**

An **Introduction**
to **People of Faith**

Teaching Activities Manual for

Break Through!

The **Bible** for **Young Catholics**

An **Introduction** to **People of Faith**

Rick Keller-Scholz and Jeannie Pomanowski with Therese Brown,
Christine Schmertz Navarro, Ann Nunes, and Chris Wardwell

Saint Mary's Press®

DEDICATION

This project is dedicated to all of the faith-filled women and men across North America who work with young adolescents in Catholic grade schools and parishes. Thank you.

♻ Genuine recycled paper with 10% post-consumer waste. 5109700

The publishing team included Christine Schmertz Navarro, development editor; Lorraine Kilmartin, reviewer; Mary Koehler, permissions editor; prepress and manufacturing coordinated by the prepublication and production services departments of Saint Mary's Press.

Printed in the United States of America

Printing: 9 8 7 6 5 4 3 2

Year: 2014 13 12 11 10 09 08 07 06

ISBN-13: 978-0-88489-908-2
ISBN-10: 0-88489-908-X

About our Principal Authors

Rick Keller-Scholz has spent the last twenty years teaching at Bellarmine Preparatory School in Tacoma, WA, and the last ten years as a volunteer junior high parish minister. Rick also teaches in the Archdiocese of Seattle Catechetical Certification Program.

Rick has been awarded "Catechist of the Year" from the Seattle Archdiocese and the Elizabeth Ann Kelley Teacher of the Year award from Bellarmine. He is a contributing author to *Pride in Our Past/Faith in Our Future: Catholic Northwest History Curriculum* (Archives of the Archdiocese of Seattle and the Catholic School's Department. Seattle: Archdiocese of Seattle, 1999), and to the *Teaching Activities Manual for "The Catholic Youth Bible®"* from Saint Mary's Press.

Rick and his wife, Nancy, live in Tacoma and have three children.

Jeannie Pomanowski has been teaching in Catholic schools for many years and has been teaching middle school religion for the last six years at Saint Leo the Great School in Lincroft, NJ. In 1999, the Diocese of Trenton awarded Jeannie the "Catholic Educator of the Year" award.

Jeannie is also a songwriter, singer, and recording artist of Christian pop and rock music and has released two albums, *Faith with an Attitude* and *Prayer Warrior,* both published by Be Attitude Music, BMI. Jeannie performs around the country and has shared her skill at the 2001, 2003, and 2005 National Catholic Youth Conference, in addition to other gatherings.

About our Contributing Authors

Therese Brown has nine years of experience with middle and high school students as a volunteer catechist and youth minister. As associate director for the National Federation for Catholic Youth Ministry, she managed the National Catholic Youth Conference, the largest regular gathering of Catholic young people in the United States. She also advocated for the needs of young people in the areas of liturgy, music, and vocations.

She has written two books, *Catechetical Sessions on Liturgy and the Sacraments* (Saint Mary's Press) and *Graced Moments: Prayer Services for the Lives of Teens,* volumes I and II, (World Library Publications), as well as sessions for *Youth Ministry Access,* a weekly online resource from the Center for Ministry Development. Therese currently holds the position of senior marketing specialist in publishing at the United States Conference of Catholic Bishops in Washington, DC.

Christine Schmertz Navarro is a senior editor at Saint Mary's Press, having taught several years in high schools and spent volunteer time with young adolescents. She is the principal author of the *Teaching Activities Manual for "THE CATHOLIC YOUTH BIBLE,"* coauthor of the *Teaching Manual for "Living Justice and Peace: Catholic Social Teaching in Action,"* and editor of several other books, all published by Saint Mary's Press.

Christine and her husband, Rudy, live in Tacoma, WA, and have an eight-year-old daughter.

Ann Nunes teaches middle school religion at the Convent of the Sacred Heart Elementary School in San Francisco. She taught parish religious education for many years and completed a master's degree in theological studies at the Franciscan School of Theology in Berkeley, CA. Her thesis addressed adolescent moral formation.

Ann has two grown children and lives in Concord, CA.

Chris Wardwell teaches theology at Saint Thomas High School in Houston, TX, his alma mater. He has twelve years of experience in youth ministry, parish religious education, and Catholic schools. He has an MA in pastoral ministries from Saint Mary's University of Minnesota and received honors for his research paper on adolescent male spirituality.

Chris and his wife, Christine, have an eight-year-old son.

TABLE OF CONTENTS

APPENDICES

INTRODUCTION

GETTING TO KNOW *BREAKTHROUGH! THE BIBLE FOR YOUNG CATHOLICS*, ITS TEACHING MANUAL, AND ITS STUDENT WORKBOOK

Thank you for picking up this exciting new Bible and its teaching activities manual! All three resources—the Bible, the teaching manual, and the student workbook—work together to familiarize the younger adolescent with the people of salvation history and to see themselves as a vital part of the Church's history.

The Bible, the teaching manual, and the student workbook do not depend on one another—they are interdependent and the use of each strengthens the positive characteristics of the other. (The teaching manual and the student workbook do require the use of a Bible, however, even if it is not *Breakthrough!*)

The *Breakthrough!* Trio

Breakthrough! is a Bible with two companions: one for the student reader and the second for the teacher's use in guiding young people who are studying it.

The Bible

Breakthrough! The Bible for Young Catholics will be your strongest resource for introducing young adolescents to the Scriptures. Every element of this Bible was carefully chosen or created to appeal to young people who are ten to thirteen years old. This starts with the choice of using the Catholic Edition of the *Good News Translation* for the Bible text. The *Good News Translation* was created with a vocabulary and reading level appropriate to the younger student. If you have been using translations with a more advanced reading level, you will notice an immediate difference in your student's ability to read and understand the Bible text.

Additionally, *Breakthrough!* provides many other tools to help young people feel more comfortable and familiar with the Bible. Forty illustrated color inserts feature "interviews" with the biblical characters. These character interviews quickly identify the important events in the biblical character's story and the role this person played in salvation history. A four-page salvation history time line at the beginning of the Bible shows how these biblical characters fit into God's big picture of salvation history.

Another key feature is the inclusion of Pray It! Study It! Live It! and Catholic Connection articles. These articles appear alongside the biblical text in forty biblical books. The forty books were chosen to provide the best overview of salvation history and a representative sampling of the different types of books found in the Bible. For these forty books, the articles provide a commentary to help young readers better understand and apply the biblical message to their life. Pray It! articles give the young reader ideas about applying the spirituality of the Bible. Study It! articles give them background so that they better understand the context of the passages they are reading. Live It! articles challenge the young people to live biblical values and teachings. Catholic Connection articles show where important Catholic teachings are found in the Scriptures.

These are some of the other features you will find in *Breakthrough!*:

* a complete list of the Sunday readings
* lists to help find important Bible stories, prayers, and teachings
* a word list with definitions of over 180 important Bible words
* nine color maps

The Teaching Manual

Although the Bible and workbook are for the young people, the *Teaching Activities Manual for "Breakthrough! The Bible for Young Catholics"* is for you! Six professionals from around the United States coauthored this manual to help Catholic middle school teachers, parish catechists, and youth ministers explore the Bible with young people.

This teaching manual gives suggestions about ways you can introduce and explore key figures in salvation history. Studying the Bible by learning the stories of its main figures interests young adolescents because they are very curious about people—themselves, their friends, their families, people they meet. People are endlessly fascinating. This holds true for Bible people as well.

Depending on their level of biblical literacy, your students will be continuing or beginning a life journey with figures from the Old and New Testaments who will inspire, challenge, and puzzle them, yet ultimately be very important in their own spiritual lives. Given the significance of these biblical people for all Catholics, it is important to talk about them with young adolescents. As they grow older, they will encounter the familiar stories anew, bringing to the stories the issues and questions that are first and foremost on their minds and hearts at that time. While few of the biblical characters that the students will encounter are their own age, their stories provide many opportunities for the young people to make connections to their own life experiences.

The Workbook

It seemed especially appropriate for the age group to provide some puzzles and worksheets to assist them in reading and reflecting on the Bible. After covering the "ABCs of Biblical Literacy," the book goes on to provide a puzzle, some background, suggested readings, suggested articles, and reflection questions for the same biblical people who are covered in the teaching manual. The workbook provides independent study opportunities for the student that can complement the work that the teacher or catechist does in the classroom. It will also be helpful for parents who are homeschooling to use in conjunction with the Bible. We envision that some parents may want their child to have a copy of *Breakthrough!* and will see the book's potential to provide some guidance to the young reader.

The puzzle about each character requires a familiarity with the character's story. Most young people will need to read or reread the passages about the figure. Up to six Scripture passages are provided per character. The article references can also help the young person get to know the person. The background in the workbook shows the reader where each biblical character "fits" in salvation history. Finally, the reflection questions invite the young person to consider how this biblical person's story sheds light on her or his own spiritual journey and life experience.

Because the teaching manual encourages mastery of the story before reflection on the character, you can use the puzzle as a diagnostic or check of understanding after doing the "Getting to Know the Story" activity and to connect the reflection questions to the "Getting to Know the Person" activities.

Even if you do not choose to purchase books for all your students, you may find it appropriate for students who have a weaker background in the Scriptures or who need to spend more time with the Bible to understand the stories.

About the Term "Young Adolescent"

You will notice that the *Breakthrough!* materials use the term *young adolescent* throughout. This term describes young people of the ages that would normally put them in grades five through eight. We intentionally use a term that describes their age rather than their status in school, which is what happens when we use "junior high" or "middle school." We all know that depending on what part of the country, state, or county you find yourself, even these terms are fluid!

We also use the terms *young people* and *student* to refer to this same group. Even though some activities may lend themselves more readily to the classroom of a Catholic grade school, all the authors wrote with both school and parish needs in mind.

Looking More Closely at This Teaching Manual

This teaching manual has many features that will help you in your ministry with young adolescents. Though the Bible itself is not a "curriculum" nor does the teaching manual provide a comprehensive curriculum for biblical study, you will find that this manual will supplement the curriculum that you are currently using.

After this introduction, the text of this book consists of forty-nine chapters covering biblical characters from the Old and New Testaments as well as four appendices. You can use these chapters in order or pick and choose as you need. In addition to inviting students to learn the stories of the people in the Bible, the material in the chapter enables you to make connections between your young people and the biblical characters. The greatest hope of this manual is that these young men and women will get to know Sarah, Samson, Isaiah, and Matthew as people—people who were chosen to play a special role in the development of our faith tradition, people through whom God spoke, people whom God called, and people who sometimes responded more completely than at other times to their own vocations. If our young people can come to see the connections between their own lives today and the lives of these biblical figures, they have a much greater chance of being able to recognize and meet God in ways that these characters do.

The next sections will explain the rationale behind the different parts of these chapters.

Preparing to Teach

Each chapter begins with a section called "Preparing to Teach." There is quite a bit of "raw material" in the first half of the chapter, such as Scripture citations, lists of *Breakthrough!* articles, connections between biblical figures and young people, and Bible quotes about God's presence. These tools are present to make it easier for you to reflect about your own students and their needs and questions and then to move quickly into a lesson or session plan that will bring the Bible and its people alive for your young people.

Instead of going through chapters sequentially, we hope that you will make the decisions about what and how to teach based on a combination of factors such as what materials you have and what you think your own students need. The following parts of the chapter should help you tailor your teaching to the needs of your students.

Overview

The overview consists of several paragraphs that introduce the biblical character and highlights ways that this biblical character *uniquely* connects with young adolescents. While several of the judges are skilled in battle, for example, the story of Gideon shows how God helps the people of Israel resist the bullying nature of their enemies. While the prophets share similar messages, it is Ezekiel who may appeal to more young people because his messages are so image-heavy and fantastic, more like the media the young people know.

This Chapter at a Glance

This short section gives you the names of the activities that are in the second half of the chapter. You will see here that each chapter provides at least one activity that helps the young people learn the story of the biblical character and one that helps them probe more deeply into the character's personality.

Scripture Passages Related to the Biblical Character

This section lists no more than twelve key passages about the character under study. Asterisks identify those that are most important to read. This section should make it easier for you to find relevant stories and to assign reading to your group.

Articles from *Breakthrough!* Related to the Biblical Character

This section lists up to twelve articles from *Breakthrough!* that are relevant to your study. The first article is almost always a reference to the interview with the character that can be found in the Bible. The Bible also features Pray It, Study It, Live It articles so that the students can learn more about aspects of the Bible, develop their prayer life, and hear challenges to live differently. These three types of articles as well the Catholic Connections can be springboards for conversation with your students. When you see the *Breakthrough!* icon in the margin, you will know that you will be directed to an aspect of *Breakthrough! The Bible for Young Catholics.*

The Biblical Character and Young Adolescents Today

This section suggests several connections between the biblical character and the young people with whom you are working. There may be more connections in a chapter than you can cover with your students. This section invites you to discern how you think God may want to speak through this biblical character to your specific group of young people today. Perhaps one or two of the connections will intuitively or obviously seem more suitable for your group now. But next year, with another group, another two may emerge as important.

Highlighting God's Presence

In this section, the authors have picked biblical quotes that describe God's action in the stories being studied about a specific person. It is our hope that students will begin to listen for and look for God in the same types of ways that God reveals himself in the Bible. While a biblical character's story is interesting in and of itself, ultimately the Scriptures bring us to God. By presenting the passages in the manual, the hope is that you will have an additional resource to bring your students to a new awareness of God.

Activities

The second half of each chapter is devoted to class or session activities. The activities section provides between one and six activities for you to choose from as you explore a biblical character with the young people. You will notice that the authors of this manual believe that it is possible to learn about the Scriptures and find God in them, while having an enjoyable, meaningful, and creative time as well!

There are two types of activities in each chapter.

- **Getting to Know the Story of the Biblical Character.** This activity exposes the young people to the *story* of the person featured in the chapter either by inviting the young people to read the Scripture passages themselves or by sharing this task with their peers.
- **Getting to Know the Biblical Character.** This type of activity presumes that the students know the character's story. The activities explore *who the biblical character is* and makes connections between his or her relationship with God and the young people's own life experience. These activities are more reflective and invite group discussion.

The Appendices: Making It Easier for You

This manual has four appendices.

Appendix 1: Additional Resources

This appendix lists other resources that could provide background for you or that could lead you to other materials for sharing the Scriptures with the students. This appendix also provides you with music and video ideas and directs you to the Saint Mary's Press Web site for links that may be helpful for your own background or for your direct work with the students.

Appendix 2: Tools for Teaching

This appendix contains some of the best and most creative activities that our authors wrote for this manual. These activities can be used with different biblical people. Look in this appendix if the recommended activity does not seem appropriate for your group or if you have had success with one of the approaches before!

Appendix 3: Answer Key for *Breakthrough!* Workbook Puzzles

This appendix contains the answers for the puzzles that appear in the *Student Activity Workbook for "Breakthrough! The Bible for Young Catholics."* This appendix does not directly connect with any materials in this teaching manual. You may choose to use this workbook to give your students additional opportunities to learn about biblical figures and their stories. This workbook is available from Saint Mary's Press, *www.smp.org.*

Appendix 4: Index of Activities by Topic

Because this manual focuses on bringing the Scriptures and the lives of students together, many topics are covered in the book that relate to their everyday lives, such as families, friendships, self-esteem, and so on. The activities are gathered and sorted under headings. In addition, activities that talk about different Catholic sacraments, feast days, or themes are also listed accordingly.

Journeying with the Young People

The authors of this manual wrote the activities here with the faces of young people in mind whom they have known and loved over the years. Some aspects of the manual will work for your group while others may not. This manual is an invitation to trust your own ability to discern the needs of your group of young people. The activities in the manual are strong because the authors did just this in the classroom and during parish gatherings.

May God give you the grace to see the everyday opportunities to teach young people about the Scriptures and the people of salvation history.

ADAM AND EVE

Preparing to Teach

Overview

Reading the story of Adam and Eve is wonderful way for the students to examine how sin affects our relationships with God and other people. Young adolescents are very conscious of their connections to others and painfully aware when relationships are broken. When we follow God's will, we become closer to him and one another, but when we sin, we separate ourselves from God and those we love. God continues his relationship with Adam and Eve after their sin, which is reassuring when students feel that they have done something wrong.

The Adam and Eve story also offers young people an opportunity to examine the place of rules in their lives and to emphasize the importance of listening to God. On the verge of greater independence, students struggle with temptation which often clothes itself as the suggestion to resist limits set by parents or school. Adam and Eve's story suggest that limits exist for our well-being.

A good way to prepare for the study of Adam and Eve is by reading the article "Uncovering the Truth" (Genesis 2:5–25) in *Breakthrough!* The Catholic understanding of the Scriptures sometimes conflicts with the literal interpretations of some other Christian denominations, especially in regard to the Creation stories. Catholics see them as symbolic stories that convey spiritual and moral truths. Knowing that this story falls into this literary genre allows us to see Adam and Eve as our predecessors who enjoyed the relationship with God before sin entered the world.

THIS CHAPTER AT A GLANCE

Getting to Know the Story of Adam and Eve

- Who Is Guilty?

Getting to Know Adam and Eve

- Hiding Who We Are
- Who Hates Rules?

Scripture Passages Related to Adam and Eve

- Genesis 2:4-17 (God creates a man and a place for him to live)*
- Genesis 2:18-20 (God creates the animals)*
- Genesis 2:21-25 (God creates a woman)*
- Genesis 3:1-6 (Adam and Eve eat the forbidden fruit)*
- Genesis 3:7-13 (Adam and Eve hide from God)*
- Genesis 3:14-24 (God punishes and banishes Adam and Eve)*
- Genesis 4:1-2 (Adam and Eve have two sons, Cain and Abel)
- Genesis 4:25 (Adam and Eve have another son, Seth)
- Genesis 5:1-32 (Adam's other descendants)

Asterisk (*) signifies key passages to cover.

Break Through! Articles from *Breakthrough!* Related to Adam and Eve

- *Breakthrough!* Interview with Adam and Eve
- Uncovering the Truth (Genesis 2:5-25)
- Original Sin (Genesis 3:1-24)

Adam and Eve and Young Adolescents Today

- Companionship is extremely important to young adolescents. God desires the companionship of human beings because he created them to walk and talk with him.
- God banished Adam and Eve from the Garden of Eden. For adolescents, companionship is so important that being left out is a difficult and feared experience.
- Young adolescents often struggle with the restrictions placed on them, as did Adam and Eve. As they struggle toward independence and responsibility, they still need rules and guidelines to assist them.
- The serpent is the master of temptation. Adam and Eve's relationship with the serpent is a wonderful model for the perils of peer pressure.
- Like Adam and Eve who try to hide from God, young adolescents often attempt to cover up their wrongdoings instead of accepting responsibility. Like Adam, they often look for someone else to whom they can point and say, "He made me do it!"
- Women's equality is still an issue in our society, and young adolescents are aware of this. In the past, this story has been used to justify the inferior status of women, so it becomes especially important to counter this misguided notion.

Highlighting God's Presence

Then the Lord God took some soil from the ground and formed a man out of it; he breathed life-giving breath into his nostrils and the man began to live (Genesis 2:7).

That evening they heard the Lord God walking in the garden (Genesis 3:8).

Getting to Know the Story of Adam and Eve

Who Is Guilty?

In this activity, students hold a trial in which the prosecutor accuses the characters in the Genesis story of bringing about the fall of humanity.

Preparation

❑ Provide students with a pen and some paper.

❑ Provide students with bibles.

1. Read Genesis, chapters 2 and 3, aloud. Explain that the objective of this activity will be to come to a verdict, trial-style, regarding who is to blame for the fall of humanity.

2. Make sure that everyone is familiar with the roles that different people play in the court. Pick one student to be the prosecutor and divide the rest of the class into four groups named "The Serpent," "Adam," "Eve," and "The Jury."

3. Tell the students to read carefully Genesis 2 and 3. Tell the first three groups to research Genesis 2 and 3 and come up with a defense for their character. (Each defendant should also try to suggest to the jury that another character is the guilty party.) The jury and prosecutor review the "evidence" in Genesis 2 and 3.

4. Take a moment to direct the students to avoid offensive sexist remarks. Because this passage has been used to oppress women, it is important that they not misrepresent this message of the story. Emphasize the need to respect all of God's creation.

5. Instruct each group to choose one person to represent them and act as its character. The prosecutor will call the representatives and give them an opportunity to tell their side of the story. The

prosecutor will then have a brief opportunity to cross-examine them. Repeat the process with the next two witnesses. The fourth group, the jury, will listen to each testimony and decide on a verdict.

6. Allow the jury a few minutes to deliberate and announce their verdict.

7. Discuss the process with the students. In this story, each character has the freedom to obey or disobey God's law. No one is completely innocent. Below are some suggested discussion starters.
- Do any of the characters ever lie to each other?
- What are the motives for each character?
- What are the immediate consequences for eating from the tree of the knowledge of good and bad?
- How does each character have a responsibility to the others? How do they ignore their responsibilities?
- Where do we see freedom misused in our everyday lives?

Getting to Know Adam and Eve

Hiding Who We Are

Students will examine how they hide their true selves in an attempt to be someone that they feel others will accept.

Preparation

❑ Have a copy of handout Adam and Eve-A, "The Fig Leaves of My Life," for each student.

❑ Make sure each student has scissors and pens, pencils, or markers.

❑ Provide magazines for cutting out pictures (optional).

This activity is appropriate if you have already established a safe environment in which students are comfortable sharing difficult emotions and experiences, and if they have a clear understanding of how to respond appropriately (and how not to respond). If not, a more depersonalized and safe version could be done by focusing on what junior high students in general do to hide themselves.

1. Read Genesis 3:1-10 aloud with the class. In your own words, make the following points:
- In this story, God makes humans who are completely happy. But the downfall comes when humans want to become something that they are not.
- Many of us are very much like Adam and Eve. Too often we are not happy with being who God made us to be. We think, "I'm too

short," or "I'm too fat," or "I'm not a good basketball player," and so on.

- Like Adam and Eve, we are ashamed to be seen without protection, and we try to hide our true selves. We might try to hang out with the cool crowd, or perhaps we try to participate in activities that we don't really like. Sometimes we avoid things that we really love in order to fit in. Like Adam and Eve's fig leaves, we try to cover up.

2. Pass out handout Adam and Eve-A, "The Fig Leaves of My Life." Have the students cut out their fig leaves and then draw or write the ways they hide who they really are. (If you brought magazines, the students could also go through them and cut and paste images that express their "fig leaves.")

3. Ask for volunteers to explain parts of their fig leaf. Below are some discussion starters.
- Why do people choose "fig leaves" over letting others see who they really are?
- Can you tell the difference when people are really being themselves versus covering up?
- What gives people the strength to be themselves?
- Are the temptations that Adam and Eve encounter similar to or different from the temptations we have today?

Who Hates Rules?

The students will engage in an activity without rules to learn their importance.

1. Have the students play a game of basketball, soccer, or some other team sport, except tell them that there are no rules. (Be sure to maintain a safe environment.) Another option would be to get a few volunteers to play checkers with you while the class looks on, but again, there are no rules!

2. After a short period of time, the students will surely start to become a little frustrated, angry, or bored. When this becomes obvious, call the game to an end.

3. Process the experience with the class. Use the following questions as discussion starters.
- How did you feel when you first heard that the game would have no rules? (Probably, excited.) So what happened?
- Did you become frustrated or angry or bored? Why?
- When you play a game, what do rules provide?

4. Read Genesis 2:15-17 aloud to the group. Present these thoughts in your own words.

- God gives human beings this rule because he cares for Adam, much as a parent gives a child the rule, "Look both ways before you cross the street." This direction given or limitation imposed is done out of love and concern.

5. Read Genesis 3:1-6. Ask, What reason does the serpent give for God not allowing them to eat from that tree? (The serpent says that God doesn't want them to be powerful like he is). Continue with the following questions.

- Why did Adam and Eve believe the serpent?
- How can young people be like Adam and Eve in their decision making?

6. Direct each student to write a list of rules they have been taught to follow and how the rules benefit people when they are followed. This could also be done in groups.

THE FIG LEAVES OF MY LIFE

Cut out this fig leaf and then draw or write the ways that you hide who you really are.

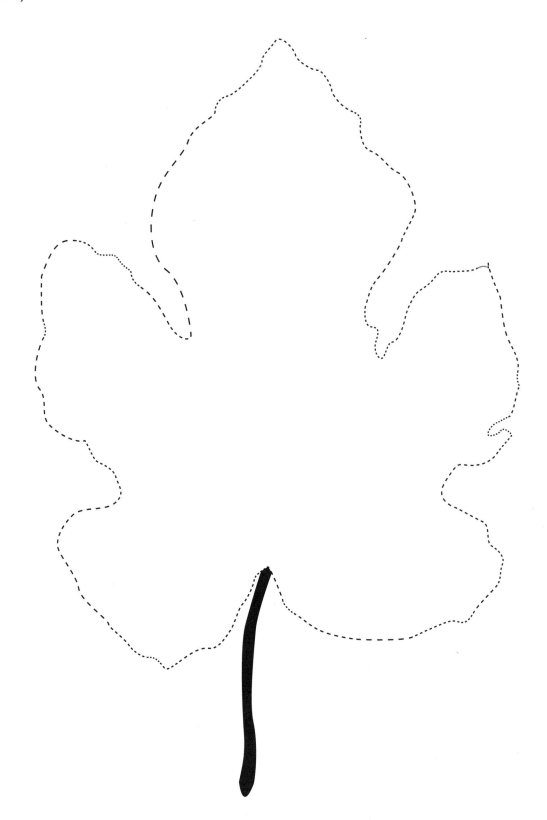

ABRAHAM

Preparing to Teach

Overview

Young adolescents can learn much about God's love for them and the power of faith through the study of Abraham. Like most young people, Abraham is an ordinary man who God calls to extraordinary faith. First, God calls Abraham to move his family, the type of transition that young people know from moving into junior high or middle school or from family moves or transitions.

Then God calls Abraham into a covenant relationship that requires something of both God and Abraham. Young people are very interested in relationships and the give and take required for those relationships. From the stories of Abraham, they can see that a good relationship requires that each party keep its commitments. They also see that even if their friends or family let them down, their God never will.

Finally, God calls Abraham to wait. Young people wait for rides, for the end of the school day, for vacation, for a friend to call. The stories about Abraham teach us that there is waiting and then there is "waiting in faith." But luckily for all of us, God gives us many chances to be faithful. Students can also see that God rewards Abraham's faith and our own.

THIS CHAPTER AT A GLANCE

Getting to Know the Story of Abraham

- Getting to the Promised Land

Getting to Know Abraham

- Moving On in Faith
- Covenants and Promises: Keeping Our Word

Scripture Passages Related to Abraham

- Genesis 11:27-32 (Abram's family of origin)
- Genesis 12:1-9 (God calls Abram to leave Ur)*
- Genesis 14:17-24 (Melchizedek meets Abram)
- Genesis 15:1-21 (God makes a Covenant with Abram)*
- Genesis 16:1-16 (Hagar gives birth to Ishmael)
- Genesis 17:1-8,15-16 (God changes Abram's and Sarai's names)*
- Genesis 17:9-13 (God asks for circumcision as a sign of the Covenant)*
- Genesis 18:1-15 (God promises to send Sarah and Abraham a son)
- Genesis 21:1-8 (The birth of Isaac)*
- Genesis 21:9-21 (Abraham sends Hagar out to the desert)
- Genesis 22:1-19 (God commands Abraham to sacrifice Isaac)*
- Genesis 23: 1-19 (The burial of Sarah)
- Genesis 25:7-11 (The burial of Abraham)

Asterisk (*) signifies key passages to cover.

Articles from *Breakthrough!* Related to Abraham

- *Breakthrough!* Interview with Abraham
- From Story to History (Genesis 11:10-32)
- An Act of Faith (Genesis 12:1-9)
- Priest of the Most High God (Genesis 14:17-20)
- Fear and Faith (Genesis 15:1-15)
- What's in a Name? (Genesis 17:1-22)
- Surprises from God (Genesis 18:1-15)
- Don't Look Back (Genesis 19:1-29)
- The Ultimate Sacrifice (Genesis 22:1-19)

Abraham and Young Adolescents Today

- God calls Abram and Sarai to move away from their familiar lives to a new territory so as to grow in their relationship with him; the young adolescent is in the midst of a transition from childhood to adolescence and can identify with the excitement and nervousness Abram and Sarai probably experienced in their move to Canaan.
- Several elements mark the of faith Abram has in God: it involves personal trust, risk, an ongoing process, and times of darkness or doubt. The student can be shown how to compare their own faith experience of God with these elements of Abram and Sarai's faith.
- Abram shows hospitality to strangers as a normal part of his family life; the young adolescent can recognize the importance of hospitality in the family home.

Highlighting God's Presence

The LORD said to Abram, "Leave your country, your relatives, and your father's home, and go to a land that I am going to show you. I will give you many descendants, and they will become a great nation" (Genesis 12:1-2).

When Abram was ninety-nine years old, the LORD appeared to him and said, "I am the Almighty God. Obey me and always do what is right. I will make my covenant with you and give you many descendants. . . . "I will keep my promise to you and to your descendants in future generations as an everlasting covenant. I will be your God and the God of your descendants. I will give to you and your descendants this land in which you are now a foreigner" (Genesis 17:1-2,7-8).

The angel of the LORD called to Abraham from heaven a second time, "I make a vow by my own name—the LORD is speaking—that I will richly bless you. Because you did this and did not keep back your only son from me, I promise that I will give you as many descendants as there are stars in the sky or grains of sand along the seashore. Your descendants will conquer their enemies. All the nations will ask me to bless them as I have your descendants—all because you obeyed my command" (Genesis 22:15-18).

Getting to Know the Story of Abraham

Getting to the Promised Land

In this activity, students review the stories about Abraham while playing a short game that helps them review the geography of the region.

Preparation

❑ Make enough copies of handout Abraham-A, "Traveling with Abraham," so that you could give one to each small group of four young people.

❑ Have a penny, a nickel, a dime, and a quarter, ideally, and markers available for each game group.

❑ Provide each group with twenty-four index cards, a pen, and a copy of the readings from "Scripture Passages about Abraham."

❑ Provide a Bible for each young person.

❑ Assemble prizes if desired. Suggestions are given below.

1. Divide the class into small groups of four people each. Have each young person take turns reading aloud the biblical passages that pertain to Abram or Abraham.

2. Give each group a set of twenty-four index cards. Instruct them to put a question about Abraham's story and then its answer below, on the same side. (An example might be the following: Question: From what city do Abram and Sarai leave? Answer: Ur)

3. After each student has made their six cards, collect each student's cards. Distribute handout Abraham–A, "Traveling with Abraham," four coins, and markers to each group. Give each a set of index card questions that another group created.

4. Provide the students with these instructions:

○ Have the oldest person at the table start. The person to his or her left takes an index card and reads the question. (Play then proceeds to the left with the next player reading the next question.) If a player answers the question correctly, he or she flips the coin. "Heads" means that the student moves one space and "tails" means that they move two spaces. A missed answer leaves the student on the same space. Arriving on the Haran spot gives the player a two-space bonus move.

For prizes, consider offering some biblical food: grapes, figs, pita bread, olives, or honey as well some contemporary refreshment.

Getting to Know Abraham

Moving On in Faith

In this activity, students explore Abram and Sarai's decision to move away from home through skits.

Preparation

❑ Make sure each student has a Bible, a pen, and paper.

1. Introduce this activity by suggesting that moving, whether to a new house, school, or soccer team, can be intense. The letting go of the known for the unknown can be exciting as well as unsettling. Discuss with the students their experiences of moving. Ask these questions:

○ What was exciting about moving and why?

○ What was difficult about moving and why?

○ How did you change as a person as a result of this move?

Through **Break** 2. Ask a student to read Genesis 12:1-9 aloud to the group. Then read the article "An Act of Faith" (Genesis 12:1-9) from *Breakthrough!* Invite students to respond to the following questions.

- Abram and Sarai, being well-established in Ur with friends and family, must have found it difficult to leave for Canaan. So, why did they go? (Because God promised them many descendants and a homeland.)

- What did having many descendants mean to them? (In the ancient world, people believed that they lived on through their descendants' memory of them. Thus, when God promises Abram and Sarai many descendants, the promise implies a certain immortality for them.)

- What does the promise of a homeland mean to Abraham and Sarai? (The promise of a homeland means that this "new people" would be associated with a place in a distinct way.)

3. Divide the class into several small groups. Ask each group to create a skit that shows Abram and Sarai explaining to family and friends why they are moving. Suggest that they might want to include dialogue about what Abram's God is like, what promises he has made to them, and how he promises to be faithful.

4. After enjoying the skits, highlight the similarities and differences between them. Have the students privately reflect on whether they have ever had to make changes in their lives that were hard for other people to understand. Ask them to consider what they might learn from Abram and Sarai's move. Ask students to reflect on ways they could invite God into the next move they make.

Covenants and Promises: Keeping Our Word

In this activity, students explore the nature of covenants, using a beanbag toss as a symbolic tool.

Preparation

❑ Each student needs a Bible, a pen, and paper.

❑ Bring beanbags to class, one for every two students.

1. Introduce this activity by explaining that God's concern for humanity reaches new heights through Abram and Sarai's lives. God makes a covenant with them and their descendants. Read Genesis 15:7-21 aloud to the class. Ask students to share what they know of covenants and how they are made. Provide them with the following information.

○ A covenant is an unconditional promise of faithfulness. Covenants are made through rituals that are public in some way. The ritual that Abram and God performed was used by the people of the Middle East to signify complete fidelity, even if it meant giving up one's own life if it was broken.

2. Move the discussion of covenant into the present day. Ask students where they see covenant-type relationships being forged today. (Possibilities include marriage, vowed religious life, swearing on a Bible in court, the oath of office the president takes, and so on) Ask, What symbols or gestures accompany these covenant events?

Note that unfortunately our human experience of covenant relationships is mixed as we see many people unable to live completely faithful to their lifelong promises. But God can be completely faithful in a way that we cannot. (In addition, emphasize that with God's help, we can live covenant relationships with greater faithfulness.)

3. Help the students distinguish between a covenant and a contract. (A covenant is unconditional in its terms; a contract has conditional terms.) Ask students to interpret the message that the ritual between God and Abram conveys. ("If either of us breaks the covenant, may we end up like the animals beside us!")

4. Discuss with the students the importance of promises. Note that a mini-covenant experience is making a promise or "giving your word." Ask the young people these questions.

○ What does it mean to give your word? (or to follow through on a commitment?)

○ How important is it to keep our promises?

○ How do you feel when someone keeps their word to you? breaks their word to you?

5. Take the students outside or to an inside open space. Divide the class in half, putting one half in a line and then putting the other half facing the line, about three feet apart. Each student should have a partner. Give each pair a beanbag. Ask them to toss the beanbag back and forth. If they do not drop the bag, have them go back a step and again throw it back and forth. The young people should do this until they are so far away that they cannot reach their partner.

6. Have the students explain to you what makes for a successful beanbag partnership and what circumstances can get in the way. Explain that throwing a beanbag back and forth can give us some

insight into covenant relationships using the following information:

- If you think of the beanbag as a symbol of a covenant, note that keeping the "covenant" afloat first requires two people. There are no one-person covenants. In addition, both parties are responsible for keeping it "afloat" or going. If one person stops focusing on the "covenant," they are more likely to drop it or throw it poorly to their partner. The farther apart the partners are also contributes to whether or not the beanbag covenant has a safe flight. Relationships that become distanced threaten any covenant that has been made.
- Both parties throwing the beanbag have hope that it will stay airborne. When one person "drops the ball," the other can be frustrated or disappointed. A key element of covenant making is covenant remaking. How do we forgive others for dropping the ball? How do we pick up the ball and resume our relationship?
- While everyday promises may not always seem earth-shattering, they form the type of person we will be when we enter into covenant relationships and the way we are in relationship with God.
- God always invite us to resume the covenant, to pick up the ball, to move closer.

7. Close this activity with the Our Father. Pray it slowly, emphasizing the importance of forgiveness we are called to share.

TRAVELING WITH ABRAHAM

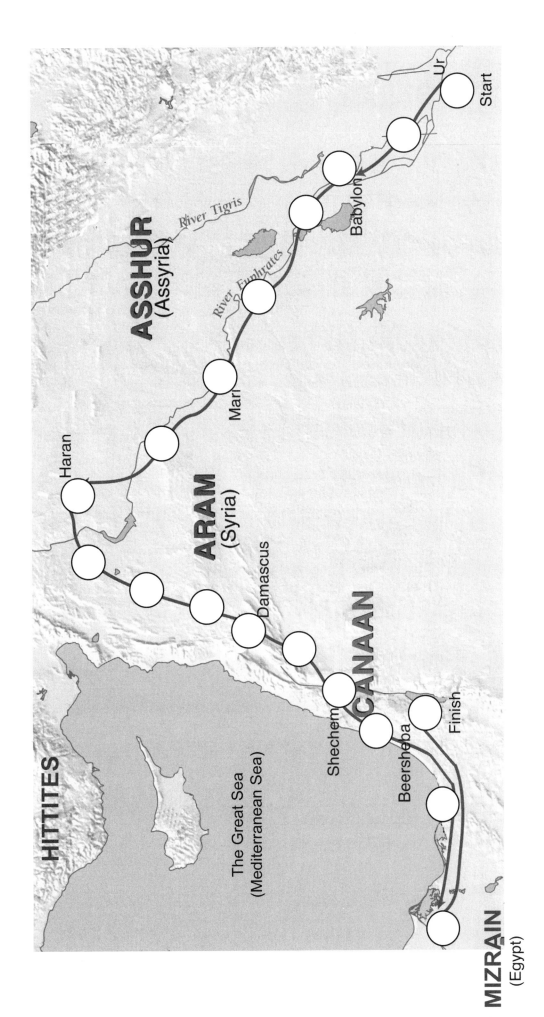

SARAH

Preparing to Teach

Overview

The power and paradoxical promises of God are revealed in the biblical story of Abraham and Sarah. The first thing we learn about Sarai (Sarah) in Genesis, chapter 11 is that she cannot have children (v. 30). This small biographical detail is significant to the unfolding story of Abram and Sarai in partnership with God. In a culture where woman were honored for their reproductive abilities, there was shame in being a woman unable to bear children. Young people also have secret or public shortcomings that make them vulnerable to feeling inferior or being made to feel lesser by their peers.

Luckily, the God of Abraham and Sarah brings honor to those whom society shames. This God is also one of loving surprises who can bring blessing out of challenge and difficulty. It is important for young people to consider that God does not see them with the critical eye of other people their age. In fact, God can strengthen and bless them if they experience being an outsider.

God's invitation to our first biblical patriarch and matriarch can be described as an invitation to trust and believe in what is possible in partnership with God—and they do, for the most part. God fulfills his promises to Abraham and Sarah, who cooperate with him. Abraham's promised son will be born only to Sarah. Sarah is significant to the fulfillment of God's promises and plan for all humankind.

THIS CHAPTER AT A GLANCE

Getting to Know the Story of Sarah

- A Paradigm of Promise: Who is Projecting the Picture?

Getting to Know Sarah

- The "Eye Popper" Activity
- Inside Out and Upside Down

Scripture Passages Related to Sarah

- Genesis 11:29-32 (Sarai enters the biblical story)
- Genesis 12:1-9 (Call of Abram and Sarai)*
- Genesis 12:10-20; 20:1-18 (Sarai, Abram's wife or sister?)
- Genesis 16:1-6 (Sarai tries to control the family plan)*
- Genesis 17:1-22 (God corrects the family plan)*
- Genesis 18:1-15 (God's promise)*
- Genesis 21:1-8 (Birth of Isaac)*
- Genesis 23:1-20 (Death of Sarah)

Asterisk (*) signifies key passages to cover.

Articles from *Breakthrough!* Related to Sarah

- *Breakthrough!* Interview with Sarah
- An Act of Faith (Genesis 12:1-9)
- What's in a Name? (Genesis 17:1-22)
- Surprises from God (Genesis 18:1-15)
- Jealousy (Genesis 21:9-21)

Sarah and Young Adolescents Today

- Sarai adapts to Abram's plans to travel with their household. Many students must adapt to new schools and neighborhoods for varied reasons—parental employment, separation, divorce, or family lifestyle changes.
- Sarah is influenced by the culture's social pressures for women to have children, which were not in keeping with God's initial plan for Sarah. Peer pressure can negatively influence young people today to conform to social expectations not in keeping with God's plan for them.
- Sarah's lack of patience with God's promise prompted her to make choices that brought pain to others and to herself. Students' impatience can cause problems for others and themselves. (See the article "Jealousy" (Genesis 21:9-21) in *Breakthrough!* to discuss this topic further with your students.)
- Sarah was pleasantly surprised to become pregnant at an advanced age. Students have both positive and negative surprises in their lives.

Highlighting God's Presence

God said to Abraham, "You must no longer call your wife, Sarai; from now on her name will be Sarah. I will bless her, and I will give you a son by her. I will bless her, and she will become the mother of nations, and there will be kings among her descendants" (Genesis 17:15-16).

Then the Lord said to Abraham, "Why did Sarah laugh, and say, 'Can I really have a child when I am so old?' Is anything too hard for the Lord? As I said, nine months from now I will return and Sarah will have a son" (Genesis 18:13-14).

The Lord blessed Sarah as he had promised, and she became pregnant and bore a son to Abraham when he was old (Genesis 21:1-2).

Getting to Know the Story of Sarah

A Paradigm of Promise:
Who is Projecting the Picture?

Sarah is the first barren woman we encounter in the Bible whom God blesses with offspring (Genesis 11:30, 21:1-2). Old Testament figures Rebecca (Genesis 25:21), Rachel (Genesis 29:31, 30:22-24), and Hannah (1 Samuel 1:1-7,19-20) are also initially barren. In the New Testament, we hear the story of childless Elizabeth, Mary's cousin, and the miraculous birth of her son, John (Luke 1:26-37,57-58).

This activity heightens the students' awareness of the kind of conditioning that society can give us, influencing the way that we see the world and God. Sarah's offering of Hagar to Abraham in Genesis, chapter 16 enables students to explore these questions: Are their actions rooted in trust in God's promises, or are their decisions based on the promises of peers, the media, and other influencing aspects of their lives? Who "conditions" the way they see their life?

Preparation

☐ Make a copy of resources Sarah-A, "The Old Woman," Sarah-B, "The Young Woman," and Sarah-C, "The Woman." The images can be either held up for the class to observe or projected on a screen. (resources A and B are pictures that "condition" the student to see a particular image in Resource C.)

1. Ask the students to take turns reading aloud the stories about Sarah from "Scripture Passages Related to Sarah."

2. Ask the students to answer this question, using a scale of one to ten one means not at all and ten signifies completely: "How much is the way you view the world influenced by the culture: media, politics, customs?" Discuss the students' answers and explain that you will return to them.

3. Divide the class in half. One half of the class will spend 30 seconds viewing resource Sarah-A, "The Old Woman" while the other half of the class closes their eyes. (The students closing their eyes can hum the theme to *Jeopardy* or another song two times to help the time pass.)

4. The students who viewed "The Old Woman" are to close their eyes (and hum), while the ones who previously had their eyes closed are to view resource Sarah-B, "The Young Woman" for 30 seconds.

5. Show resource Sarah-C, "The Woman," to all of the students and discuss what the image looks like. Ask, "Is the woman in the picture old or young? What are some of her physical characteristics?"

(If the students have never done this exercise, they should describe the woman as old or young according to the image that they viewed previously for 30 seconds. Those who looked at resource-A will likely describe an old woman and those who observed resource-B will likely describe a young woman.)

6. Tell the students that you just "conditioned" them to see the picture in a particular way. Then show resource-A to the group that viewed resource-B, and vice versa. Discuss what image they initially saw when they viewed resource-C. Highlight that this conditioning only took 30 seconds! Ask students to react to this experience, especially in light of their response in step 2.

7. Ask the students to think about some of the things that condition them to see the world a particular way. Television, film, magazines, advertising, and friends all influence the way young people see themselves and the world around them. Note that they spend much more time than 30 seconds with these influences! Discuss these questions with the students.

- Do people and things condition you to see the world in a certain way? Can you prevent this?

- Do people and things condition you to see God in your lives?

- What conditions you to have trust in God's promises and plans for you?

8. Ask the students to consider the way that Sarai acts in Genesis 16:1-6. Ask these questions.

- What kind of conditioning does Sarai seem to have received?

- Did Sarai not trust God's promise that she and Abram would have children or was she conditioned by the culture around her when she offered her servant girl, Hagar, to Abram?

- To what extent does social conditioning affect our own ability to listen to God?

9. Conclude the discussion with comments about the importance of giving God time to condition the way we see our relationships with God, self, others, and the world around us.

Getting to Know Sarah

We encounter a God of loving surprises when we discover the God of Abraham and Sarah. In these two activities, students can see that God sends blessings in unexpected, surprising ways.

The "Eye Popper" Activity

In this activity, students use the surprising nature of the party favor "eye poppers" as a way of talking about the surprising nature of God.

Preparation

❑ Purchase a bag of "eye poppers" party favors at a party supply store or from an online vendor. The theological idea in this activity can be communicated with just one eye popper, but students enjoy the surprise of having a handful of poppers thrown into the air for them to catch! Tell the students to keep them as a reminder that God is full of surprises.

1. Introduce the students to the God of Abraham and Sarah, a God of surprises, by reading the stories listed under "Scripture Passages Related to Sarah," highlighting Genesis 11:30 and Genesis 12:1-4. Explain that God's promise to make Abram's name great meant that God would bless him and his wife with children. Then ask the students why God would choose this particular couple in God's mission to bless the world. With that introduction, throw a handful of eye poppers into the air for the students to catch, and let the students enjoy the chaos.

2. Let the students play with these poppers for a couple minutes, turning them inside out and upside down on a flat surface and waiting for the surprise jump into the air. Settle the class and ask what theological lessons can be drawn from this exercise of inversion and surprise? Guide the conversation toward some of these themes.

- God reverses our understanding of the way things should work, and this is sometimes called the "divine reversal" (Several other biblical passages point to this reality: Hannah's Prayer [1 Samuel 2:1-10], the Magnificat [Luke 1:46-55], and the Beatitudes [Matthew 5:3-11]).
- "You [God] choose the weak and make them strong in bearing

witness to you, through Jesus Christ our Lord" (from "Preface of Martyrs," *Sacramentary*, page 483). There are numerous biblical narratives and stories of the saints that support this paradoxical promise.

*   God's love knows no bounds. The Spirit of God moves as the Spirit wills. We need to be ready and willing to encounter divine love, which is often revealed in unexpected and surprising ways.

3. Bring closure to this activity by having a student read Genesis 22:17. Share the following insights in your own words.

*   Abraham is considered the father of faith for three world religions: Judaism, Islam, and Christianity so his spiritual descendents are today as numerous as the stars. God reveals in the story of Abraham and Sarah that nothing is impossible when you are willing to follow a God of surprises!

Inside Out and Upside Down

Students may be familiar with the song *Spinnin' Around,* by Jump5. (Find on *The Very Best of Jump5,* by Jump5 (Sparrow/Emd, 2005.) This tune captures a sense of the paradoxes and surprises of God. Sarah and Abraham's journey with God kept them "spinnin' around," and when they kept their eyes and heart on God, it was a joyful journey enriched by laughter!

You could either listen to the song in class and have the students make connections between the concepts of the biblical story and the lyrics of the music, or you could make the connections on your own and bring these ideas into discussion in class. You might suggest that the students interject God as a replacement for the "you" of the song.

THE OLD WOMAN

THE YOUNG WOMAN

(From *The Seven Habits of Highly Effective People: Restoring the Character Ethic,* by Stephen R. Covey (New York: Free Press, 1989), pages 25–26. Copyright (c) 1989 by Stephen R. Covey. Used with permission.)

THE WOMAN

Isaac

Preparing to Teach

Overview

Isaac's story connects with the lives of young adolescents in several areas. His life, with its up and downs, can challenge the misconception that biblical characters' lives are so very different from ours. Just as God was present in the up and down moments of Isaac's life, God is also present in the ups and downs of our own lives.

Isaac is the promise that God made to his parents, Abraham and Sarah. In a culture today that often says you are important for what you do, wear, or for how you look, Isaac's birth reminds us that each person is important because he or she is a promise of God. The word *promise* is used in different ways in our society so it is important to sort out what type of promise God's promise is.

Isaac was also tested. Young people experience various challenges, big and small. It is important that they realize that God is close in all challenges they face.

THIS CHAPTER AT A GLANCE

Getting to Know the Story of Isaac

- Isaac's Ups and Downs

Getting to Know Isaac

- Isaac Is a Promise
- Being Tested

Scripture Passages Related to Isaac

- Genesis 21:1–8 (Isaac's birth)*
- Genesis 21:9–13 (Isaac plays with Ishmael)
- Genesis 22:1–19 (Abraham leads Isaac to sacrifice)*
- Genesis 23:1–19 (Sarah dies)
- Genesis, chapter 24 (Isaac's servant brings Rebecca to Isaac)*

- Genesis 25:1-6 (Abraham remarries, has children, and leaves all to Isaac)
- Genesis 25:19-26 (Rebecca gives birth to their sons, Esau and Jacob)*
- Genesis 25:27-34 (Isaac's family dynamics)*
- Genesis, chapter 26 (Isaac and Abimalech)
- Genesis 27:1-29 (Isaac gives Jacob a blessing rather than Esau)*

Asterisk (*) signifies key passages to cover.

Articles from *Breakthrough!* Related to Isaac

- *Breakthrough!* Interview with Isaac
- What's in a Name? (Genesis 17:1-22)
- Surprises from God (Genesis 18:1-15)
- Jealousy (Genesis 21:9-21)
- The Ultimate Sacrifice (Genesis 22:1-19)
- A Match Made in Heaven (Genesis 24:57-67)
- Thanks for Siblings (Genesis 25:19-34)

Isaac and Young Adolescents Today

- Isaac came from ancestors and from parents. He has a lineage as do the students.
- Isaac's name has a special meaning. Students have been given names for particular reasons and this makes up part of their identity.
- Isaac's birth is a promise to Abraham. Each person's birth is a promise and a gift.
- Isaac has a half brother, Ishmael, and experiences the joy and tension of a blended family. Some students are part of blended families. (See "Jealousy" (Genesis 21:9-21) in *Breakthrough!* for a discussion of this dynamic in Isaac's family.)
- God's request to Abraham to sacrifice Isaac was a test for Isaac. Students face tests of various types in their lives.
- Isaac loses his mother and his father remarries. Some students have lost loved ones.
- Isaac's own sons are rivals with one another and experience favoritism from their parents. Some students have these family dynamics at home.

Highlighting God's Presence

"Don't hurt the boy or do anything to him," he said. "Now I know that you honor and obey God, because you have not kept back your only son from him" (Genesis 22:12; the angel of the Lord).

Laban and Bethuel answered, "Since this matter comes from the L ORD, it is not for us to make a decision" (Genesis 24:50).

Because Rebecca had no children, Isaac prayed to the L ORD for her. The L ORD answered his prayer and Rebecca became pregnant (Genesis 25:21).

Getting to Know the Story of Isaac

Isaac's Ups and Downs

In this activity, students review or learn about the story of Isaac and focus on the high and low points of his story.

Preparation

❑ Create a time line for the Isaac story on butcher paper or on the blackboard prior to meeting as a class. You can subdivide the time line with the headings "birth," "youth," "adulthood," and "old age." The space above the time line should indicate a high point, the line itself an "average point in life," and below the line is a "low point."

❑ If you would like to give the students the poem "Footprints," make enough copies of handout Isaac-A, "Footprints," on nice paper to hand out to the students.

❑ Make sure that students have a Bible.

1. Divide the class into six groups and assign each group one of the biblical stories that has an asterisk in "Scripture Passages." For each biblical story, tell the students to do the following tasks.
- Write down what chapter and verse in Genesis corresponds to the story.
- Summarize the plot of the story.
- Decide whether or not this story describes a low, average, or high point in Isaac's life and why. (If the story has more than one type of experience, ask students to identify them all in terms of highs and lows.)
- Look for God's presence in the story. If God is directly mentioned, what does God do or say, either himself or through a messenger? (Note that God can be working whether he is mentioned by name or not.)

2. Go through the Isaac stories in order, asking each group to share the summary of the story. After each group shares the summary, instruct a representative to go up to the board and pick a spot to put the story on the time line, explaining the group's choice. Invite comment or discussion.

3. Ask students whether or not they think that Isaac had a pretty typical life, or one that was characterized by many highs and lows.

4. Return to the stories, in order, and ask each group to share whether or not they saw God acting in the stories. Have a volunteer map God's presence on the time line while the groups share. (The volunteer might use an adjective to describe God's presence in a given situation such as "testing" or "reassuring," for example.)

5. Conclude by discussing that God is present in our lives all the time. The poem "Footprints" is a helpful illustration of God's presence whether visible or invisible. Pass out the copies of "Footprints" to the young people and invite them to reflect on what it means.

Getting to Know Isaac

Isaac Is a Promise

In this activity, students contemplate the meaning of the word *promise* and then consider themselves as God's promise.

Preparation

❑ Students will each need a Bible, a piece of paper, and a pen or pencil.

❑ Make copies of handout Isaac-B, "Promises," for every participant.

❑ Review Genesis, chapter 21.

1. Distribute handout Isaac-B, "Promises," to the young people and go over the directions with them. Give them 5 or more minutes to put several answers in each of the boxes on the handout.

2. Put the headings from the handout chart on the board. Then ask students to share their answers while a student volunteer records them.

3. Ask these questions about the different areas on the board.

○ What happens when these different types of promises are kept?

○ What happens when they are broken? (Play devil's advocate, if necessary, to encourage students to explore the concept of promise more deeply.)

4. Ask a student to read Genesis, chapter 21 aloud. What type of promises does God make? Ask, what are God's promises like?

5. Conclude by asking the young people to consider this question: "What does it mean for you to be a promise of God or the fulfillment of God's promise, as was Isaac?"

Being Tested

In this activity, students look to see that God is present when life tests them, just as he was there when Isaac was tested.

1. Put students into groups of three and have them read Genesis 22:1–19, with each person taking a role: Abraham, Isaac, or the angel of the Lord. Afterward, ask each group to prepare a short role-play of this reading. Encourage the students to reflect on the feelings that they imagine each of the figures had and to communicate those feelings not just in the tone of voice they use during the role-play but also in the gestures, speed of walking, and facial expressions that they use. You may want the students to write up a script first.

Another possibility would be to use the already-made skit for "Abraham and Isaac" from *Ready-to-Go Scripture Skits . . . That Teach Serious Stuff,* by Michael Theisen (Winona, MN: Saint Mary's Press, 2004).

2. Invite several groups to present their role-plays. Afterward, ask, "What is similar in these role-plays? What is different?" Ask each group to explain their own depiction. Note the types of emotions that emerge in this story.

3. Give the students a few moments of silence and ask them to think privately about times when they have felt the kinds of emotions on the board. Ask, "When have you been tested? What did you do?" Invite students to share as they feel comfortable.

4. Conclude the discussion of Isaac's test with these thoughts in your own words:
• All of us go through times that feel very much like the journey that Abraham and Isaac took. Even people who are following the will of God sometimes feel alone and scared. It is important to remember that God is with us and that God wants us to come through our test with feelings of hope and joy like Isaac and Abraham did

Variation

Have the students read the *Breakthrough!* article "The Ultimate Sacrifice" (Genesis 22:1–19) to discuss the parallels between Abraham, Isaac, and Jesus.

FOOTPRINTS

One night a man had a dream about walking along the beach with the Lord. The sky flashed scenes from his life. For each scene, he noticed two sets of footprints in the sand: his and the Lord's.

After the last scene flashed before him, he looked at the footprints, noticing that at the most difficult times in his life there was only one set of footprints.

"Lord, you said you'd walk with me all the way if I followed you. But during the most troublesome times in my life, there is only one set of footprints. Why did you leave me when I needed you most?"

The Lord replied, "I love you and would never leave you. In your times of trial and suffering when you only see one set of footprints, that was when I carried you."

Author Unknown

One night a man had a dream about walking along the beach with the Lord. The sky flashed scenes from his life. For each scene, he noticed two sets of footprints in the sand: his and the Lord's.

After the last scene flashed before him, he looked at the footprints, noticing that at the most difficult times in his life there was only one set of footprints.

"Lord, you said you'd walk with me all the way if I followed you. But during the most troublesome times in my life, there is only one set of footprints. Why did you leave me when I needed you most?"

The Lord replied, "I love you and would never leave you. In your times of trial and suffering when you only see one set of footprints, that was when I carried you."

Author Unknown

PROMISES

Describe the kind of promises that are made in the following areas, giving several examples for each one.

Friends	Family
School	Government

What are the characteristics of God's promises? Circle the promises above that most resemble God's promises.

_____

_____

_____

_____

_____

JACOB

Preparing to Teach About Jacob

Overview

Jacob is a complex figure. His initial deceit in cooperation with Rebecca to obtain Isaac's blessing is a tough story for many young people. They ask, "How did he become such an important person in the Bible if he did that?" Clearly, God still blesses people even when they fail in living moral lives. This subtlety can help young people see that not just "the really good kids" can be people through whom God works; everyone can!

Esau's forgiveness of Jacob is also a powerful witness to the way that people can overcome damage that has been done to them and grow because of it. Esau's example challenges students to expect more from themselves (with God's help) and to be able to hope that reconciliation can occur in some of their own troubled relationships.

Jacob's love for Rachel is beautiful. Despite the way that Laban treats him, he is willing to stay on with him because of her. Young people search for models of what "true love" is. In addition, they can easily imagine the jealousy between the two young wives who both want to bear children and be seen as special in Jacob's eyes.

Do family patterns repeat themselves? Although this part of Jacob's story is usually covered in the study of Joseph, it is interesting that after suffering from parental favoritism that Jacob himself has a favorite son. This choice causes him much pain, but again God works through it all. If the young people could come away from Jacob's story saying, "God can work through it all," they would have learned an important and relevant lesson.

THIS CHAPTER AT A GLANCE

Getting to Know the Story of Jacob

- Comic Book Life of Jacob

Getting to Know Jacob

- Jacob's Extended Family and Our Own
- Jacob's Transformation at Peniel
- Jacob and Reconciliation

Scripture Passages Related to Jacob

- Genesis 25:19-26 (The birth of Esau and Jacob to Isaac and Rebecca)
- Genesis 25:27-34 (Esau sells rights as firstborn son)*
- Genesis 27:1-45 (Rebecca and Jacob deceive Isaac, and Jacob receives blessing)*
- Genesis 28:10-22 (Jacob's dream at Bethel)*
- Genesis 29:1-14 (Jacob arrives at Laban's house)
- Genesis 29:15-30 (Jacob marries Leah and Rachel)*
- Genesis 29:31—30:24 (Birth of Jacob's children)
- Genesis 31:1-55 (Jacob flees from Laban)
- Genesis 32:22-30 (Jacob receives the name Israel)*
- Genesis 33:1-20 (Jacob meets Esau)*
- Genesis 35:16-21 (Rachel's death)
- Genesis 35:22-25 (A list of the sons of Jacob)*

Asterisk (*) signifies key passages to cover.

Articles from *Breakthrough!* Related to Jacob

- *Breakthrough!* Interview with Jacob
- Thanks for Siblings (Genesis 25:19–34)
- Esau's Dilemma (Genesis 27:1–29)
- An Imperfect Believer (Genesis 30:25–43)
- Jacob's Wrestling Match (Genesis 32:22–32)
- A Moment of Great Power (Genesis, chapter 34)
- The Tribe of Judah (Genesis 49:8–12)
- To Be Continued (Genesis, chapter 50)

Jacob and Young Adolescents Today

- The story of Jacob revolves around troubling family dynamics: each parent favors a different child over the other and the two children are rivals. Students also experience difficult dynamics in their families.
- The story of Isaac's blessing of Jacob demonstrates the power of the spoken word in ancient cultures. Students also can see how the words they use build up or hurt people.
- The story of Jacob is about reconciliation especially in families. Young people need and have experienced reconciliation within their families.
- The story of Jacob is about positive transformations that can happen in our lives through memorable events, even hard ones. Students also carry the memories of significant experiences in their lives.

• The story of Jacob emphasizes the importance of our extended families. Students have experiences of extended families.

Highlighting God's Presence

And there was the LORD standing beside him (Jacob). "I am the LORD, the God of Abraham and Isaac," he said. "I will give to you and to your descendants this land on which you are lying. They will be as numerous as the specks of dust on the earth" (Genesis 28:13-14).

"Your name will no longer be Jacob. You have struggled with God and with men, and you have won; so your name will be Israel" (Genesis 32:28; the man wrestling with Jacob).

God said to Jacob, "Go to Bethel at once, and live there. Build an altar there to me, the God who appeared to you when you were running away from your brother Esau" (Genesis 35:1).

Getting to Know the Story of Jacob

Comic Book Life of Jacob

In this activity, students use comic strips to familiarize themselves with the story of Jacob and to share the story with one another. For the first part of this activity, follow the four steps that can be found in appendix 2, "Tools for Teaching," under the heading "The Comic Book Approach," on page 325. Use the readings for Jacob under the heading in this chapter "Scripture Passages Related to Jacob." (Continue here at step 5 after the comic strips are completed and shared.)

5. After students have created and shared their comics with each other, ask the students to think about the whole Jacob story and then to reflect on one or more of these questions:
• What is the moral of this story?
• If this comic was made into a movie, what would the title for it be?
• What does Jacob learn from his life?

These are other questions you may want to pose to your students:
• How is God's promise to Abraham and Isaac continued in the life of Jacob?
• What does the saying "What goes around, comes around" mean?
• How is this saying true in the life of Jacob, and what about Jacob's story challenges its truth?

Getting to Know Jacob

Note to Teacher. To help you prepare for this section, it is strongly recommended that you read a book titled *Son of Laughter,* by Frederick Buechner (New York: HarperCollins, 1993). This book is a fictionalized account of the biblical character Jacob, the son of Isaac, whose name means "laughter." These pages, in particular, bring the biblical story to life for students.

- pages 73–75 (Rebecca discusses her plan with Jacob)
- pages 80–86 (Isaac blesses Jacob)
- pages 164–166 (Jacob and Esau meet again)

Jacob's Extended Family and Our Own

Preparation

❑ Make sure that students have a Bible, paper, and a pen.

❑ Make copies of handout Jacob-A, "The Patriarch Family Tree," for each student.

❑ Have a visible map of the United States on a bulletin board, a globe, and thumbtacks.

❑ If you are not familiar with family trees, look on the Internet where there are quite a few sites with information about them.

1. Invite young people to read aloud Genesis, chapters 29 through 31, the parts of Jacob's story that relate to his Uncle Laban's family.

2. In pairs or individually, have the students fill in handout Jacob-A, "The Patriarch Family Tree."

3. After reviewing the trees as a class, examine the part of the tree that includes Jacob, Leah and Rachel, and Laban. Discuss these questions with the students:
- How well do Jacob and Laban relate?
- How well does Jacob relate with Rachel and Leah?
- What does Jacob learn about himself after twenty years with his extended family?

4. On a separate piece of paper, have students create their own family tree going back at least to their grandparents. (Get a reading from your group as to whether or not they need to go home and gather information or if they can complete the assignment during the same session.)

5. When the trees are complete, invite the students to share something about their family tree with the class. They might want to show the class where they fit on the tree, identify their favorite relatives, share family customs, and definitely talk about where their relatives live. Have a large map of the United States and of your own state on a bulletin board or a similar surface and have students put thumbtacks in the areas of the state and country where their relatives live. (International family members can be listed on the board or found on a globe.)

6. After students have shared their family trees, go back to the story of Jacob and Esau's reconciliation (Genesis 33:1–20). If time allows, invite students to share a story of reconciliation from their own family if appropriate.

Jacob's Transformation at Peniel

Preparation

❑ Make sure that each student has a Bible, paper, and a pen.

1. Have students read the account of Jacob wrestling with the angel (Genesis 32:22–30). Ask, "What do you think would have been Jacob's wrestling strategy in wrestling someone all night?"

2. Set up a thumb wrestling situation. Pair up the students and have them first write down a strategy for successfully thumb wrestling this opponent and the reasons why they would take that approach.

Then ask the pair to engage in thumb wrestling. After the competitors have wrestled a bit, ask them if their strategy was successful or not and why.

3. Then have several of the students, using their thumbs as characters, rewrite the dialogue from the Genesis account and perform the scene for the rest of the class, using their thumbs as characters. (Definitely allow for some humor.)

4. Ask a student to read "Jacob's Wrestling Match" (Genesis 32:22–32) from *Breakthrough!* Ask the students to privately consider the question, "Where are you personally wrestling with God?"

Break Through!

Jacob and Reconciliation

Preparation

❑ Make sure that students have a Bible, paper, a pen, and markers.

❑ Provide cutout pictures of human faces from newspapers, magazines, and other sources (or simply the sources themselves).

1. Have students read Genesis 33:1-20 and ask these questions:

   ○ How is Jacob expecting to be received by Esau?

   ○ What does Jacob do to prepare for this meeting and why?

   ○ How does Esau receive him and why?

2. After discussing these questions with the students, ask them to reflect on this question:
   - At the meeting with Esau, Jacob says, "To see your face is for me like seeing the face of God." (Genesis 33:10). Given what just happened to Jacob the previous night, what does this mean?

3. Have the students consider how faces convey meaning. Pass out the newspapers and magazines you have brought. Have the students find six different facial expressions in magazine pictures. (If some of the young people are artistic, allow them to draw the faces.) Ask them to share their images and talk about what feelings they associate with each face. Then ask them to make the parallel with the story in Genesis and to consider what Esau's face must have looked like for Jacob to associate it with God.

THE PATRIARCH FAMILY TREE

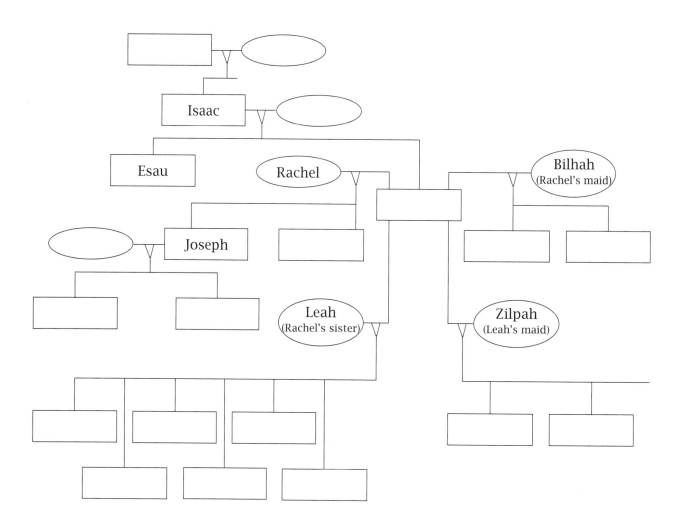

Adapted from "My Own Genesis," in *Faith Works for Junior High: Scripture- and Tradition-Based Sessions for Faith Formation,* by Lisa-Marie Calderone-Stewart (Winona, MN: Saint Mary's Press, 1993.) Copyright © 1993 by Saint Mary's Press. All rights reserved.

Leah and Rachel

Preparing to Teach

Overview

Though Jacob steals the spotlight in chapters 29-31 of Genesis, Rachel and Leah play important roles in fulfilling God's promise to Abraham that his descendents will be as numerous as the stars. As the students learn more about the story of Leah and Rachel, they will see how God is a part of Leah and Rachel's lives.

Leah and Rachel share the vulnerability of women in their era. Their father makes decisions for them. Neither Leah nor Rachel has a say in the way that their relationship with Jacob takes shape. In some ways, their lack of power contributes to their jealousy as they try to stay "even" in childbearing, another area in which they have no control.

Young people can relate to feeling vulnerable because many of them do not have very much say in the direction that their own lives take right now. Perhaps the story of these sisters can show them that petty rivalries can stem from having little control. Leah can bear children but Rachel is beautiful. This type of comparison is the type of reality that they know in their families and among their peers. Noticing how God helps both Leah and Rachel in their struggles and strategizing about not comparing themselves to others will hopefully bring these students some peace during what can be turbulent years.

This Chapter at a Glance

Getting to Know the Story of Leah and Rachel

- The Diaries of Two Sisters

Getting to Know Leah and Rachel

- Sibling Rivalry

Scripture Passages Related to Leah and Rachel

- Genesis 29:1–14 (Rachel meets Jacob for the first time)*
- Genesis 29:15–20 (Jacob works seven years to marry Rachel)*
- Genesis 29:21–30 (Jacob marries Leah; Jacob marries Rachel in exchange for another seven years of work)*
- Genesis 29:31–35 (Leah bears four sons)*
- Genesis 30:1–21 (Leah and Rachel's maidservants bear more children in the wives' names)*
- Genesis 30:22–24 (Rachel gives birth to Joseph)*
- Genesis 31:1–21 (Rachel and Leah flee with Jacob, family and flocks.)*
- Genesis 31:22–42 (Laban chases Jacob, wives, and family)*
- Genesis 35:16–20 (Rachel dies in childbirth with Benjamin)

Asterisk (*) signifies key passages to cover.

Break Through! Article from *Breakthrough!* Related to Leah and Rachel

- *Breakthrough!* Interview with Leah and Rachel

Leah and Rachel and Young Adolescents Today

- Rachel tends the sheep for her father. Many students are responsible for specific household chores like Rachel's shepherding.
- Jacob greets Rachel with an unexpected kiss. Because they are not children anymore, students have to deal with the occasional kiss or hug from parents, relatives, or strangers when they say hello, even if they are uncomfortable with the practice.
- Of the two sisters, Rachel is the beautiful one. Students may feel like teachers, parents, coaches, and friends compare them with their brothers and sisters.
- Jacob pays a lot of attention to Rachel, who is clearly his favorite. Students sometimes feel like their parents, teachers, or friends play favorites.
- Laban secretly marries Leah to Jacob instead of Rachel, his promised bride. Students feel disappointed when they do not get what they expect or promised from someone.
- When Rachel finally becomes pregnant with her son Joseph, she praises God for helping her. When students overcome a difficult task or time, they thank and praise God for his help.

Highlighting God's Presence

When the LORD saw that Leah was loved less than Rachel, he made it possible for her to have children, but Rachel remained childless (Genesis 29:31).

God answered Leah's prayer, and she became pregnant and bore Jacob a fifth son (Genesis 30:17).

Then God remembered Rachel; he answered her prayer and made it possible for her to have children (Genesis 30:22).

"All this wealth which God has taken from our father belongs to us and to our children. Do whatever God has told you" (Genesis 31:16; Leah and Rachel).

Getting to Know the Story of Leah and Rachel

The Diaries of Two Sisters

Preparation

❑ Make sure students have one piece of lined paper each and pens or pencils.

❑ Have enough bibles available for every two people.

❑ Post three pieces of blank newsprint so that the students can see them. Label one piece, "Facts," and the others, "Insights-Leah" and "Insights-Rachel." (Have some additional newsprint on hand.)

❑ Provide four sheets of newsprint and a marker for each small group of four people.

1. Divide the students into four groups of no more than eight people. For larger student groups, divide them into eight groups of four or more people. (The number of small groups must be a multiple of four.) Hand out bibles, paper, and pens or pencils.

2. Divide the characters and stories among the groups. Half of the groups represent Leah and half represent Rachel. In a four-group model, instruct one Rachel group and one Leah group to read the first five passages in "Scripture Passages Related to Leah and Rachel." Assign the other two groups to read the last four readings. Tell students to write on the paper which character they are writing about and their assigned Scripture passages.

Leah and Rachel

3. Provide the small groups with the following instructions using your own words:

- Each of your groups is assigned the character of either Leah or Rachel. Read the passages aloud from the Bible that talk about them and their lives. Think about how your "sister" acted, felt, talked, and what she did in the story. If your character is not in a particular story, imagine what she thought, felt, talked about, or did when she heard someone tell her that story.

- After you have read each passage, quietly write a diary entry on your piece of paper that goes with the Bible reading from the perspective of your character.

4. Distribute four sheets of newsprint and a marker to each small group. When the small groups are finished writing, ask them to share their diary entries with each other. Using one piece of the newsprint per Bible passage, ask each small group to come up with a common diary entry for each Bible passage based on what each person wrote individually.

5. Gather the small groups together into the large group. Beginning with Genesis 29:4-14, ask the students to list the facts about Leah and Rachel's lives. Write down their responses on the newsprint labeled, "Facts." Make sure that they put the facts in the right order and that each listing is complete.

6. After getting the facts straight, starting with the first Bible passage, invite the small groups that represent Leah and Rachel to share their diary entries with the rest of the group. With input from the whole group, fill the newsprint pages with insights about Leah or Rachel that come from the diary entries.

7. Share the following information about women characters in the Scriptures:

○ The Bible often focuses on the motherhood of female characters. Like many other women in the Old Testament, Leah and Rachel are an important part of the realization of God's promise to Abraham—that Abraham's descendants will be a numerous as the stars. Leah and Rachel have twelve sons who become the leaders of the tribes of Israel and Judah. We hear about the tribes of Israel and Judah even in the Gospels.

8. Ask the students the following questions:

○ Who do you know who is like Leah? like Rachel? Give examples.

○ In what ways do you see God acting through these people?

Getting to Know Leah and Rachel

Sibling Rivalry

Preparation

- ❑ Make sure each person has a Bible.

- ❑ Provide paper, and pens or pencils.

- ❑ Have masking tape on hand.

- ❑ Ahead of time, write down the two discussion questions from step 2 on the newsprint, using a marker.

- ❑ Bring as many pieces of white card stock as there are members of your group. Print one of the nine statements below on a piece of card stock. Repeat as needed so that there are cards for one half of the group.
  - I'm beautiful.
  - I'm smart.
  - I'm athletic.
  - I'm tall.
  - I'm funny.
  - I'm fun.
  - I'm nice.
  - I'm sensitive.
  - I'm happy.

- ❑ Print one of the following statements on nine pieces of card stock. Repeat the statements as necessary so that there are cards for the remaining half of the group.
  - I'm the beautiful one's sister or brother.
  - I'm the smart one's sister or brother.
  - I'm the athletic one's sister or brother.
  - I'm the tall one's sister or brother.
  - I'm the funny one's sister or brother.
  - I'm the fun one's sister or brother.
  - I'm the nice one's sister or brother.
  - I'm the sensitive one's sister or brother.
  - I'm the happy one's sister or brother.

1. Tape the signs to the backs of the students, asking them to close their eyes while you do it. Give them the following instructions:

- ○ Everyone has a sign that says "who they are." The object of this game is to guess who you are. The signs say one of two things. They either describe a characteristic that *you* have or they say that *you are the brother or sister of someone else in the room.*

For example, someone might be wearing the sign that says, "I'm silly." Someone else might be wearing the sign that says, "I'm the silly one's brother or sister." More than one person may have the same sign.

Leah and Rachel

○ As you encounter each person, say one or two sentences that indirectly point to the information that is on their back. For example, if a person is tall, you might say, "It was good to see you at basketball practice" or "Could you reach that book off the top shelf?" Because the statements should be indirect, a number of different people will be helping you figure out what the sign on your back says.

○ Once you have guessed who you are, move the sign to the front of your shirt.

Give the young people 5 to 10 minutes to do this exercise.

2. When the exercise is complete, divide the students into two groups: those who wore signs saying, "I'm . . ." and those who wore signs saying that they were a brother or sister. Show them the following questions on the newsprint and ask them to discuss them in their smaller groups.
• How did people treat you?
• Was one group treated better than the other? worse than the other? Why?

3. In the large group, ask the groups to share some of their responses. Ask representatives from the "I'm . . ." group and the sibling group to share how they felt they were treated by those giving them hints about what their sign said. Ask these questions:

○ In what ways did people treat you nicely because you had a certain trait?

○ In what ways did people treat you nicely because you were someone else's brother or sister.

○ How were you treated differently than the other group?

4. Read Genesis 29:15-30 aloud. Highlight the text's description of Leah and Rachel. Note that Rachel is Jacob's favorite and explain what he does in order to marry her. Ask the group the following questions based on the reading:

○ How do you think Rachel felt under the circumstances about her relationship with Jacob and Leah? Why?

○ How do you think Leah felt under the circumstances about her relationship with Jacob and Rachel? Why?

○ Which sister had it "easier"—Rachel or Leah? Why?

5. Lead a discussion on sibling rivalry using the following questions as needed. Highlight the responses that focus on siblings being different from each other.

- What is sibling rivalry?
- Why are sister and brothers sometimes rivals?
- Why were Rachel and Leah rivals?
- Is being different from your brother or sister good? bad? Why or why not?
- Is there a polite way to share with someone else that you prefer not to be compared with your brother or sister? How?

Leah and Rachel

JOSEPH

Preparing to Teach

Overview

The story of Joseph is a biblical story about a family and God's action within it as well as about two nations, Israel and Egypt.

Joseph's very birth is the result of Rachel's prayer to have a child. Interestingly, the fact that Joseph is Rachel's son is pivotal in his story. Jacob's love for Joseph because he is Rachel's son and Joseph's use of his own gifts lead his brothers to a jealousy that prompts them to sell Joseph into slavery. Young people can empathize with the brothers' jealousy but can be somewhat horrified by the brothers' decision. They too know the pain that can come from sibling rivalry, especially when the gifts of some family members are valued more than the gifts of others.

Despite Joseph's dire situation, God works through him during his time in Egypt. It is important for young people to understand that God is with them and can work through them in any situation to heal and touch others. This type of knowledge counters the phrase seen on T-shirts that "it is all about me."

The story of the brothers' visit to Egypt to get grain and then Joseph's complicated response is very human. Joseph's heart is touched when he sees that Judah regrets the pain that he caused Jacob and would substitute himself for Benjamin rather than put Jacob through this again. It is good for young people to hear such a powerful story of reconciliation because they know that family hurts can be very painful and seem impossible to overcome.

Joseph saves both the nation of Egypt through his stewardship of their resources and the nation of Israel by welcoming his family to share in Egypt's wealth and escape from famine.

THIS CHAPTER AT A GLANCE

Getting to Know the Story of Joseph

- Audiovisual Overviews of Joseph's Story
- Joseph Book Covers

Getting to Know Joseph

- Dreams and Gifts
- Good Luck, Bad Luck, Who Knows?

Scripture Passages Related to Joseph

- Genesis 37:1-11 (Joseph's relationship with his brothers)*
- Genesis 37:12-36 (Joseph's brothers sell him into slavery)*
- Genesis 39:1-6 (Joseph works for Potiphar)
- Genesis 39:7-19 (Potiphar's wife falsely accuses Joseph)*
- Genesis 39:21-23 (Joseph in jail)
- Genesis 40:1-23 (Joseph interprets prisoners' dreams)*
- Genesis 41:1-36 (Joseph interprets Pharaoh's dreams)*
- Genesis 41:37-57 (Joseph becomes governor of Egypt)
- Genesis 42-45 (Joseph's brothers journey to Egypt)
- Genesis 46 (Jacob and his family come to Egypt)

Articles from *Breakthrough!* Related to Joseph

- *Breakthrough!* Interview with Joseph
- Favored Sibling (Genesis, chapter 37)
- Joseph's Tough Times (Genesis 39:1-6)
- Catching Dreams (Genesis 41:1-36)
- The Great River of Blessings (Genesis 42:1-11)
- The Way to Peace (Genesis, chapter 45)
- To Be Continued (Genesis, chapter 50)

Joseph and Young Adolescents Today

- Joseph is one of the two youngest brothers in the family. Students have feelings about their place in the family, either as an older sibling with younger ones, in the middle, as a younger child with older siblings, or as an only child.
- Joseph has special gifts of dream interpretation. Students have gifts and may be encouraged (or discouraged) to use them.
- While being a slave challenged Joseph's trust in God, later experiences helped him see how God used this to bring about a greater good for himself and his family. Students can experience confusion about the meaning of family events but later may gain clarity about God's role in their family.
- Joseph is placed in a position of responsibility. Students have positions of responsibility. They need guidance in understanding themselves as role models for others.
- Joseph changes over fourteen years such that his brothers do not recognize him. Students are changing in their own eyes and in the eyes of others.
- Joseph must decide how to deal with those closest to him who have abandoned him and he must choose forgiveness or revenge. He chooses forgiveness. Students experience similar instances of

being let down by friends and family, especially because there is much turmoil in the lives of young adolescents. They struggle with revenge and forgiveness as well.

Highlighting God's Presence

But the LORD was with Joseph and blessed him, so that the jailer was pleased with him. . . . The jailer did not have to look after anything for which Joseph was responsible, because the LORD was with Joseph and made him succeed in everything he did (Genesis 39:21,23).

"It was really God who sent me ahead of you to save people's lives. . . . God sent me ahead of you to rescue you in this amazing way and to make sure that you and your descendants survive. So it was not really you who sent me here, but God" (Genesis 45:5,7–8).

Joseph

Getting to Know the Story of Joseph

Audiovisual Overviews of Joseph's Story

Joseph, the Musical

An engaging way to introduce the story of Joseph is to listen to parts or the entire CD of *Joseph and the Amazing Technicolor DreamCoat, 1993 Los Angeles Cast* (Andrew Lloyd Webber, Decca, US, 1993). As they listen, ask the young people to reflect on these questions:
* How does the music portray Joseph?
* At the end of the musical, why does Joseph end up forgiving his brothers?

Joseph, King of Dreams

Show the movie, *Joseph: King of Dreams* (Dreamworks, 2000; NR, 74 minutes) to the students in part or in full. Ask the students to notice if there are segments of the movie that do not appear in the biblical text and to assess why pieces were added. Students should also look to see if the movie misses any of the key parts of the story and assess that too. (This movie is fairly close to the biblical account.)

Joseph Book Covers

Because of the length of the Joseph stories and the number of years the stories cover, the activity "Character Book Covers" from appendix 2, "Tools for Teaching," page 325, is well suited for this activity.

Getting to Know Joseph

Dreams and Gifts

In this activity, students recognize the gifts that God gave Joseph as a way of understanding what their own gifts are.

Preparation

❏ Outline one jacket or trench coat on a piece of butcher paper about the size that would fit one of your students. (The group will only use one jacket outline.)

❏ Provide scraps of cloth or paper in various colors and sizes, so that every student can have two or three scraps and a sufficient number to fill in the "coat." Provide fabric markers, glue or tape, and markers for the students to use. (If using these materials is not feasible, create a handout with a rough outline of a coat on it, large enough for the young people to write in. Make a copy for each person.)

❏ Have a CD of some reflective instrumental music on hand and a CD player.

❏ Each student needs a Bible, paper, and a pen.

1. Ask students read Genesis 37:3-11. Pose these questions to the students:

   ○ Why does Jacob love Joseph best?

   ○ Why do his brothers not like him?

   ○ What are the gifts that Joseph receives in this passage?

2. Note that while Joseph's father gifts him with a coat, it is God who gives him a gift that cannot be taken away—that of interpreting dreams. Play some music for the students and give them some time to write down their own gifts, both the kinds that are visible and then those that are within them on scratch paper.

3. Pass out the craft materials or the handout. Ask students to write down one of their gifts on each piece of paper or cloth (or within the image of the coat on the handout.) When students have completed their scraps, ask them to attach them inside the outline of the coat on the butcher paper.

4. When all of the scraps are on the coat, ask students to share their impressions of the coat. Ask, "Do you see this coat as meant for one person in the class?" Suggest that this coat is powerful because unlike Joseph's, this one symbolizes the gifts of a class of students.

5. You may want to make the connection between the class's coat and the description that Paul gives of the Body of Christ in 1 Corinthians 12:12–31. Just like this coat would have a lesser impact with fewer students, the community loses when the gifts of every person are not appreciated and brought forth.

6. Conclude the activity with a prayer of thanks for the gifts of the members of your youth group or class.

Good Luck, Bad Luck, Who Knows?

Preparation

❑ Students need to have a Bible, a straightedge, paper, and a pen.

❑ Read over the story for this activity and consider it in light of Joseph's story.

1. Ask a student to read Genesis 39:1–22 aloud to the class. Then read the following story:

> There is a Chinese story of an old farmer who had an old horse for tilling his fields. One day the horse escaped into the hills and when all the farmer's neighbors sympathized with the old man over his bad luck, the farmer replied, "Bad luck? Good luck? Who knows?" A week later the horse returned with a herd of wild horses from the hills and this time the neighbors congratulated the farmer on his good luck. His reply was, "Good luck? Bad luck? Who knows?" Then, when the farmer's son was attempting to tame one of the wild horses, he fell off his horse and broke his leg. Everyone thought this very bad luck. Not the farmer, whose only reaction, was "Bad luck? Good luck? Who knows?" Some weeks later the army marched into the village and conscripted every able-bodied youth they found there. When they saw the farmer's son with his broken leg they let him off. Now was that good luck? Bad luck? Who knows? Everything that seems on the surface to be evil may be a good in disguise. And everything that seems good on the surface may really be an evil. So we are wise when we leave it to God to decide what is good luck and what bad, and thank him that all things turn out for good with those who love him.
> (Anthony De Mello, *Sadhana: A Way to God*, pp. 85–86)

2. Ask the young people to consider these two stories side-by-side. Ask the students to share their observations about the story and its relationship to the Joseph story. Then ask the young people to reflect about whether or not they have seen the truth of this story in their own lives.

3. Give the young people these directions about creating a personal time line.

- Begin the time line at birth and have it extend to the present moment.
- Break the time line into year units.
- Above the line and corresponding to the years in which they happened, write down three positive aspects or times in life.
- Below the line and corresponding to the years in which they happened, write down three negative aspects or times in life.
- See whether or not there is any relationship between the positive times and the negative times and illustrate the connection on the time line by drawing a line. (Draw the line even if the positive event does not necessarily cancel out the negative one. For example, your parents have divorced and while your real dream has been for them to remarry and reform your original family, you have baby brothers and sisters from your mother's remarriage whom you love.)

4. Give the young people a few minutes to reflect in writing on the answer to this question, "In your life experience so far, do you think that God can bring good out of situations that can be very negative? Why or why not?"

5. Conclude with observations such as these:

- The meaning of suffering is a question that Christians and people from all religions have struggled with since the dawn of time. Because of Christ's life, suffering, death, and Resurrection, however, Christ has conquered death for all of us which means that death is never the last answer.
- God is present in all parts of life, good and bad, and brings good out of horrible tragedy. We need to be open to God when tough times come our way and try not to get caught up in "Why am I suffering?" but in "How, with God's help, will I get through this suffering? Where will God bring good here?"

Joseph

MOSES

Preparing to Teach

Overview

There has never been a prophet in Israel like Moses; the LORD spoke with him face to face. No other prophet has ever done miracles and wonders like those that the LORD sent Moses to perform against the king of Egypt, his officials, and the entire country. No other prophet has been able to do the great and terrifying things that Moses did in the sight of all Israel.

(Deuteronomy 34:10-12)

Moses is a central figure in the Bible yet he is also someone with whom the students can relate. The very fact that Moses has very human moments reminds us that it is truly God who is working through him in amazing events such as the ten plagues, the parting of the Red Sea, and the receipt of the Ten Commandments.

Moses is born in the midst of nonviolent protest as the midwives refuse to kill baby Israelite boys. His background, an Israelite, and his experience of growing up in the royal Egyptian household prepare him for his role as negotiator between these two peoples.

When God first reveals himself in the burning bush, Moses expresses only insecurities and hesitations about why he would take on such a role. Young people are very familiar with insecure thoughts and feelings. If they listen carefully to this passage, they will hear that God is one who expresses confidence in his people. Prayer is a very good place for them to take such fears.

It could very well be that Moses's own weaknesses enable him to cope with the fragile beliefs of the Israelites who seem to fall back into fear regularly during their escape and sojourn in the desert. When reading Exodus, it is easy to ask, "Why don't the people just trust in God?" Young people will easily relate to the kind of fear that makes it difficult to trust others and God. God, however, is constant throughout the journey despite the doubts and fears of the people, just as he is with Moses.

Because he doubts God, Moses does not enter the Promised Land although God shows it to him. It is clear that Moses is a model to follow not because he is perfect but because he opens his life to God's work.

THIS CHAPTER AT A GLANCE

Getting to Know the Story of Moses

- The Life of Moses: A Chronology
- *The Prince of Egypt*

Getting to Know Moses

- Moses: A Calling
- The Plagues
- The Ten Commandments
- "Holy Ground"

Scripture Passages Related to Moses

- Exodus 2:1-10 (The birth of Moses)*
- Exodus 2:11-25 (Moses escapes to Midian)
- Exodus 3:1-22 (God calls Moses)*
- Exodus 4:1-17 (God gives Moses miraculous power)
- Exodus 4:18-31 (Moses returns to Egypt)
- Exodus 5:1-21 (Moses and Aaron before the King of Egypt)
- Exodus 7-11 (The plagues)
- Exodus 12:1-4 (The Passover)*
- Exodus 14:1-31 (Crossing the Red Sea)*
- Exodus 20:1-17 (The Ten Commandments)*
- Exodus 32:1-35 (The golden calf)*
- Deuteronomy 6:1-9 (The Great Commandment)
- Deuteronomy 34:1-12 (The death of Moses)

Asterisk (*) signifies key passages to cover.

Articles from *Breakthrough!* Related to Moses

- *Breakthrough!* Interview with Moses
- Standing Up for Right (Exodus 2:11-17)
- A God of Many Names (Exodus 3:14)
- Moses's Problem (Exodus 4:1-17)
- *Now* What? (Exodus 5:1-22)
- Not Me, Lord! (Exodus 6:12-13)
- On Being Stubborn (Exodus 8:5-19)
- Promise Breakers and Promise Keepers? (Exodus 9:13-35)

Moses and Young Adolescents Today

- Moses experiences fear, doubt, and concern when he considers the enormity of God's calling. Adolescents are often overwhelmed with the responsibilities of school, social life, and family obligations.
- Moses displays great courage when he approaches Pharaoh with a request to let the Israelites go free. Young people display courage as they move into the adult world.
- The Israelites have faith that is immature. Because of this they complain of the hardships that they experience after being freed from bondage. Students' faith is developing and they will often question why God allows "bad" things to happen.
- God gives Moses the Ten Commandments. These commandments are the framework by which we show love and justice to others.

Moses

Highlighting God's Presence

God said, "Do not come any closer. Take off your sandals, because you are standing on holy ground" (Exodus 3:5).

God said, "I am who I am. You must tell them: 'the one who is called I AM has sent me to you'" (Exodus 3:14).

God spoke, and these were his words: "I am the LORD your God who brought you out of Egypt, where you were slaves.
    Worship no god but me." (Exodus 20:1-3

The LORD said, "I will go with you, and I will give you victory" (Exodus 33:14).

"I, the LORD, am a God who is full of compassion and pity, who is not easily angered, and who shows great love and faithfulness" (Exodus 34:6).

Getting to Know the Story of Moses

The Life of Moses: A Chronology

In this activity, students read or review the story of Moses as they determine the correct chronology provided on a handout.

Preparation

❑ Reproduce enough copies of handout Moses-A, "The Life of Moses: A Chronology," so that each student will have one.

❑ Make sure each student has a Bible.

1. Pass out handout Moses-A, "The Life of Moses," to each student. Give students quiet time to browse through the Book of Exodus so as to be able to put the events listed on the handout in the correct chronological order. Explain that students should also put down the chapter and verse from Exodus that corresponds to each event.

2. After students have finished the activity, divide the class into groups. Assign each group one or two of the events from the handout to explore further. Have the groups summarize the event for a brief oral presentation for the class.

3. Conclude by reviewing the relationship God had with Moses and the Israelites for each event on the handout. Using a scale of one through five (in which one is a distanced relationship and five is a very close relationship), ask the students to rate how close Moses was to God during the major events of this story. (This can be done in the large group, in pairs, or individually.)

Share the following insights with the students in your own words:
- Moses and the Israelites were closest to God when they were following the instructions that God gave them. It might seem that God's instructions and the Ten Commandments limited what the Israelites could do. In reality, the rules helped the Israelites live in freedom.

The Prince of Egypt

Preview and then show students parts of or the entire film *The Prince of Egypt* (Dreamworks, 1998, 99 minutes, rated PG).

In this film, the screenwriter and producer make interesting choices about staying close to the story line. There is quite a bit of imagination given especially to the adolescent relationship between Moses and the Pharaoh's son. Ask students to assess why the filmmakers added material or left it out. They may want to suggest some changes they would make if they were in the position to do so.

Getting to Know Moses

Moses: A Calling

In this activity, students see that God responds with care to Moses's concerns about his own abilities, and to their own now.

Preparation

❑ Make sure each student has a Bible.

1. Share the story about the burning bush as told in Exodus 3. You may want to have three students read the story aloud: a narrator, Moses, and God from the bush.

2. Ask students to list the doubts, fears, and concerns that Moses had about his calling. Have the young people call out what is on their list and make a chart on the board listing these concerns. Next to each concern, ask students to name what the Lord said and did to address Moses's concerns.

3. Give students some quiet time to write about a time in their lives when they experienced doubts about their abilities and have felt inadequate. Did they go to God? How did they handle their fears? Does God promise to help us as he did Moses?

Break Through!

4. In closing, share some of the verses from "Highlighting God's Presence," on page 70 of this manual, to emphasize that God is always with us in difficulty. (See the *Breakthrough!* article "Moses's Problem" for an affirming presentation of God's love for us despite our shortcomings!)

(Adapted from "What If They Won't Believe Me?" in *Old Testament: Seminary Student Study Guide*, p. 43)

The First Nine Plagues

In this activity, students use the genre of cave paintings to illustrate the first nine plagues.

Preparation

❑ Review chapters 7 through 11 in the Book of Exodus and write down the verses that correspond with each plague.

❑ If necessary, provide paper and markers for students.

❑ Find pictures of cave drawings, if possible, to help the students create their own drawings. (An Internet search of "cave paintings" or "pictographs" yields quite a few examples.)

1. Tell the students to imagine that they are cave painters and that they are to draw symbols that represent the plagues sent upon the Egyptians. (In fact, this will be their only way to pass this important story on to future generations so the pictures need to be clear.)

2. Divide the class into nine groups and assign each group a different plague, providing the corresponding verses. Have the students in each group read the passage of Exodus that describes their plague. Next, ask each group to draw a symbolic representation

of their assigned plague in a way that resembles ancient cave drawings. Suggest that they portray a story from left to right, with the first event on the left.

3. When all groups are finished, have them make a display for the classroom, arranging the pictures in proper sequence as they happen in the Scriptures. (You may want to have groups exchange pictures to see if they can interpret the drawings.) If not, you may want a representative from each group to interpret their cave drawings for the class.

4. Ask students to consider the way that God interacts with the Egyptians. What was God's approach? Conclude by highlighting God's mercy when dealing with the Egyptians. He could have immediately destroyed them but he kept giving them many opportunities to acknowledge him and his power. God wants all his children to be faithful and gives us all many chances.

5. After reviewing the first nine plagues, read over the tenth plague with the students, noting both its distinction from the other plagues and its ongoing significance in Judaism.

The Ten Commandments

In this activity students translate the words of the Scripture passage as found in Exodus, chapter 20, into a present-day interpretation of the Ten Commandments.

Preparation

❑ Make sure students have a Bible, paper, and pens or pencils.

❑ You may want a copy of the *Catechism of the Catholic Church.*

1. After reading Exodus, chapter 20, with the class, have the students list God's commands to the Israelites as found in verses 1 through 17 on a piece of paper. Next to each verse, have each student write the commandment in today's language, with a present-day interpretation.

2. Ask students to share their different versions of each commandment, making notes on the board about them. If you would like to, use the index in the *Catechism* or flip through the section called "Life in Christ," to show students how that section of the *Catechism* thoroughly explores what each commandment means personally and socially in a modern context. It is likely that some of their modern translations will be captured in the *Catechism.*

3. Conclude the activity with the following thought:

• God made us in his image and likeness; we each posses a free will. By giving us commandments to live by, God is assisting us in making the right choices in life.

"Holy Ground"

Play the song "Holy Ground" from the CD *Prayer Warrior* (Jeannie Pomanowski, Chesapeake Music Works, 2004, Be Attitude Music, BMI). By appreciating the awesome beauty of God's creation and his presence among us, we can come to realize that like Moses we too are standing on holy ground.

THE LIFE OF MOSES: A CHRONOLOGY

Number the following events in the correct chronological order. After each event, note the chapter and verse from Exodus that describes the event.

_____ The Israelites worship a golden calf.

_____ God calls Moses from a burning bush.

_____ The Passover occurs.

_____ Pharaoh's daughter finds Moses in a basket.

_____ The Israelites cross the Red Sea.

_____ Moses receives the Ten Commandments at Mount Sinai.

_____ Moses kills an Egyptian and escapes to Midian.

_____ God causes problems for Egypt by sending plagues.

_____ The tabernacle is built and dedicated.

_____ Moses begins a confrontational series with Pharaoh by asking for the release of the Israelites.

Aaron

Preparing to Teach

Overview

Aaron, the brother of Moses, is presented in the Scriptures as a true servant of God, second only to Moses in his obedience. When God calls on Moses to lead his people to freedom, Aaron shows his obedience to God and love for his brother by coming to Moses's aid as a spokesperson. Many students will identify with this act of sibling support.

Aaron later succumbs to peer pressure and leads the Israelites in idol worship. Because peer pressure exists in the lives of adolescents, it is important to stress the need to guard our relationship with God rather than succumb to temptation.

This Chapter at a Glance

Getting to Know the Story of Aaron

- All About Aaron

Getting to Know Aaron

- Would You Like Aaron as Your Brother?
- Research on Priestly Clothing

Scripture Passages Related to Aaron

- Exodus 4:14-16,27-30 (God speaks to Moses and Aaron)*
- Exodus 5:1-4 (Moses and Aaron before the King of Egypt)*
- Exodus 7:1-13 (The Lord's command to Moses and Aaron)
- Exodus 29:1-17 (Priestly ordination of Aaron and his sons)*
- Exodus 32:1-35 (The golden calf)*
- Numbers 12:1-16 (Aaron and Miriam are jealous of Moses)
- Numbers 20:22-29 (The death of Aaron)

Asterisk (*) signifies key passages to cover.

Articles from *Breakthrough!* Related to Aaron

- *Breakthrough!* Interview with Aaron and Miriam
- *Now* What? (Exodus 5:1–22)
- The Ten Commandments (Genesis 20:1–17)
- Vestments (Exodus, chapter 28)
- Sinful but Forgiven (Exodus, chapter 32)

Aaron and Young Adolescents Today

- Aaron was the elder brother of Moses and shared in the responsibilities of the Exodus. Adolescents share responsibilities within their own families.
- Aaron displayed courage when addressing Pharaoh. God assures us the same courage when we speak the truth in love.
- Aaron succumbs to peer pressure and erects a golden calf for worship. Peer pressure plays a significant role in the lives of young adolescents.
- God in his infinite mercy forgives Aaron for idol worship. Young people need to believe that God is always ready to forgive us our sins if we are sincere in our sorrow and are willing to repent.
- Aaron and his sister display jealousy toward Moses over his relationship with God and the Israelites. Sibling rivalry and jealousy exist in families.
- Aaron was rewarded for his faith and obedience by being anointed high priest. God rewards us for our faith and obedience with everlasting life.

Highlighting God's Presence

The LORD said, "I am going to make you like God to the king, and your brother Aaron will speak to him as your prophet. Tell Aaron everything I command you and he will tell the king to let the Israelites leave his country" (Exodus 7:1–4).

Moses, Aaron, Nadab, Abihu, and seventy of the leaders of Israel went up the mountain and they saw the God of Israel. Beneath his feet was what looked like a pavement of sapphire as blue as the sky (Exodus 24:9–10).

Getting to Know the Story of Aaron

All About Aaron

In this activity students will identify various terms relating to Aaron's life.

Preparation

☐ Make a copy of handout Aaron-A, "All About Aaron," for each student.

☐ Complete this handout yourself before meeting with the students.

1. Share the scriptural passages below with the students by asking students to take turns reading aloud.
- Exodus 4:14-17,27-31
- Exodus 5:1-5,7:1-7
- Exodus 15:19-20
- Exodus 16:5-7,29-34
- Exodus 28:1
- Exodus 29:38-40

Have the students do a Scripture search of these passages using handout Aaron-A, "All About Aaron." You can have the students do a Scripture search as a whole-class activity, in groups, or on their own. Check the students' answers as a group.

Answers to handout: 1. D; 2. F; 3. E; 4. A; 5. B; 6. C; 7. (H or I); 8. G; 9. (H or I)

Getting to Know Aaron

Would You Like Aaron as Your Brother?

In this activity, students assess Aaron's strengths and weaknesses as a brother. They then reflect on their own strengths in this area as siblings. (For those students who do not have siblings, extend the conversation to include cousins or close friends.)

1. Discuss the relationship Aaron had with his brother, Moses. You may want to include the following questions to spark class discussion:
- Aaron is older than Moses, yet Moses is the leader. Is that fair?
- Moses reprimands Aaron for making an idol and leading the people in worshiping a false god. Was Moses justified in doing this? Why or why not?
- How would you rate Aaron as a brother? Why?
- Which stories about Aaron support the statement, "Aaron is a great brother," and which stories support the statement, "Aaron let Moses down as a brother"?

2. Conclude by having students discuss their sibling relationships. Are they in any way similar to the relationship Moses had with Aaron? Does God's treatment of the brothers shed light on the way brothers and sisters should act today?

Research on Priestly Clothing

Have your students research the clothes that priests wore during
Aaron's time (Exodus, chapter 28) and those that are worn by Roman
Catholic priests during Mass. Explore these questions:

- Are there similarities or mainly differences between the priests'
  clothing?
- What is similar? What is different?
- Why is it important for priests to wear special clothing when
  leading religious rituals?

Aaron

ALL ABOUT AARON

Each of the following items has something to do with Aaron. For each of the numbered items in column A, select a matching lettered item from column B. Place the appropriate letter in the space next to the number.

Column A

1. ＿＿ Temple sacrifices and worship

2. ＿＿ Son who became high priest after Aaron's death

3. ＿＿ Exit or departure

4. ＿＿ Relative of Aaron

5. ＿＿ Tribe from which Aaron was a member

6. ＿＿ Used for the atonement of sin

7. ＿＿ Book containing journey to Canaan

8. ＿＿ Major Jewish holy day

9. ＿＿ Book containing journey to Canaan

Column B

A. Miriam (Exodus 15:19-20)

B. Levi

C. Burnt offering (Leviticus 16:5-7)

D. Priestly duties (Exodus 29:38-46)

E. Exodus

F. Eleazar (Exodus 28:1)

G. Day of Atonement (Leviticus 16:29-34)

H. Deuteronomy

I. Numbers

MIRIAM

Preparing to Teach

Overview

The Exodus is very much a family affair. Brother Aaron and sister Miriam are very important to Moses's success in leading the people out of Egypt. Moses is not the only leader, however. The prophet Micah quotes the Lord as saying, "I sent Moses, Aaron, and Miriam to lead you" (Micah 6:4) to the people of Israel.

Miriam and Aaron can be kindred spirits to many young adolescents who may not be the class leader but do play important roles in school, clubs, teams, and in their families. The importance of being a team player is evident as Miriam helps to save her brother Moses from death.

In addition, as a prophet, Miriam leads the Israelites in their first joyful expression of worship with song and dance that celebrates that Israel was freed *from* slavery *for* worship. Song and dance were, and are today, characteristic expressions of praise and thanksgiving. Far from engaging in solitary worship, it is she who helps unite the people in praise of God.

THIS CHAPTER AT A GLANCE

Getting to Know the Story of Miriam

- Choosing Life and Love

Getting to Know Miriam

- Freedom *From* and Freedom *For!*

Scripture Passages Related to Miriam

- Exodus 2:1–10 (Miriam helps to save baby Moses)*
- Exodus 15:19–21 (The Song of Moses and Miriam) *
- Numbers 12:1–16 (God punishes Miriam for being jealous of Moses)*
- Micah 6:4 (God calls Miriam an Israelite leader)

Asterisk (*) signifies key passages to cover.

Articles from *Breakthrough!* Related to Miriam

- *Breakthrough!* Interview with Aaron and Miriam

Miriam and Young Adolescents Today

- In the Exodus story, Miriam contributes to a rescue effort to save Moses from Pharaoh's decree of death for infant boys. Young people today can relate to the familial experience of doing the right thing for the good of the family.
- Miriam leads the liberated Israelites in expressing their joyful feelings of freedom. Adolescents have probably experienced feelings of freedom in moments of their lives—the first day of summer break, for example.

Highlighting God's Presence

Miriam sang for them:
"Sing to the Lord, because he has won a glorious victory;
  he has thrown the horses and their riders into the sea."

(Exodus 15:20)

They [Moses, Aaron, and Miriam] went and the Lord came down in a pillar of cloud, stood at the entrance of the Tent, and called out, "Aaron! Miriam!" The two of them stepped forward, and the Lord said, "Now hear what I have to say!" (Numbers 12:4-6).

Getting to Know the Story of Miriam

Choosing Life and Love

Miriam is a team player and this activity depicts the efforts of five women working together to bring life to baby Moses, who grows up to save their people. This activity will explore the concept of fear and the actions of Miriam, Moses's mother, Pharaoh's daughter, and the midwives.

Preparation

❑ Write on the board, "I am now giving you the choice between life and death, between God's blessing and God's curse, and I call heaven and earth to witness the choice you make. Choose life" (Deuteronomy 30:19).

1. Read Exodus 1:8—2:10 with the students. Discuss the actions of the midwives (1:15-22). Ask the young people these questions about the story:

○ Do you think that Pharaoh would punish the midwives if he found out what they were doing?

○ Might Pharaoh punish his own daughter for disobeying his command?

○ Could Miriam and her mother fear for their lives?

○ What empowers all of them to choose life for this child?

2. Explore the idea of being "God-fearing" with the students. Have them distinguish between a healthy and an unhealthy fear of God. (For example, respect and awe versus being scrupulous.) Note that options besides being God-fearing would be to be fearful of other human beings, the natural world, or the future. Ask the students to explain why Pharaoh was asking that the boys be killed.

3. Have a young person read aloud "Doing the Right Thing" (Exodus 1:15-22) in *Breakthrough!* Ask the students to think of situations that challenge them to rise above immediate fears and respond in brave, life-giving ways. Note that when one fears God in a healthy way, the fears of other things in life diminish and take their proper perspective. (For example, if we do not revere God and live by his values, it might be unthinkable to risk capture like the midwives do. But, because they value life and believe in God, they believe that the risk is well worth it.)

4. Explain that the passage written on the board was part of Moses's farewell address to the people of Israel before they enter into the Promised Land. Make these comments in your own words:

• The fear of God goes with life and blessing while fears of other types go with death and curse. They fit together this way because a misunderstanding of what is really important (God and life) can lead us to excess fear of this world, to disguise true blessing, and to mistake what is true life. Moses is able to lead the people of Israel to freedom because there were women who conquered fear in order to do the right thing. In choosing life, they changed the world!

Getting to Know Miriam

Freedom *From* and Freedom *For!*

This activity emphasizes that God wants freedom for us as he does for the Israelites in Exodus. In addition, God does not simply want us to be free from enslavement but wants us to be free to be in joyful relationship with him.

1. Read Exodus 5:1-21. Emphasize that the Lord says, "Let my people go, so that they can hold a festival in the desert to honor me" (5:1). Paraphrase this request like this: "*Free* my people from slavery so that they will be *free for* a festival."

2. Discuss with the students some of the reasons why God would have wanted them freed for a celebration that honors God. Pose these types of questions.

- Does *God need* the worship of the Israelites, or rather, do the *Israelites need* to worship God? Why?
- Does *God need* our worship at Mass, or rather, do *we need* to worship God at Mass? Why?

3. Refer back to Genesis 2:1-3 and the concept of Sabbath rest. Engage the students in a discussion about the value of a period of rest. Ask: "How does rest enable us to experience the freedom of being unconditionally loved by God? What about daily life can take away our freedom to be with God?" Ask students to mention elements of our society that have the potential to enslave us and list them on the board.

Ask these follow-up questions:

○ From the reading of Exodus, does God desire for us the enslavement that can happen in our busy weeks?

○ Does God desire the freedom of rest on Sunday when Christians practice the Sabbath?

○ What happens when we take the business of the week and do it on Sunday?

Paraphrase the following thoughts in closing:
- The Exodus story teaches us that not only does God want to free the Israelites and us from different forms of being enslaved, but that God wants us to be free for a celebratory relationship with him. In fact, after the Israelites cross the Red Sea, Miriam is the one who takes out the tambourine to celebrate (Exodus 15:20-21).

4. Ask each student to choose a contemporary song (not necessarily a "church" song) that expresses for them a sense of joyful freedom, of rest, a sense of God's unconditional, liberating love, a sense of goodness and grace in their lives—freedom that makes us want to celebrate!

5. On the board create a CD or play list from the songs that the students chose. With the students, give this class CD or play list a name, for example, "Joy in God's Freedom: Songs of Love and Liberation." Invite them to think of these songs when they feel burdened by stress or do not feel free in some way

Miriam

JOSHUA

Preparing to Teach

Overview

Joshua is portrayed in the Scriptures as a thoroughly heroic character. He leads the successful military conquest of Canaan with a combination of shrewd tactical strategies, complete faith in God, and a charismatic personality. By the end of the Book of Joshua, it is evident that he is an inspiration to others to recommit themselves to God's Covenant.

In some ways, young adolescents may regard Joshua as more legendary in character than in real life. He is portrayed as someone who is very in tune with God, able to discern what God wants the people to do, and courageous enough to lead them. His motto might be for young people, "When going into new situations, take God with you or follow God in."

Young people may be more familiar with the story of Jericho than with Joshua's farewell address and his renewal of the Covenant. But young people can take some of his statements to heart and apply them to their own lives.

> "Any one of you can make a thousand men run away, because the LORD your God is fighting for you, just as he promised. Be careful, then, to love the LORD your God." (Joshua 23:10-11)

> "Now then," Joshua continued, "honor the LORD and serve him sincerely and faithfully. . . . If you are not willing to serve him, decide today whom you will serve, the gods your ancestors worshiped in Mesopotamia or the gods of the Amorites, in whose land you are now living. As for my family and me, we will serve the LORD." (Joshua 24:14-15)

In the first passage, Joshua reminds the Israelites how much God is on their side, working for them, wanting their success. Young people do not always remember that they can count on support from God in whatever they are doing. In the second passage, Joshua challenges the people of Israel to make a commitment, a commitment to serve God. While young people may want to serve God, they may not know what they even mean by that. All Christians need to stop and reflect upon the direction they are going.

Joshua has many heroic qualities. Because of this, he carries some of the credibility of heroes in our own day and age. Young people need to get to know a hero who sees God as his strength and is single-minded in his devotion to him.

THIS CHAPTER AT A GLANCE

Getting to Know the Story of Joshua

- Pictures from the Road: Joshua

Getting to Know Joshua

- Joshua, the Hero
- Permanent as a Rock
- *Josh and the Big Wall*

Scripture Passages Related to Joshua

- Joshua 1:1-9 (God commands Joshua to conquer Canaan)*
- Joshua 3:9-17 (Crossing the Jordan River)
- Joshua 6:1-27 (The fall of Jericho)
- Joshua 7:1-29 (The sin of Aachan and the defeat at Ai)
- Joshua 8:1-29 (The capture of Ai)
- Joshua 11:16-23 (The extent of Joshua's conquest)*
- Joshua 23:1-16 (Joshua gives his farewell address)
- Joshua 24:1-28 (Joshua leads the renewal of the Covenant)*
- Joshua 24:29 (Joshua dies)

Asterisk (*) signifies key passages to cover.

Articles from *Breakthrough!* Related to Joshua

- *Breakthrough!* Interview with Joshua
- Introduction to the Book of Joshua
- Big Shoes to Fill (Joshua 1:1-9)
- Remember When . . . (Joshua 3:14-17)
- The Angel's Promise (Joshua 5:13-15)
- Whose Power Won? (Joshua 6:1-20)
- Courage (Joshua 8:1-2)
- Conquering Canaan (Joshua, chapter 12)
- Older and Wiser (Joshua 13:1-7)
- Remembering God's Goodness (Joshua 24:1-15)

Joshua and Young Adolescents Today

- Moses picks Joshua to be his successor. Joshua is a leader in ways that are both similar to Moses but also different. The young adolescent needs to see a variety of models of heroic faith.

- Joshua's faith in God is shown clearly in his attitudes and actions, despite difficult circumstances and even resistance from others. The student will see from examining Joshua's story of faith the utter faithfulness of God to bring about his promises.
- After the conquest of Canaan Joshua is shown as an equitable leader in his fair distribution of the land to the different tribes. It reminds the reader that we have a responsibility to be fair in all of our dealings with others especially when we are in positions of advantage over them.
- At the end of the book, Joshua convenes the whole people together at Shechem to review their history of salvation. He challenges them to recommit themselves to the Covenant seeing how faithful God has been in the conquest of Canaan. He says, "As for me and my family, we will serve the LORD" (Joshua 24:27). The student can be challenged to ask, "What values does my family stand for? Who or what do we serve in our lives and why?"

Highlighting God's Presence

After the death of the LORD's servant Moses, the LORD spoke to Moses's helper, Joshua, son of Nun. He said, "My servant Moses is dead. Get ready now, you and all the people of Israel, and cross the Jordan River into the land that I am giving them. . . . Joshua, no one will be able to defeat you as long as you live. I will be with you as I as was with Moses. I will always be with you; I will never abandon you" (Joshua 1:1–2,5).

While Joshua was near Jericho, he suddenly saw a man standing in front of him, holding a sword. Joshua went up to him and asked, "Are you one of our soldiers or an enemy?"

"Neither," the man answered. "I am here as the commander of the LORD's army."

Joshua threw himself on the ground in worship and said, "I am your servant, sir. What do you want me to do?"

And the commander of the LORD's army told him, "Take your sandals off; you are standing on holy ground." And Joshua did as he was told (Joshua 5:13–15).

So the LORD gave to Israel all the land that he had solemnly promised their ancestors he would give them. When they had taken possession of it, they settled down there. The LORD gave them peace throughout the land, just as he had promised their ancestors. Not one of all their enemies had been able to stand against them because the LORD gave the Israelites the victory over all their enemies. The LORD kept every one of the promises that he had made to the people of Israel (Joshua 21:43–45).

Getting to Know the Story of Joshua

Pictures from the Road: Joshua

In this activity, small groups of students represent the city or regional news papers that Joshua passes through. See "Pictures from the Road," page 324 in appendix 2, "Tools for Teaching," for the necessary preparation and steps for this activity.

Divide the class into five small groups and assign each group one of the following cities and the story that goes with it:

- The Negev, Wilderness of Zin (Numbers 13:16-31, 14:6-10)
- Mount Nebo, Moab (Deuteronomy 34:5-9)
- Jordan River near Gilgal (Joshua 3:9-17)
- Jericho (Joshua 6:1-27)
- Schechem (Joshua 24:1-28)

Getting to Know Joshua

Joshua, the Hero

In this activity, students identify the qualities that make Joshua a hero and then compare them to other heroes they know.

Preparation

❑ Make sure each student has a Bible.

❑ Prepare for this lesson by looking for examples of heroes in the movies currently showing in theatres and by thinking back over movies that students may have seen recently. Compare them to Joshua in order to draw a modern day comparison and contrast to this hero. If you have access to a VCR or DVD player, you may want to show clips of some of these heroes to liven the discussion.

1. Have students review the major stories in the Book of Joshua and list on paper what heroic qualities he possesses. As a large group, create a list on the board.

2. Divide the class into groups of three and ask students to come up with three to five people who are considered heroes (or heroines). They can be historical figures, currently living people, or heroes portrayed in film or literature. Direct students to make a chart with at least four columns. In the left-hand column, list characteristics they or the class developed for Joshua. Joshua's name should top this list. At the top of three other columns, tell students to place the other heroes that they chose. Have students write plus signs when

their chosen hero has one of Joshua's qualities and minus when he or she does not. (If the chosen heroes have positive qualities not demonstrated by Joshua, they can also make a note of these.)

3. Conduct a discussion around these questions:
- How do these heroes resemble Joshua?
- What could each of these heroes teach each other?
- Are there people that are considered heroes that do not act like heroes?

Have students select the "must have" hero qualities from their list, adding any qualities that students did not see in Joshua. Suggest that they give some modern-day heroes the "hero test" to see if they really qualify.

4. Close by asking a student to read Hebrews 4:8-10 where Joshua's leadership is considered a foreshadowing of Christ's leadership. Ask the students how Joshua inspired his people to keep trusting God? How does Christ inspire us to keep trusting God today?

Permanent as a Rock

Preparation

❑ Find stones at least three inches in diameter, index cards, and markers. Provide twelve stones for every group of two students.

❑ Students need a Bible, paper, and a pen.

❑ Search the Internet for images of monuments to use when talking about stone commemorations.

1. Ask a young person to read Joshua 4:1-24. Emphasize these verses:

And he said to the people of Israel, "In the future, when your children ask you what these stones mean, you will tell them about the time when Israel crossed the Jordan on dry ground. Tell them that the LORD your God dried up the water until you had crossed, just as he dried up the Red Sea for us. Because of this everyone on earth will know how great the LORD's power is, and you will honor the LORD your God forever." (Joshua 4:21-24)

2. Have the students think of stone monuments that they have seen or know of. Many of the monuments may be local but others may be national or international monuments. Ask students why the monuments were there and how they felt looking at the monument and reading any writing that goes with it.

There are many monuments in Washington, DC, that commemorate people or events that happened before the young people were born: the Lincoln Memorial, the Vietnam Veterans Memorial, the U.S. Holocaust Memorial Museum, the U.S. Marine Corps War Memorial Iwo Jima. If you have been to any of these monuments or are able to research them online, you can illustrate the value of monuments by telling the young people "what these stones mean" (Joshua 4:21). By this discussion it is possible to awaken the awe that people feel before a monument that commemorates an important event.

3. Put the students in pairs and pass out twelve rocks to each pair as well as an index card. Give the following instructions in your own words:

- We don't know what kind of memorial the Israelites made, but it was meant to help them remember God. Arrange the rocks that you have into a pattern that stands for God that would help you remember something important you know about God or that God does for us. Write an explanation of what these rocks mean on the card.

4. After the students have prepared and explained their rock patterns to the class, explore the following aspects of the symbolism of rock. Note that rock is powerful for commemorating something because it is so permanent. Rock is also used to refer to faith and God. (Consider reading Matthew 7:24-27, the story of the two house builders, to the students as a New Testament parallel.) Before they clean up the rocks, give students time to say a quick private prayer asking for God to strengthen their faith.

5. In closing, make the following observations:

- In the Book of Joshua, the symbolism of rocks as permanent and solid objects challenge us to think of the way we commemorate important events and to remind us of God's constant presence.

Josh and the Big Wall

Preparation

❑ Obtain a copy of *Josh and the Big Wall* (Warner Home Video, 2003, NR, 30 minutes).

❑ Have a VCR or a DVD player on hand.

1. Ask students to read quietly the account of the fall of Jericho (Joshua 6:1-27) and then view the "Veggie Tales" version of the story. Ask the young people these questions:

  ○ What is the moral of the biblical story?

  ○ What is the moral of the "Veggie Tales" version?

  ○ What can we learn from looking at them side by side?

DEBORAH

Preparing to Teach

Overview

Deborah, a woman of God, is a judge and the type of person to whom people come for advice. She has great faith in what God tells her to do and passes along the Lord's instructions to Barak who leads his troops to victory just as God promises.

Deborah is very confident and is willing to accompany Barak even though she is just as happy to allow him to get all of the credit for the victory. Both she and Barak immediately praise God together upon winning.

For young adolescents, especially young women, Deborah is a reminder that it is God that chooses to speak through people even when cultural norms usually assign these roles to men. Like Joshua, she is in tune with God, secure in what God says, and very appreciative of what he does for her people. She is a good example of a wise, balanced, and faith-filled woman.

THIS CHAPTER AT A GLANCE

Getting to Know the Story of Deborah

- Extra, Extra! Read All About It!

Getting to Know Deborah

- Getting to Know God

Scripture Passages Related to Deborah

- Judges 4:4-5 (Introduction to Deborah, the prophetess and judge)*
- Judges 4:6-9 (Deborah calls on Barak to lead the army)*
- Judges 4:10-16 (Deborah sends Barak to defeat Sisera's army)*
- Judges 4:17-24 (Jael kills Sisera)*
- Judges 5:1-31 (Deborah and Barak sing God's praises)*
- Judges 5:31 (Victory leads to peace in the land for forty years)

Asterisk (*) signifies key passages to cover.

Articles from *Breakthrough!* Related to Deborah

- *Breakthrough!* Interview with Deborah
- A Brave and Wise Woman (Judges 4:1–8)
- Sing a Song (Judges, chapter 5)

Deborah and Young Adolescents Today

- Deborah frequently sits under her favorite "quiet spot," a palm tree where others come to talk to her. Many students have a special place to go where they can think, pray, or relax.
- Deborah's kin and others, including Barak, respect her insights and orders. Students have relatives and friends—parents, grandparents, aunts, uncles, a friend's mom—whom they listen to because they value their perspective.
- Deborah praises and thanks God for the Israelites' victory over the Canaanites. Students thank God for the great and small "victories" in their lives like passing a test or overcoming a fear.

Deborah

Highlighting God's Presence

"The Lord, the God of Israel, has given you this command: 'Take ten thousand men from the tribes of Napthtali and Zebulun and lead them to Mount Tabor'" (Judges 4:6; Deborah to Barak).

Then Deborah said to Barak, "Go! The Lord is leading you! Today he has given you victory over Sisera" (Judges 4:14).

That day God gave the Israelites victory over Jabin, the Canaanite king (Judges 4:23).

Getting to Know the Story of Deborah

Extra, Extra! Read All About It!

Preparation

❑ Supply at least twelve sheets of newsprint.

❑ Provide seven markers, one for the leader and one for each small group.

❑ Make sure each small group has a Bible.

❑ Before the session, write each of the following headings on its own sheet of newsprint:
  • Headline and news story
  • Interview with Deborah
  • Question and answer interview with Barak
  • Question and answer interview with Jael
  • Summary of the battle with Sisera (in bullet form)
  • Analysis of Deborah's canticle
After writing, tear off the six pieces of newsprint and set aside.

1. Divide the class into six small groups. Distribute one piece of newsprint with a heading, one marker, and one Bible to each small group.

2. Instruct the small groups to read the story of Deborah (Judges, chapters 4 and 5) aloud within their group.

3. Tell the small groups that they are going to create a special section of a newspaper on the story of Deborah. Assign one topic to each small group and tell them to write it on the top of the piece of newsprint they received. (There is a second sheet for each group if needed.) Instruct the young people to create and write their news story. Give them 5 to 10 minutes to complete this step.

4. Gather the students back into the large group. Invite someone from each small group to come forward to present their news story. Have them present the stories in the order found above under "Preparation." Ask follow-up questions as necessary.

5. To conclude, note that Deborah was a wise person who was highly regarded by the Israelites. She was wise because she listened carefully to God to learn how the people were to act.

Getting to Know Deborah

Getting to Know God

Preparation

❑ Make sure that each student has a pen, pencil, or thin-line marker.

❑ Make a copy for each student of handout Deborah-A, "Getting to Know God."

1. Note that the Israelites come to Deborah's palm tree when they want to talk to her. It is a special place where she goes to pray to, listen to, talk to, or wait for God. Distribute handout Deborah-A,

"Getting to Know God," and the pens, pencils, or markers to the students and review the directions with them.

2. Give the young people 5 to 10 minutes of quiet time to work on the handout. When they are done, have them gather with two to three people near them, and share their answers, as they feel comfortable.

3. In the large group, ask students to share some of their group's responses. Then ask the entire group the following questions:

○ Which places do you think are the best for being with God? Why?

○ Why is it important to find a good place to pray to, listen to, talk to, or wait for God?

○ Does one place work equally well for relating to God or is it good to find several spots for this relationship?

Deborah

GETTING TO KNOW GOD

For each of the following four statements, list a different place (even if you can relate to God in more than one way in the places). Then, in the same box, write down the reasons you have listed this particular place.

"Pray to God"

"Listen to God"

"Talk to God"

"Wait for God"

GIDEON

Preparing to Teach

Overview

The Scriptures present us with a picture of Gideon as someone who tests God's will. This behavior is quite bold considering God's omnipotence! Young adolescents can display this type of boldness with adults through attitude and appearance and may relate to the character of Gideon.

As Gideon gets to know God and trust him, and as God allows Gideon to come to know him, Gideon grows in trust and acceptance of God's will. Through dialogue with God, Gideon eventually discovers God's plan for his life and then sets out to accomplish this knowing that God will come to his aid. Through prayer students will also come to know God's plan for their lives.

THIS CHAPTER AT A GLANCE

Getting to Know the Story of Gideon

- Gideon the Prayer Warrior

Getting to Know Gideon

- Gideon and God: A Dialogue and Call
- Bullying

Scripture Passages Related to Gideon

- Judges 6:1-11 (The Israelites' relationship to the Midianites)*
- Judges, chapters 11-40 (Gideon asks God for proof)*
- Judges 7:1-25 (Gideon defeats the Midianites)
- Judges 8:1-28 (The final defeat of the Midianites)
- Judges 8:29-35 (The death of Gideon)

Asterisk (*) signifies key passages to cover

Articles from *Breakthrough!* Related to Gideon

- *Breakthrough!* Interview with Gideon
- But Lord . . . (Judges 6:11–16)
- Miracles (Judges 6:17–22,36–40)
- I Will Not Rule Over You (Judges 8:22–23)
- Prayer of a Humble Leader (Judges, chapter 9)

Gideon and Young Adolescents today

- Gideon tests God's will; young adolescents test their parents' wills.
- The people of Israel are fearful of the bullying Midianites. Students fear peers who bully.
- The Lord orders Gideon to rescue Israel but Gideon doubts his ability. Students experience doubt about their abilities.
- The Lord gives Gideon assurance that he will be able to conquer the Midianites. God empowers us to face the difficulties in life with certainty.

Highlighting God's Presence

"The LORD is with you, brave and mighty man!" (Judges 6:12; The Lord's angel speaking to Gideon).

Then the LORD ordered him, "Go with all your strength and rescue Israel from the Midianites. I myself am sending you" (Judges 6:14).

Getting to Know the Story of Gideon

Gideon the Prayer Warrior

In this activity, students familiarize themselves with the story of Gideon and consider the role of prayer in Gideon's military efforts.

Preparation

❑ Make sure each young person has a Bible, paper, and a pen.

1. Divide the class into three groups and assign them each one of chapters six, seven, or eight. Give each group the task of writing a summary of the story of Gideon the warrior as found in their assigned chapter of the Book of Judges. Ask that each summary include a list of the characteristics or qualities that Gideon displays when instructed by God to rescue Israel from the Midianites.

2. Compare and contrast each group's findings. Use these questions for discussion:

- Do Gideon's reactions to God's commands change throughout the story or stay the same?
- Does God influence Gideon's actions? If so, how?

3. Explain to the students that to pray is to talk with God, which makes Gideon's dialogue a prayer. Ask students to discuss how we can be God's warriors. Invite them to identify what makes it possible to accomplish this. Suggest that prayer enables us to become God's warriors. As "prayer warriors" we can work in defeating sin and evil in the world.

Getting to Know Gideon

Gideon and God: A Dialogue and Call

In this activity students will explore the relationship God had with Gideon.

Preparation

❑ Make sure each person has a Bible, paper, and a pen.

❑ Make copies of handout Gideon-A, "Gideon and God: A Dialogue," one per participant.

1. Distribute a copy of handout Gideon-A, "Gideon and God: A Dialogue," to every student. Have students individually fill in Gideon's reply to God's statements by writing down verses from Judges 6:1-40 on the handout.

2. When students are finished, call on them to read their answers aloud. Ask them to summarize Gideon's changing relationship with God. (At first Gideon tests God, and then he becomes obedient to God's will.)

Discuss the following questions with the students:

- How do we respond to God's calling?
- What types of work can we be called to do in order to carry out God's plan? (teachers, priests, nurses, doctors, mothers, fathers)
- How might a dialogue with God look today?

Conclude the activity by asking students in pairs to create an e-mail dialogue with God. What are the similarities and differences between the e-mail dialogue and Gideon's conversation?

Variation

Have students read the article "But Lord . . ." (Judges 6:11-16) in *Breakthrough!* to initiate discussion about what happens when we doubt our own abilities to do what God wants. Ask, "Do you think that saints ever feel that way?"

Bullying

In this activity students draw a comparison between Israel's relationship with the Midianites and the practice of bullying today.

1. Summarize Israel's relationship with the Midianites in Judges, chapter 6.

2. Ask students to suggest words that would describe what is going on in that chapter. (The Midianites were bullying the Israelites.) Have the students define bullying, using their own words.

3. Discuss the following questions with the students:
- How did the Midianites bully the Israelites?
- What was the Israelites' reaction to being bullied? Did they react the same way throughout Gideon's story? (Judges, chapters 7 and 8)
- Did the confrontation that took place between Gideon and the Midianites (Judges 7:19—8:17) come as a result of bullying?
- From this story, what does God's stand on bullying seem to be?

4. Talk with the students about bullying today, using these questions:
- Does bullying exist among your peers?
- Why do people choose to be bullies? Do they have to be or is it a choice?
- Where can you look for God's presence in a situation of bullying?
- How can God help you if you have this experience?

Conclude the discussion with words such as these:
- In the Gideon story, we can see that God defends the Israelites when they are bullied by the Midianites. In addition, God is actively helping Gideon and his men because they certainly do not defeat the Midianites through numbers. In a similar way, God can give you courage to stand up for what is right and to speak out against injustices. When one speaks out against injustices he or she becomes a hero.

GIDEON AND GOD: A DIALOGUE

Read each Scripture passage as stated and then fill in Gideon's response from the passage.

1. Read Judges 6:14–15.
   Gideon's reply:

2. Read Judges 6:16–17.
   Gideon's reply:

3. Read Judges 6:25–27.
   Gideon's action:

4. Read Judges 7:4–8.
   Gideon's action:

5. Read Judges 7:9–18.
   Gideon's action:

Fill in the blanks using the following citation: Judges 8:28.

So _____ was defeated by the _____ and was no longer a threat.

The land was at _____ for _____ years, until Gideon died.

SAMSON

Preparing to Teach

Overview

The story of Samson is a rousing story of a one-man army taking on Israel's enemies, the Philistines. He is heroic but out of control at times as he tries to protect God's people. Young people may be equally horrified and impressed at the violence displayed by this man of God. Once again, the story of Samson is one of growth. It seems that he does not really "get it" until the last moments of his life.

While Samson carries out his spiritual authority to defeat the Philistines primarily through his astounding physical strength, it is not until he is on the verge of losing his life that he realizes that all of his strength comes from God alone and that to God alone he must submit his will. At this point, the powerful Samson asks God very sincerely and humbly for help.

> Then Samson prayed, "Sovereign Lord, please remember me; please, God, give me my strength just this one more time, so that with this one blow I can get even with the Philistines." (Judges 16:28)

As young adolescents mature, the difference between them in size and strength becomes more apparent. Adolescent males, especially, hope to appear masculine and strong. Samson's final realization is a reminder to all of us that physical strength is secondary to the strength we find in faith.

THIS CHAPTER AT A GLANCE

Getting to Know the Story of Samson

- Samson Posters

Getting to Know Samson

- Samson's Anger: Getting Even or Getting Over?
- Fashions for God's Ambassadors

Scripture Passages Related to Samson

- Judges 13:1-24 (An angel announces Samson's birth to his parents)*
- Judges 14:1-20 (Samson marries a Philistine woman who betrays him)
- Judges 15:1-8 (Samson burns down the Philistines' orchards and fields)
- Judges15:9-20 (Samson defeats the Philistines with a donkey's jawbone)*
- Judges 16:4-22 (Delilah betrays Samson)*
- Judges 16:23-31 (The death of Samson and the defeat of the Philistines)*

Asterisk (*) signifies key passages to cover.

Articles from *Breakthrough!* Related to Samson

- *Breakthrough!* Interview with Samson
- A Sneak Preview (Judges 13:2-24)
- Samson in Trouble (Judges 14:15—15:8)
- Be Careful Whom You Trust (Judges 16:4-22)
- Prayer in Despair (Judges 16:23-31)

Samson and Young Adolescents Today

- While it is an angel who tells Samson's parents that their son will be a special person to the people of God, they are likely disconcerted at the way that this plays itself out. Young adolescents want their own parents to have faith in them despite the different phases they go through.
- Samson becomes aware that his strength comes from God. When he forgets the true source of his strength and begins to do things his own way, he gets into trouble. For the young adolescent, this is a cautionary tale of what can happen when one is too focused on one's own strengths and not on God as the source of strength.
- Samson turns to God in his weakest moment and asks God to give him the strength to still serve God's people despite his previous behavior. God's response can be very reassuring for young adolescents who know they can count on God even if they have not recently made the best choices.
- In many ways Samson behaves like an adolescent because he is impetuous, strong-willed, swaggering, and sensual. In his relationships he likes teasing people with jokes and riddles. The young adolescent may easily identify with much of his personality. Young people should see what the cost of such a life can be if it is not left behind in adolescence.

Highlighting God's Presence

The woman gave birth to a son and named him Samson. The child grew and the LORD blessed him. And the LORD's power began to strengthen him while he was between Zorah and Eshtaol in the Camp of Dan (Judges 13:24-25).

Suddenly, the power of the LORD made him strong, and he broke the ropes around his arms and hands as if they were burnt thread (Judges 15:14).

Then Samson prayed, "Sovereign LORD, please remember me; please, God, give me my strength just this one more time, so that with this one blow I can get even with the Philistines" (Judges 16:28).

Getting to Know the Story of Samson

Samson Posters

Preparation

❑ Each student needs to have a Bible.

❑ Copy the readings from "Scripture Passages Related to Samson" onto the board.

❑ Provide the following items for each small group: a large piece of poster board, markers, glue, copy paper, construction paper, and optionally, old magazines, scissors, and stickers.

1. Divide the class into small groups of six people and assign each member of each group one of the reading sections on the board so that within each group, the entire story can be shared. (Adapt the group number, if necessary.)

2. Instruct each student to write a brief summary of their section and then tell the other group members what happens in the story. (These summaries will be attached to the poster later.)

3. Introduce this activity by sharing some thoughts such as these:
• The Book of Judges describes Samson in very dramatic terms. He is physically imposing and dominates all of his war adversaries! In some ways he sounds like a successful professional wrestler or boxer.

4. Distribute to the small groups the supplies you have gathered. Using the general metaphor of a prize fighter, have the students

design a poster presenting the star of the "Biblical Wrestling Association." Each poster should have the following items.

- The letters "BWA" need to appear at the top in some logo design.
- Samson's name and his "wrestling persona" and image need to be in the center of the poster board.
- Biblical citations that describe Samson and some other aspects of the story need to be in the background of the poster.
- A title needs to communicate something of his nature as a judge such as "Judge Samson, the Wild and Woolly Man of God." If you have provided magazines for the students, encourage them to use images or words or letters from magazines as well drawing with markers.
- The "Life of Samson" should be briefly summarized on copy paper with dark markers using a strong headline at the top of each section. (The individual summaries can be cut and pasted together, or rewritten or retyped as one.) If there is not room on the poster itself, these sheets can hang off the sides.

5. Ask a volunteer to summarize the life of Samson and then ask other students to fill in any gaps. Then have each group share their posters and explain the symbols contained within them. If any of the symbols raise questions or issues about the stories, pursue them with the young people.

Getting to Know Samson

Samson's Anger: Getting Even or Getting Over?

Preparation

❑ Each student needs to have a Bible, a pen, and paper.

1. Introduce the activity by noting that the results of Samson's anger present an important lesson for us to learn: just because we feel deeply upset about something does not mean we must react furiously with our anger. Ask the young people these questions:
- Does the Samson story teach us that reacting in anger is the way to solve problems?
- Or does it suggest that striking against others who make us angry causes more problems than it solves?

2. Have a student read Judges 14:5—15:8 aloud to the group and discuss these questions:
- Why is Samson angry and does his angry response solve the problem at hand?

- What in your experience suggests that the "getting even" approach solves problems? How?
- What in your experience suggests that the "getting even" approach does not solve problems? How?
- Can "getting even" create even more problems?

3. Ask the young people to imagine that they are newspaper advice columnists and that Solomon has written in and basically said that he has no idea how to control his anger and to please give advice. Give each student a half a page of copy paper. At the top of the page the student is to finish the phrase "When I feel angry . . ." some way. It should be in large letters, but leaving room in the middle for a picture or image. Below the picture, have the student write a short prayer about using this means of resolving their anger.

4. Create a small book called "When I feel angry, I . . ." based on their responses. After all students have finished the pages collect them, photocopy them, and assemble them in a cover for each student. Distribute the prayer book to other grades if it seems appropriate.

5. After the students have read over each other's ideas, conduct a general discussion about ways to handle anger. Note that anger is often "a secondary emotion." What this means is that we are often angry at something or someone because some deeper emotion has been stirred first: we feel angry because we feel hurt, discouraged, inadequate, betrayed, and so on. To resolve our anger often means resolving another level of feelings too.

Fashions for God's Ambassadors

See the activity by this name on pages 118-119 of this manual. This activity invites students to explore the impact on Samuel of being a nazirite and can be adapted for Samson.

RUTH

Preparing to Teach

Overview

The story of Ruth is a beautiful story of generosity and blessing. Ruth's decision to accompany Naomi back home starts a chain reaction of these blessings, culminating in her marriage to Boaz. Ruth is an ordinary woman, just like the young people who will be studying her, but her example invites all readers to strive for the harmony and kindness demonstrated in her story.

The Kingdom of God is often described as an "already, not-yet" reality. The Book of Ruth beautifully depicts the "already" Kingdom of God in its story of an inclusive, caring, and compassionate community—a people who live in the divine image. This community can be described by the Hebraic term *hesed*, which means "genuine love and kindness." Divine *hesed* is revealed and made incarnate through the loving thoughts, words, and deeds of this human community.

The story can challenge young people to think about whether or not we can create such a wonderful "already" environment in our schools and communities. Could ordinary people doing extraordinary things transform people so completely?

Because Naomi's sons marry foreigners, Ruth is not Jewish. It is interesting that Ruth is one of the ancestors of King David even though she herself is not a descendant of Jacob. The story of Ruth depicts ethnic diversity in the family tree of Israel.

Because many young people are open to people of diverse backgrounds, it may not seem surprising to them to see Ruth's participation in David's heritage. Is her inclusion an invitation to make greater efforts to celebrate everyone's gifts?

THIS CHAPTER AT A GLANCE

Getting to Know the Story of Ruth

- The "Already" Kingdom of God

Getting to Know Ruth

- A Talking Tapestry
- Inside Out and Upside Down

Scripture Passages Related to Ruth

- Ruth 1:1-5 (Introducing the people and the places)*
- Ruth 1:6-22 (Naomi's sad situation and Ruth's generous response)*
- Ruth 2:1-23 (Ruth gathers grain in Boaz's field)*
- Ruth 3:1-16 (Ruth seeks to marry Boaz)*
- Ruth 4:1-12 (Ruth marries Boaz)*
- Ruth 4:13-22 (Boaz and Ruth's descendants)

Asterisk (*) signifies key passage to cover.

Articles from *Breakthrough!* Related to Ruth

- *Breakthrough!* Interview with Ruth
- Introduction to the Book of Ruth
- When Bad Things Happen (Ruth, chapter 1)
- Caring for Poor People (Ruth 2:1-3)
- A Good Reputation (Ruth 2:11-12)
- Marriage Then and Now (Ruth 4:1-12)

Ruth and Young Adolescents Today

- Ruth enters a new environment and the members of the community warmly welcome her. Young people may have experienced being a new member of a community or welcoming someone into their cluster of school or neighborhood friends.
- Ruth remains loyal to a family member in a difficult situation. It may be easier for Ruth to respond in a different way, but her character guides her decision making. Young people may have had situations in which defending a family member would have proved difficult. Their character guides their response to the situation. See "A Good Reputation" in *Breakthrough!*
- Naomi feels that God has "dealt harshly" with her because of the death of her husband and sons. Difficult situations can prompt similar feelings in the life of a young person. See "When Bad Things Happen" in *Breakthrough!*
- Ruth and Naomi are dependent on the compassion and care of a community when difficulties necessitate their move to Bethlehem. The face of poverty and homelessness is familiar to many students through the news media or direct experience.

Highlighting God's Presence

Some time later Boaz himself arrived from Bethlehem and greeted the workers, "The Lord be with you!"

"The Lord bless you!" they answered (Ruth 2:4).

The leaders and the others said, "Yes, we are witnesses. May the LORD make your wife become like Rachel and Leah, who bore many children to Jacob. May you become rich in the clan of Ephrath and famous in Bethlehem" (Ruth 4:11).

So Boaz took Ruth home as his wife. The LORD blessed her, and she became pregnant and had a son (Ruth 4:13).

Getting to Know the Story of Ruth

The "Already" Kingdom of God

Preparation

❏ Students need bibles and pens or pencils.

❏ Write across the top of the board the words, "Ordinary to Extraordinary."

❏ Draw on the board a large hexagon. Allow enough room so that you could add an outside triangle to each facet of your hexagon and not go off the board. Putting one outside triangle on each facet of the hexagon will create the Star of David. Do not reveal this but allow the students to discover it. Write in the center of this hexagon the name of your school, church, or civic community.

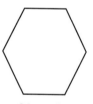

❏ Make each student a copy of handout Ruth-A, "Extraordinary Blessings."

1. Read the Book of Ruth aloud to the students. Note that Ruth by going with her mother-in-law exceeds what would have been culturally expected, and that her action initiates a biblical book about blessings.

2. Pass out handout Ruth-A, "Extraordinary Blessings," to the students. Ask them each privately to look up the passages on the top half of the handout and follow the directions provided. Check the students' answers with them when they are done.

The answers for the handout: Naomi blesses and looks out for Ruth (1:8-9). Ruth, in turn, blesses and attends to the needs of Naomi (1:16-18, 2:17-18). Boaz extends blessing and kindness to Ruth (2:5-16, 3:10-13). Ruth responds to Boaz (2:13, 3:9-10). Boaz provides for the needs of Naomi (3:17). Naomi blesses and plays "matchmaker" for Boaz and Ruth (2:19-20, 3:1-4). The people of Bethlehem extend blessings and kindness to each other (2:4, 4:11-17).

3. Note that Ruth's determination to be loyal and loving shines through the biblical pages as an example for ordinary people to respond in extraordinary ways. Engage the students in a discussion about community life and the everyday, ordinary activities that create a sense of goodness within us.

4. Bring the students' attention to the hexagon on the board and on their handouts. Solicit from the students six ways that a person can bless the community. Along the lines inside of this hexagon write each of the six activities that bless a community. (An example of this would be to pick up one's own litter and dispose of it properly.) Invite the students to copy the same activities onto their handouts.

5. Choose one activity from the hexagon out of the six, such as "picking up one's own litter," and draw a triangular shape as shown below. Ask the students to take each of the six actions or characteristics, which would be considered ordinarily good, and go further with it to make it extraordinary. Some ideas for the litter example might be (1) picking up the garbage that others have left behind, (2) taking the time to place recyclables in assorted receptacles, or (3) working on a beautification project. Write the ideas of your students within the boundaries of the triangle.

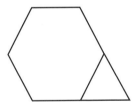

6. Repeat step 2, adding five additional triangles to your hexagon until you have created a shape that depicts the Star of David. Note to the students that this star began in the ordinary actions of a community. The beams of light that extend from the star are filled with extraordinary good deeds that reflect God's love in the world today.

Note that the triangle is also a symbol of our Trinitarian God, in whose image we are created. Our understanding of God is that of three "persons" who dynamically give and receive love. God is a community of love. We "image" God when we give selflessly to others and receive their love in turn.

7. Offer the image often used by theologians that the kingdom of God is an "already, not-yet" reality. Close with these thoughts:

○ On the one hand, we are clearly "not yet" in heaven, but there are times, such as when an ordinary person does extraordinary things, that we experience the Kingdom of God as "already" here.

Getting to Know Ruth

A Talking Tapestry

Preparation

❏ See the Saint Mary's Press Web site for links that will allow you to familiarize yourself with stories of some of the immigrants to the United States or do an Internet search using "Ellis Island."

❏ Find the poem "The New Colossus," by Emma Lazarus, which is easily found on the Internet. One place to look is the National Park Service Web site.

❏ **Something to Consider.** This activity talks about ancestors and their arrival in America. While many students of European descent and from other places arrived through Ellis Island, the topic of ancestors coming to America can be painful for those students whose forbearers were forced to come here because of slavery, persecution, or perhaps are illegally here. If you sense that this conversation might affect students quite differently, you might consider either addressing that difference head on by focusing on the different ways that people are received in a new land or you might want to spend your time emphasizing the diversity aspect of this activity.

1. Students should be familiar with the Statue of Liberty, Ellis Island, and the idea of the United States as a "melting pot" of cultures. Suggest that today, we might more appropriately engage the metaphor of a "tapestry" that is richly woven with multihued cultural threads indicative of the diversity of American society. This tapestry can be imaginatively seen through the stories of human experience.

2. Read "The New Colossus," by Emma Lazarus, to your students and focus on the line that states, "give me your tired, your poor, your huddled masses."

3. Engage the students in dialogue about the experience of being an immigrant to the United States. Ask the students the following types of questions:

- Do you have relatives, neighbors, or friends who have come to the United States from another country?
- When did your family come to this country? How did they come?
- Did these people experience a warm welcome and blessings as Ruth did in the biblical story? What kind of effect did that have on their experience?
- What is the value of welcoming people of different ethnicities into our national story?
- How is the United States enriched by people of other lands?

4. Ask the students to get into groups and discuss ways that the United States can live out the biblical ideal of hospitality and welcome illustrated in the Book of Ruth. The biblical story says that the whole town became excited at Naomi's return with Ruth (Ruth 1:19) and Boaz welcomed the foreigner, Ruth, with advice and a means of work (Ruth 2:5-17). After 5 to 10 minutes of small group discussion, bring the larger group together and write their ideas on the board using an assortment of colored markers or chalk.

5. Bring closure to this activity by discussing why God chose a foreign-born woman to play a significant role in the story of Israel, and by extension, the Christian story (Matthew 1:2-6). The Book of Ruth introduces a brilliant and blessed ethnic thread into the tapestry of Judeo-Christian history.

Inside Out and Upside Down (see activities in "Getting to Know Sarah")

This activity from the chapter on Sarah can be revisited for the story of Ruth. Once again, God is revealed as a God of surprises who invites a foreign woman to play a significant role in the story of salvation. Ruth is the only book of the Bible that is named for a foreign (not Israelite) woman.

EXTRAORDINARY BLESSINGS

Look up the following passages in the Book of Ruth and briefly explain how one person blesses another in these verses. (There may be more than one blessing going on at one time!)

Ruth 1:8-9
Ruth 1:16-18, 2:17-18
Ruth 2:5-16, 3:10-13
Ruth 2:13, 3:9-10
Ruth 3:17
Ruth 2:19-20, 3:1-4
Ruth 2:4, 4:11-17

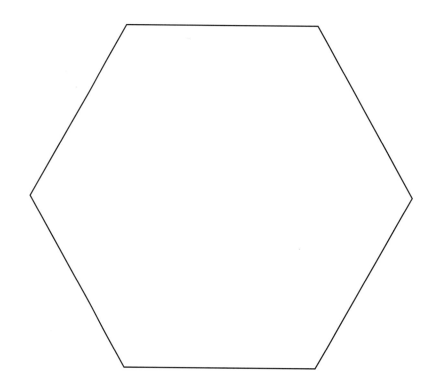

SAMUEL

Preparing to Teach

Overview

Samuel is a wonderful biblical figure with a beautiful call from God and an important role in the transition from the era of the judges to the kingdom. His in-tune connection with God and courage to do God's will provides young adolescents with a figure who "does it really right."

His true commitment to God and to the people he serves is very impressive. He is very fair, a quality that many young people value especially in the adults with whom they come into contact. He is also very upfront about who he is because he follows the nazirite rules of not cutting his hair and avoiding alcohol. Young people can admire Samuel because he "walks his talk" or stands up for what he believes.

Although God does not want Israel to have a king, God allows the people to make this decision that eventually comes back to haunt them. Samuel must stand aside and watch this happen. (His own sons disappoint him, however, which is part of what leads Israel to ask for a king.) He must also communicate God's displeasure to Saul whom he first anoints as king. Students will be able to empathize with the disappointment Samuel must have felt after Saul proved not to be a good king.

Samuel's upright conduct, prayerful connection with God, and courage to rely on God as his strength brings much good during his lifetime. Young people need to be reminded that they can only control their own actions and attitudes. What goes on outside them is often out of their control.

THIS CHAPTER AT A GLANCE

Getting to Know the Story of Samuel

- A Samuel Time Line Game

Getting to Know Samuel

- Dedicated to God
- Fashions for God's Ambassadors

Scripture Passages Related to Samuel

- 1 Samuel 1:1-18 (Hannah prays for a son)*
- 1 Samuel 1:19-28 (Samuel is born and Hannah brings him to the house of the Lord)*
- 1 Samuel 2:18-21 (Hannah's visits to Samuel)
- 1 Samuel 3:1-18 (The Lord appears to Samuel)*
- 1 Samuel 3:19-21 (Samuel becomes known as a prophet)
- 1 Samuel 7:2-14 (Samuel prays for victory over the Philistines)*
- 1 Samuel 7:15-17 (Samuel as judge)
- 1 Samuel 8:4-21 (The people ask Samuel for a king)*
- 1 Samuel 10:17-25 (Samuel announces Saul as king)
- 1 Samuel 12:1-25 (Samuel's final address to the people)*
- 1 Samuel 15:10-11 (God rejects Saul as king)
- 1 Samuel 16:1-13 (Samuel anoints David as king)

Asterisk (*) signifies key passages to cover.

Articles from *Breakthrough!* Related to Samuel

- *Breakthrough!* Interview with Samuel
- Introduction to First Samuel
- I'm Praying Really! (1 Samuel 1:12–18)
- Two Women at Prayer (1 Samuel 2:1–10)
- Speak, Lord (1 Samuel 3:1–10)
- Stealing Has Consequences (1 Samuel, chapter 5)
- Who's the King? (1 Samuel, chapter 8)
- Being Anointed (1 Samuel 10:1)
- A Simple Choice (1 Samuel 12:13–15)
- Who Do You Think You Are? (1 Samuel 15:17–25)
- The Heart of the Matter (1 Samuel 16:1–13)

Samuel

Samuel and Young Adolescents Today

- Samuel has a distinctive grooming pattern of long, uncut hair that marks him as one dedicated to God. Young adolescents are very fashion-conscious and are figuring out what they like to wear and at times are experimenting with the effect that these clothes have on other people.
- Samuel's sorrow over Saul's departure from God's path resembles the young adolescent's experience of watching friends take a wrong turn.
- Samuel was widely hailed in Israel for his fairness in settling disputes. Young adolescents prize fairness and justice in others, though they may not be so consistent in being that way themselves.

Highlighting God's Presence

In those days, when the boy Samuel was serving the LORD under the direction of Eli, there were very few messages from the LORD, and visions from him were quite rare. . . . Before dawn, while the lamp was still burning, the LORD called Samuel. He answered, "Yes, sir!" and ran to Eli and said, "You called me, and here I am."

But Eli answered, "I didn't call you; go back to bed." So Samuel went back to bed.

The LORD called Samuel again . . .

The LORD called Samuel a third time . . .

Then Eli realized it was the LORD who was calling the boy, so he said to him, "Go back to bed; and if he calls you again, say, 'Speak, LORD, your servant is listening.'" So, Samuel went back to bed.

The LORD came and stood there, and called as he had before, "Samuel! Samuel!"

Samuel answered, "Speak; your servant is listening" (1 Samuel 3:1-10).

Then he [Samuel] prayed to the LORD to help Israel, and the LORD answered his prayer. While Samuel was offering the sacrifice, the Philistines moved forward to attack; but just then the LORD thundered from heaven against them. They became completely confused and fled in panic (1 Samuel 7:9-10).

But the LORD said to him [Samuel], "Pay no attention to how tall and handsome he is. I have rejected him, because I do not judge as people judge. They look at the outward appearance, but I look at the heart" (1 Samuel 16:7).

Getting to Know the Story of Samuel

A Samuel Time Line Game

Preparation

❏ Write the twelve citations about Samuel from "Scripture Passages Related to Samuel" on the board or in a visible place.

❏ Each student needs to have a Bible and a pen.

❏ Provide enough index cards so that each group of three young people can have twelve cards.

1. Introduce Samuel by noting that the Scripture passages about him cover his childhood, parts of his adulthood, and parts of his old

age. Explain that to help them learn something about all the parts of his life, the young people will make a card game based partly on the card game known as "Concentration" or "Memory."

2. Divide the class into groups of three participants. Make sure there are twelve index cards per group. Ask the students to read each of the twelve Scripture passages on the board. Instruct them to summarize each of the twelve readings on the cards provided. The other side of the cards should remain blank.

3. After each group has created their "deck" of the twelve events, have them shuffle the cards and then exchange decks (face down) with another group so that each group has a new set of cards. Each group then lays out the twelve cards face down in a three by four rectangle on their table.

4. Explain the object of the game, which is to find TWO pairs of matching cards that describe Samuel's boyhood, ONE pair of matching cards that describes an event from his adulthood, and TWO pairs of matching cards that record events from when he is old. Players should take turns turning over pairs of cards to find ones that match the categories, but they must find the cards in chronological order from Samuel's boyhood through his adulthood to his old age!

If a player guesses incorrectly, he or she replaces the card and gives the next player a chance. Players can only turn over one pair of cards each time, even if they get one match right. The winner, of course, is the first one to get the right number of matched cards from all three parts of Samuel's life.

Note: The boyhood cards are the first four Scriptures listed (1 Samuel 1:1—3:18); the adult cards are the next three listed (1 Samuel 3:19—7:17); the old age cards are the final five (1 Samuel 8:4—16:13).

Getting to Know Samuel

Dedicated to God

Preparation

❑ Each student needs to have a Bible, some loose-leaf paper, and a pen.

1. Have the students read 1 Samuel 1:1-28. Review the reading with these questions:
- What is Hannah praying for?
- What is her promise if her prayer is answered?
- What does Samuel's name mean?
- What does Hannah do with Samuel to fulfill her promise?

2. Make these observations in your own words:

- Samuel's early life is based on a promise that his mother makes before God. She tells God that if she conceives a child, she will "dedicate" or hand over the child to God's service. Hannah is pretty amazing to say, "God, I really want to have a baby so I give him to you!" This idea of dedicating or committing oneself to God is commendable but also daunting.

3. Ask the young people to discuss the following questions:

- What does it mean for Hannah to dedicate Samuel to the Lord?
- To what do people dedicate themselves to today? Why?
- What are the signs that they are dedicating themselves?
- Are you dedicated to anything?
- How would someone know if you are?

4. Instruct the students to examine the contents of their wallets or purses. (If they do not have one of these with them, have them think of their backpack, pencil case, a drawer at home, or another location that holds valuables.) After they have done a thorough inventory of what these contained, ask the young people to consider these questions privately or to share depending on the environment of the group:

- What would be the hardest thing from your wallet or purse for you to willingly surrender to someone?
- Would it be easier to give it up if that someone promised you "something better in return" (even if they did not tell you what that would be)?
- Why would it be hard to dedicate that particular item to another person?
- Under what conditions would it be possible for you to surrender it?

5. Have the students briefly reflect in writing about what they hope to dedicate or commit their lives to in the future and why they might want to do this. After they have written the reflections, either invite them to share their reflections or you, the teacher, can share your own sense of being dedicated to God or surrendered to his will. Share these types of thoughts:

- At this time in your life, you are mainly on the receiving end of things as you depend on your parents and teachers to guide and support you as you grow up. As a family member, a team member, a participant in a dance troupe, or a part of a school, you are learning what it means to hand yourself over for the sake of others. Hannah is a wonderful model of someone who loves selflessly enough to share a baby she desires so much and can be a model of the person we all want to become.

6. Close by reading parts of Hannah's prayer of gratitude, 1 Samuel 2:1-10.

Fashions for God's Ambassadors

Preparation

❑ Each student needs a Bible, loose-leaf paper, plain copy paper, markers, and a pen.

❑ Bring in some fashion magazine ads or ask the young people to bring them in if they do not mind having them cut up.

1. Have the students read 1 Samuel 1:9-11, 2:24-28. Ask the young people the following questions to check their understanding of the passages:

○ What kind of son does Hannah want to raise? (A nazirite. Being a nazirite means having no hair cuts and no alcohol. One completely dedicates oneself to God.)

○ How do you imagine nazirites were able to take care of their hair?

○ What else does Samuel wear to show he is a nazirite? (Samuel wears a sacred linen apron his mother makes for him.)

2. Share some of the following thoughts in your own words:

- Samuel's hair, apron, and lifestyle clearly identify him as one living a vowed life to God. One would observe by his hair and realize by his avoidance of alcohol that he is one specially set apart for God's service.

- A nazirite could not pretend that he was not one of God's "ambassadors" in the world. People could expect you to live a faithful life because of how you looked. The expectation is probably similar to the one people have for a priest wearing a clerical collar or a sister wearing a habit.

- We communicate something about our values in the way that we dress and groom ourselves. Our clothes and appearance can be seen by others as a sign that we respect or do not respect ourselves. We must be careful, however, about stereotyping people based on how they look.

3. Ask the young people to write down their favorite piece of clothing that is not a T-shirt and to explain why it is their favorite in two to three sentences. Then ask them to do the same with their favorite T-shirt. Afterward, ask students to answer this question: "When I wear this piece of clothing in public, do other people receive a message about what I value or who I am?"

4. Pass out the magazines that you have brought in so that the young people can look at them in twos and threes. (Make sure that there are sufficient examples of men's fashions if you have both sexes in your group.) Have the young people pick three advertisements for clothing or hair products. On the loose-leaf paper, have them answer these questions for each advertisement:

- What values are promoted by these hair and clothing choices?
- How do these fashion choices affect how people look at those who use them?

5. Share some of the following ideas with the young people:

- Samuel's appearance and alcohol avoidance clearly reveal his values as someone dedicated to God. Whether or not you believe that other people receive messages about you from what you wear, the fact is that they do.
- God tells Samuel that he is not to judge solely by appearance for God judges the heart rather than by outward appearance. Clothing should not determine your assessment of another person.
- The clothing industry is not promoting Christian values in clothing but rather is trying to make money through sales. Given that, you might need to make an extra effort to communicate your Christian values through your clothing purchases.

6. Ask the young people to suggest ways that they know that another person is Christian from their clothing. (The answers might include Christian jewelry, T-shirts with Christian logos, and so on.)

7. Pass out the markers and copy paper to the students. In pairs, ask the young people to design a piece of Christian clothing or jewelry. (Challenge them to take their favorite pieces of clothing and give it a Christian twist.) After designing their piece of clothing or jewelry, have the students explain their images to each other.

8. Conclude the activity with the following questions:

○ Can a follower of Jesus be fashion-conscious and faith-conscious?

○ Might you make some wardrobe changes in order to fit both descriptions?

SAUL

Preparing to Teach

Overview

The story of King Saul is somewhat difficult to read since it narrates the failure of a man called by God. While Saul does not seem to be a bad person initially, as he moves away from God, he continues to slip into more unusual behavior and finally takes his own life.

Young adolescents are beginning to learn about the characteristics of a strong leader. Cleary, a biblical leader such as Joshua keeps his eyes on God at all times and listens to prophets sent to him. Saul allows his jealousy of David to take over. God's spirit is with David but it departs from Saul.

It appears that mental illness may contribute to Saul's failure rather than simply sinful choices. Because we do not know for sure what led him to suicide, Saul's story becomes an opportunity to talk with young people about mental illness, its signs, and what a person can do if they see such signs in themselves or others.

THIS CHAPTER AT A GLANCE

Getting to Know the Story of Saul

*   The Rise and Fall of Saul

Getting to Know Saul

*   From Nobody to King—The Perils of Fame
*   Music and the Soul

Scripture Passages Related to Saul

*   1 Samuel 9:1-18; 10:1,17-24 (Samuel encounters Saul and anoints him as king)*
*   1 Samuel 13:1-14 (Saul's disobedience over the sacrifice)
*   1 Samuel 15:1-26 (Saul is rejected as king)*
*   1 Samuel 16:14-23 (David in Saul's court as harpist)*

- 1 Samuel, chapter 17 (David defeats Goliath)
- 1 Samuel 18:6-16 (Saul is jealous of David)*
- 1 Samuel 22:1-22 (The slaughters of the priests)
- 1 Samuel 24:1-23 (David spares Saul's life)*
- 1 Samuel 26:1-25 (David spares Saul's life again)
- 1 Samuel 28:3-19 (Saul consults a medium)
- 1 Samuel 31:1-11 (Saul commits suicide)*

Asterisk (*) signifies key passages to cover.

Articles from *Breakthrough!* Related to Saul

- *Breakthrough!* Interview with Saul
- "Do Whatever You Think Best" (1 Samuel, chapter 14)
- Who Do You Think You Are? (1 Samuel 15:17-25)
- The Power of Music (1 Samuel 16:14-23)
- Taking a Big Risk (1 Samuel, chapter 17)
- The Jealousy Monster (1 Samuel, chapter 19)
- Innocent Blood (1 Samuel, chapter 22)
- Respect (1 Samuel, chapter 22)
- Calling Up the Dead (1 Samuel, chapter 28)
- A Tragic End (1 Samuel, chapter 31)

Saul and Young Adolescents Today

- As king, Saul struggled to make the right leadership decisions. Students may be in positions of responsibility and find themselves struggling to do the right thing. Through examining Saul the student observes qualities that make a good leader and a poor leader.
- Saul's impatience gets him into much trouble. Students struggle with being patient as well.
- Saul is jealous of David's success and fame among the people of Israel. He even tries to kill David! Students struggle with feelings of inferiority, especially when they initially have established themselves with some confidence within a certain group. Students need tools to effectively deal with feelings of inferiority and jealousy.
- Saul lets his temper get the best of him; he even knows he should not be so obsessed over hunting down David, but he cannot help himself. The Bible says that "an evil spirit" comes upon him. Students know how wildly their own moods can swing. Students need guidance so they don't feel powerless in the face of their intense feelings.

Saul

- Saul commits an act of unprovoked aggression against the priests of Nob and the innocent inhabitants. This may or may not surprise young adolescents who witness quite a bit of violence on television and in movies.
- Saul consults a witch about his fate. Saul discovers the occult to be a dangerous and despairing source of spiritual exploration. Young adolescents need to be made aware of the dangers of the occult, but in a matter-of-fact and low-key way.
- Saul's despair and suicide, unfortunately, may not be too far removed from the experience of some students. The topics of suicide and mental illness should be seen in the light of God's love and mercy.

Highlighting God's Presence

The LORD said to Samuel, "I am sorry that I made Saul king; he has turned away from me and disobeyed my commands" (1 Samuel 15:10).

The LORD said to Samuel, "How long will you go on grieving over Saul? I have rejected him as king of Israel" (1 Samuel 16:1).

Saul was afraid of David because the LORD was with David but had abandoned him (1 Samuel 18:12).

Getting to Know the Story of Saul

The Rise and Fall of Saul

In this text, students create a living time line representing Saul's life and his downfall.

Preparation

❑ Each student needs to have a Bible, the list of readings from "Scripture Passages Related to Saul" which you may want to place on the board.

❑ Bring in enough index cards so that each young person can have eleven.

❑ Each student needs a pen and paper.

1. On a white board or butcher paper, draw a long, downward curving line like this:

2. Ask the students to quietly read the eleven sections you have written on the board. After reading the eleven sections, the students should write a brief description of the action for that section. Indicate that eventually, a group of students from the class will place one of the eleven cards describing the downfall of Saul on the correct chronological spot on the line but first every student will organize their own timeline individually. Students can also read *Breakthrough!* articles about Saul for more background.

Break Through!

3. After each student has determined the order in which they would place their cards on the time line, assign eleven students to a team and give each one the task of representing one of the eleven readings.

Ask the members of the team to line themselves up from Saul's high point to his low point without using any of the index cards or sneaking any peeks at their own materials. (If a student goes out of order, ask for a volunteer from those sitting to put the next event in!) Each representative should tell the part of the story that they represent.

Talk with the students about how Saul's life, circumstances, and mental state go downhill.

4. Conclude the activity by asking the students these questions:

○ What is a tragedy? One definition is "a medieval narrative poem or tale typically describing the downfall of a great man" (*Merriam Webster's Collegiate Dictionary*, 11th ed., s.v. "tragedy").

○ What makes a character a "tragic figure"?

○ Does Saul's tragedy have to end as it does? Why or why not?

○ What are some modern-day tragedies?

○ Are there ways to recognize and then stop contributions that we make to tragedies whether for ourselves or others?

Variation

Review David's life, showing how David's life rises rather than declines. Use another line on the board, only make it start low and cross over Saul's life at a critical event: David's defeat of Goliath. See "Life on the Road with David" on pages 128–129 of the next chapter for a similar journey approach to the life of Israel's King David.

Getting to Know Saul

From Nobody to King—The Perils of Fame

In this activity, students use Saul's story in order to contemplate the potential perils of having celebrity status.

Preparation

❏ Students will need a Bible, paper, pens, scissors, and glue.

❏ Provide the students with magazines such as *Teen People*, *People*, and other publications that feature movie celebrities. You could also ask the young people to bring in magazines if they do not mind cutting them up.

1. Ask students to read 1 Samuel, chapters 9, 13, and 15 quietly to themselves. Then ask the students to reflect in writing on the question, Why do you think Saul does what he does in these chapters?

2. Ask students to suggest characteristics of these different lifestyles and list their responses on the board.

                Ordinary Life   Celebrity Life

3. Encourage students to reflect on these questions in a large-group discussion:
- Which of these terms best describes Saul's life? Why?
- Does Saul use his fame well or not? Why?
- The biblical concept of leadership involves listening to God and serving God's people. Does Saul fit this description or not? How do you know?

4. Distribute a magazine to each student. Have them find pictures that fit each of the characteristics on the board. Ask the students these questions:

    ○ What are the risks of celebrity life?

    ○ What does it cost to be famous?

    ○ How would this magazine be different if all the people in it were leaders according to God's definition?

Music and the Soul

Preparation

❏ Each student needs a Bible, a pen, and paper.

❏ Bring in CDs with a variety of musical styles on them and a CD player.

❑ Invite students to bring in instruments if they are musicians, or bring in your own.

1. Read 1 Samuel, chapter 16 aloud to the students. Note that David plays the harp to ease Saul's troubled mind. Suggest that music has a profound effect on us and that the effect differs depending on the type of music.

2. Ask your students to number a piece of scrap paper with the number of musical styles you have prepared plus those of any students who have brought their instruments.

3. Play selections from the different CDs in the order that students wrote them down. As you present several different types of music, ask the students to write down how they feel when they hear each piece of music next to the selection number on their scrap paper.

4. Return to the passage about Saul and David. Ask this question:
• Of the selections that we heard today, which ones do you think would have eased Saul's mind and would have been the type of music David might have played for him. Why?
Invite discussion from the students about the impact of music on the spirit, utilizing the expertise of the student musicians present.

5. Have students write down five to ten songs that bring them joy or hope. (Suggest that they include some of the Christian popular music that they may know or Catholic liturgical music.) Invite students to keep such music close at hand, if possible at home, for days that are struggles.

Saul

DAVID

Preparing to Teach

Overview

David is one of the Bible's most colorful and charismatic figures. He fights Goliath with God's strength, is a musician whose playing calms souls, is an accomplished soldier, and yet is a sinner like us.

When David dodges Saul's efforts to kill him, he tries to reconcile his respect for Saul as God's anointed one with his own safety. David has experienced Saul's instability.

In King David, young people can see a leader who is sinful despite his greatness but also one who repents of his sin and accepts its consequences. While his crime against Bathsheba and Uriah is very wrong, he accepts that he will lose a loved one as a just consequence for his actions. It is this sincere remorse for the failures in his life that makes David so appealing to us.

During his reign as king, David needs to align his plans with God's plan. At one point David expresses a desire to build a temple. God's plans for David do not include the building of a temple. In a similar way, it is important for young people to pray and see if their own plans fit in with God's plan for them.

THIS CHAPTER AT A GLANCE

Getting to Know the Story of David

- Life on the Road with David

Getting to Know David

- David and Goliath
- Psalms and Rap

Scripture Passages Related to David

- 1 Samuel 16:1-13 (Samuel anoints David as king)*
- 1 Samuel 17:41-54 (David defeats Goliath)*

- 1 Samuel 18:1-16 (Jonathan and David become friends; Saul is jealous of David)
- 1 Samuel 24:1-22 (David spares Saul's life)
- 2 Samuel 2:1-7 (David is made king of Judah)*
- 2 Samuel 5:1-16 (David becomes king of Israel and Judah)*
- 2 Samuel 7:1-17 (Nathan's message to David about a temple)*
- 2 Samuel 11:1-27 (David seduces Bathsheba)*
- 2 Samuel 12:1-15 (Nathan's message and David's repentance)
- 1 Kings 2:10-12 (The death of David)

Asterisk (*) signifies key passages to cover.

Articles from *Breakthrough!* Related to David

- *Breakthrough!* Interview with David
- Torn Apart (2 Samuel 1:1-12)
- Jerusalem, the Holy City (2 Samuel 5:6-9)
- It's a Party! (2 Samuel 6:12-23)
- An Eternal Kingdom (2 Samuel 7:12-29)
- Facing the Truth (2 Samuel, chapters 11-12)
- Fathers and Sons (2 Samuel 13:1-21)
- If Only (2 Samuel 18:33)
- The Man Whom God Made Great (2 Samuel, chapter 14)
- Good Advice (1 Kings 2:1-4)
- Grandparents' Prayer (1 Chronicles 17:16-27)

David and Young Adolescents Today

- David is a musician. Many teens may be musicians in their own right or find pleasure from listening to music.
- Saul and David are rivals due to Saul's jealousy of David. Students encounter rivalry and jealousy in their lives.
- David defeats Goliath because he looks to God for his source of strength. Students have their own "Goliaths" which they look to overcome.
- David has plans and aspirations for his life that at times do not mirror God's plan for his life. Students have plans and ambitions for their own lives that need prayerful consideration and proper discernment.
- David and Jonathan share a special friendship. Loyal friends are a blessing in the lives of teens.
- David's life is that of a repentant sinner. Students can identify with the sinful David who loves God enough to ask for mercy.

Highlighting God's Presence

The LORD said to Samuel, "This is the one—anoint him!" Samuel took the olive oil and anointed David in front of his brothers. Immediately the spirit of the LORD took control of David and was with him from that day on (1 Samuel 16:12-13).

David answered, "You are coming against me with sword, spear, and javelin, but I come against you in the name of the LORD Almighty, the God of the Israelite armies, which you have defied" (1 Samuel 17:45).

David led his men in battle and was successful in all he did, because the LORD was with him (1 Samuel 18:13-14).

And so David realized that the LORD had established him as king of Israel and was making his kingdom prosperous for the sake of his people (2 Samuel 5:12).

"So tell my servant David that I, the LORD Almighty, say to him, 'I took you from looking after sheep in the fields and made you the ruler of my people Israel. I have been with you wherever you have gone, and I have defeated all your enemies as you advanced. I will make you as famous as the greatest leaders in the world. I have chosen a place for my people Israel and have settled them there, where they will live without being oppressed any more. Ever since they entered this land, they have been attacked by violent people, but this will not happen again. I promise to keep you safe from all your enemies and to give you descendants. When you die and are buried with your ancestors, I will make one of your sons king and I will keep his kingdom strong. He will be the one to build a temple for me, and I will make sure that his dynasty continues forever'" (2 Samuel 7:8-13).

Getting to Know the Story of David

David

Life on the Road with David

Using the image of a road, students fill in a time line of David's life, indicating the successes and rough spots in his journey. They then compare this journey to their own.

Preparation

❑ Refer to the readings listed in the "Scripture Passages Related to David" section.

❑ Provide a pack of index cards and a roll of tape for this activity.

❑ Each student will need a copy of the Bible.

1. Divide the class into ten groups and assign each group a scriptural passage listed in "Scripture Passages Related to David" of this chapter to read and summarize on the index card provided. (Students should include a title and citation in the summary.)

2. While students are reading, draw a road on the chalkboard. The first section of the road should be straight. Somewhere at midpoint have the road make a sharp left turn and continue left. Then have another turn so that the road continues in a parallel to the beginning section. Label the road with a beginning and an end.

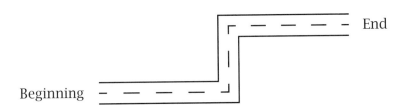

3. Have a discussion with the students about what they read. Include in the discussion how David at first displays traits of a model king and then because of his sinful behavior his life went in a different direction.

4. Have each group read their summary aloud and place their index card on the road where they think it belongs. Continue describing events in David's life until his death. Events that show sinful ways can be marked with "bumps" in the road. After each group takes a turn, discuss the events in David's life that caused him to sin. In each case, discuss what he should have done instead of what he did. (One event in particular is looked on by God with disdain—his relationship with Bathsheba.)

5. Conclude with the class doing a choral reading of David's Psalm 51 (A Prayer for Forgiveness). Discuss the sincerity in David's remorse. How can we show God we are truly sorry for our sins?

Getting to Know David

David and Goliath

In this activity, students compare David and Goliath to gain insight into David's victory.

Preparation

❑ Each student will need a copy of the Bible and a pen or pencil.

❑ Make copies of handout David-A, "Measuring Up David and Goliath," for the students or put the chart from the handout on the board to complete the exercise as a class.

1. Have students read 1 Samuel, chapter 17 individually and then do the following activity.

 2. Pass out handout David-A, "Measuring Up David and Goliath," Allow time for the students to complete the chart and then discuss their findings. Ask the following questions:

○ Based on the chart you have just filled in, which person would you side with? Why?

○ Who was most likely to win the battle?

○ Why do you think David won?

○ What are some "Goliaths" that we might need to overcome in our lives? (Explain that "Goliaths" are any situations in life that seem insurmountable.)

○ What is the faith message in the story of David and Goliath?

○ How can we apply this message to our own lives?

Conclude by saying that the story of David and Goliath testifies to the truth of the statement by the angel Gabriel, "For there is nothing God cannot do" (Luke 1:37).

Psalms and Rap

Preparation

❑ Each student will need a copy of the Bible and a pen or pencil.

❑ Make copies of handout David-B, "Choices," for the students.

❑ If possible, play the CD *Prayer Warrior* (Jeannie Pomanowski, Chesapeake Music Works, 2004, Be Attitude Music, BMI).

1. To begin this activity, share the following thoughts with your students in your own words:

• The Book of Psalms is a book of both prayers and hymns. Many of the Psalms were written by David, were used by Jesus, and continue to be a source of worship today. In this activity we will analyze the twenty-third Psalm for its lyrical content and use its inspiration to create a modern-day rap. Of all the Psalms, this one is the best known.

2. Have the class do a choral reading of Psalm 23. Then ask the students the following questions:

- ❍ What do you think is the intent of the Psalmist (David)?

- ❍ Think of a time when you experienced anxiety, fear, or distress. Can you picture it in your mind?

3. Ask the students to each rewrite the twenty-third Psalm in reference to the experience they pictured. Guide the students in the following ways. Have them use the same beginning (The Lord is my shepherd). As they read through each line, they should write their own version next to the original so as to keep to the same form and intent. The following is an example:

The Lord is my shepherd	The Lord is my shepherd
I have everything I need	My life is complete
He lets me rest in fields of green grass	I rest in his loving arms

At this time you may want to play the song "Choices" from the CD *Prayer Warrior*. Pass out handout David–B, "Choices." In the song "Choices" is a verse that raps lyrics describing God's mercy when we fail to make good choices that ultimately lead to sin. Listening to the song will inspire the students to create their own rap when rewriting Psalm 23. Some students will be able to rap without any music if you do not have a recording.

4. When students are finished with their composition call upon volunteers to rap their prayer or hymn. (Some students may want to practice at home first before they present it to the class.) Conclude the activity with these comments:

- ❍ Psalms were written to be sung. By creating modern translations of the Psalms, students will gain insight into the purpose of the Psalms, which is to interact with God in prayer asking for what one needs.

- ❍ The project also emphasizes that all types of music can praise God.

David

MEASURING UP DAVID AND GOLIATH

Fill in this chart using the story of David and Goliath, 1 Samuel 17:41–54. Then answer the questions below. Use the back of this page for writing if necessary.

Tools	Goliath	David
armor		
weapons		
occupation		
relative age		
reward for winning battle		
past warrior experience		
source of strength		

Based on the chart you have just filled in, which person would you side with? Why? Why was David victorious?

Can you think of any "battles" (injustice, temptation) you may have faced or may face in the future?

In what ways can David's victory influence the outcome of your battles?

CHOICES

Verses 1 and 4
There isn't anything we do that God won't forgive
Making choices in life it's all relative
You've got to be a little more demonstrative and just pray

Verse 2
We all make mistakes that are indicative
Of situations in the past that make us sensitive
We've got to try not to be so negative and just pray

Chorus
Life is a series of choices we make
It doesn't matter to Him if we make a mistake
There's a prodigal son that wants to come home
It doesn't make any sense to continue to roam

Verse 3
I'd like to be a little more informative
About the healing of the heart 'cause it's imperative
You simply musn't be like a fugitive, just pray

Rap
I made a few mistakes in the past you see
I was feelin' pretty bad, it was getting to me
Nobody around me could understand
So with my back against the wall I turned to the Man
Jesus said the truth will set you free
So I poured out my heart to the almighty
I tell you this ditty 'cause I want you to know
The only way to live life is to let your guilt go

(Lyrics and music by Jeannie Pomanowski,
Prayer Warrior, Chesapeake Music Works, 2004,
Be Attitude Music, BMI)

SOLOMON

Preparing to Teach

Overview

Solomon's story explains the nature of wisdom and how wisdom can be corrupted. The story is a study in contrasts between Solomon as a king who actively serves God through his commitment to the Temple and Solomon, as a king who later foolishly turns to other gods. On the one hand, he is a model to young adolescents, and on the other hand, he also shows them that even model human beings can fall if they do not keep their focus on what is important.

In his early years, God asks Solomon what he would like God to give him and he answers, "wisdom" (1 Kings 3:9). As young people grow up and realize that many of life's events are out of their control, they will likely value wisdom even more than they do now. It is a good gift to ask God for at any stage of life. Spending some time in the Book of Proverbs can help them flesh out what wisdom means.

One of Solomon's huge accomplishments is the construction of the Temple in Jerusalem. If some of the students have been to Jerusalem or traveled abroad in Europe and have been able to see some of the great cathedrals, ask them to share what they are like. Explore why human beings want to build beautiful and lofty monuments to God.

Human beings, no matter how wise, are still vulnerable to sin, as we see with Solomon, who turns to gods other than the Lord. By focusing on his wisdom and learning from his downfall, we can gather that it is important always to keep our focus on God.

THIS CHAPTER AT A GLANCE

Getting to Know the Story of Solomon

- The King Is Dead! Long Live the King!

Getting to Know Solomon

- The Wisdom of Solomon
- Temple Building, Building Faith
- Stuck on Proverbs

Scripture Passages Related to Solomon

- 1 Kings 2:1–4 (David gives final instructions to Solomon)
- 1 Kings 3:4–15 (Solomon prays for wisdom)*
- 1 Kings 3:16–28 (Solomon decides wisely for the mothers)*
- 1 Kings 6:1–38 (Solomon builds a temple)*
- 1 Kings 8:54–61 (Solomon prays)
- 1 Kings 10:1–13 (The Queen of Sheba visits)
- 1 Kings 11:1–13 (Solomon turns away from God)*

Asterisk (*) signifies key passages to cover.

Articles from *Breakthrough!* Related to Solomon

- *Breakthrough!* Interview with King Solomon
- Introduction to the First Book of Kings
- Good Advice (1 Kings 2:1–4)
- Not a Perfect Person (1 Kings 3:6–9)
- Three Thousand Proverbs! (1 Kings 4:20–34)
- A Place to Worship (1 Kings, chapters 5–6)
- God in a Box? (1 Kings 8:27)
- A Royal Visit (1 Kings 10:1–13)
- Too Many Gods . . . or Wives? (1 Kings 11:1–8)

Solomon and Young Adolescents Today

- In Solomon we see a very modern image of success because he is very wealthy, a shrewd business man, and a skillful politician. What is the source of his success? The Scriptures portray Solomon as one whose heart is completely turned toward God. Students have their own ideas of success that are shaped by family, culture, and Church.
- Solomon desires to honor God by building a beautiful temple to house the ark of the Covenant. Students have encountered sacred objects and sacred spaces.
- Solomon turns his heart from God and chooses idolatry. He loses his focus on God, the source of his wisdom and right behavior. This turn of heart destroys his kingdom. Students turn toward God and turn toward sin, trying to figure out which spirits to trust and follow.
- Solomon shows wisdom and foolishness regarding his possessions and power. Students have ideas about the value of power and possessions that are shaped by family, culture, and Church.

Highlighting God's Presence

The LORD was pleased that Solomon had asked for this (wisdom), and so he said to him, "Because you have asked for wisdom to rule justly, instead of a long life for yourself or riches or the death of your enemies, I will do what you have asked" (1 Kings 3:10-12).

The LORD said to Solomon, "If you obey all my laws and commands, I will do for you what I promised your father, David. I will live among my people Israel in this Temple that you are building, and I will never abandon them" (1 Kings 6:11-13).

Getting to Know the Story of Solomon

The King Is Dead! Long Live the King!

Preparation

❏ Each student should have a Bible, a pen, and paper.

❏ If you have computer access, you can invite the students to use Word Publishing to access a newsletter template that would be useful for this exercise.

❏ Before class write the list of readings from "Scripture Passages Related to Solomon" in a visible place.

❏ If you have completed this or a similar activity in the past, you may want to provide students with examples to jumpstart their thinking. Perhaps you could show copies of newspapers that carried special editions after John Paul II passed away (April 2005). These accounts not only give a sense of format but also show them how the death of a wise man might be celebrated in print.

1. Divide the class into groups of seven. Ask the members of each group to divide the assigned sections about Solomon among themselves and read them.

2. Propose the following scenario to the students:
• Imagine that as a group, you are publishing a front-page report on the life of Solomon on the occasion of his death. Each of you should prepare one column (headline and then article) based on your section of the reading.

3. Have the students first write out their column on paper, discussing how they would like to present their passage with the others in the group. (One might want to do a "here on the scene" while another may want to do a letter to the editor or a "spotlight on Solomon," and so on.) Then have the students transfer their columns to the front page of a newspaper layout, complete with the name of the paper and assorted other newspaper items. At this point, students can further their creativity by "posting a list of events at the temple," creating an advertisement for "wisdom," and so on.)

4. After each group has completed their newspaper, make copies and distribute them to each group to read. At the end, have each student write a letter to the editor explaining how successful they think Solomon was as king.

Getting to Know Solomon

The Wisdom of Solomon

Preparation

❑ Students will need a Bible, a pen, and paper.

1. In a large class discussion, have the students define the word *wise*. Ask, How is it different from being intelligent? How does one get wisdom?

2. Have the students read 1 Kings 3:1–10 quietly to themselves. Ask these questions about the reading:

   ○ Why is Solomon's request of God a wise one?

   ○ What would you have asked for? Why?

3. Have the students read 1 Kings 3:16–28. Process this story with them by asking these types of questions:
   • How does Solomon demonstrate wisdom in this story?
   • Can you think of any situations in today's world that might benefit from this type of wisdom?

4. Divide the class into small groups and invite each group to present a skit that would provide an updated version of this story. Each skit will need to feature two competing parties and one "King Solomon" figure. (Encourage students to move beyond the roles of two mothers into the business world, school, home, and so on.)

5. After students have presented their skits, ask them to look for common themes or insights that emerge. Have students skim the Book of Proverbs and, as a class, phrase their own wisdom into a proverblike formula.

Temple Building, Building Faith

Preparation

❏ Students need a Bible, a pen, and paper.

❏ Bring in material to build a replica of Solomon's Temple. Bring several different materials and the means to put them together: glue, tape, and so on. Wooden blocks, Legos, cardboard, and paper can be used.

❏ Make a copy of a picture of Solomon's Temple for each student.

❏ A representation of Solomon's temple can be found in the *Saint Mary's Press® Essential Bible Dictionary* or on page 1263 of the *New Jerome Biblical Commentary* (see appendix 1). An Internet search also yields several possibilities.

1. Ask students to read 1 Kings 6:1–14. Divide the class into small groups and assign each group a type of building material.

2. Using some building material, ask them to build a version of the Temple on this scale: 11 inches long by 5.5 inches high by 4 inches wide. (This is not to the actual scale of the Temple itself.)

3. After building a model of the temple, allow the young people to walk around and appreciate the work of the other groups. The students can then begin to compare and contrast the Temple to a church. Ask these questions:

○ Why does Solomon want a temple?

○ Does his desire for a Temple resemble a Christian's desire for a church? How so? How not?

4. See Solomon's prayer for his people. Ask students to copy 1 Kings 8:22–30 and tape it to the model Temple. Ask these types of questions:
*   How strong is this building?
*   Is it building materials or people who strengthen the Temple or a parish community today?

5. Ask the students to imagine a seesaw with the Temple model on one side. Read I Kings, chapter 11 aloud to the students and ask these questions:
*   What undoes Solomon's wisdom?
*   What would go on the other side of this seesaw that would counterbalance Solomon's faith in God (unfaithfulness, idols)?
*   How does a leader's downfall affect others?

Stuck on Proverbs

In this activity, students take passages from the Book of Proverbs and create bumper stickers for them.

Preparation

❑ Provide markers and sheets of 8.5-by-11-inch paper for the students.

❑ Students will need bibles.

1. Begin the activity by talking about the types of things we read in traffic on the bumpers of cars: bumper stickers and those sayings that are put on license plate holders. Share some of your favorite bumper stickers and then ask the students to mention any appropriate bumper stickers they have liked.

2. Ask, What are the qualities of clever bumper stickers or license plate holders? (They often have a message that appeals to a number of people; they are succinct; they are catchy so that it is hard to forget them.)

3. Explain that the Book of Proverbs is attributed to Solomon's wisdom. Have students look through the Book of Proverbs and pick out a proverb they like. Instruct the students to design a bumper sticker from one of their favorite proverbs. Have them connect the proverb to the present day by the way they letter it and illustrate it.

4. Share the bumper stickers.

Solomon

ELIJAH

Preparing to Teach

Overview

Elijah is one of the great prophets of the Old Testament. He is a bold, courageous spokesman for God whose words are often accompanied by miraculous events. Even his name declares his message as *Elijah* literally means "Yahweh is God!" Despite his insistent call to the people of Israel back to a faithful observance of the Covenant with God, his work is met with stiff resistance from the kings and queens of the northern kingdom of Israel. Young people can identify with the experience of meeting with resistance.

The Bible portrays Elijah as having great spiritual power to affect the lives of others, while at the same time suffering greatly at the hands of political leaders who wish to resist this spiritual power. Like many prophets, Elijah functions as the conscience to the king and the nation. Elijah sees the reality of Israel's present situation (characterized by disregard for the poor, idolatry, and political intrigue) with the clarity of God's eyes. He can thus predict that if things do not change, Israel will be destroyed! Only by a faithful return to God, Elijah predicts, can Israel save itself. Young people may have an easier time seeing the decadence of life in the northern kingdom than in modern society today.

Elijah is a complicated biblical figure. We see the tenderness of his relationship with the widow, his boldness in confronting the prophets of Baal, and his discouragement that leads him into the wilderness. This humanity makes it easier for us to see that Elijah, like the other prophets, is not a "superman" but rather a human being who is dedicated completely to God.

THIS CHAPTER AT A GLANCE

Getting to Know the Story of Elijah

- Elijah Action Figure Design Project

Getting to Know Elijah

- Calling Down the Fire
- Going to the Cave: Listening for God

Scripture Passages Related to Elijah

- 1 Kings 17:1-7 (Call of Elijah)
- 1 Kings 17:8-24 (Elijah goes to see the widow of Zarephath)*
- 1 Kings 18:1-40 (Elijah, King Ahab, and the prophets of Baal)*
- 1 Kings 19:1-8 (Elijah encounters God in a cave on Mount Sinai)*
- 1 Kings 19:19-21 (Elijah calls Elisha)
- 1 Kings 21:1-28 (Elijah and Naboth's vineyard)
- 2 Kings 2:1-15 (Elijah departs in a flaming chariot)*

Asterisk (*) signifies key passages to cover.

Articles from *Breakthrough!* Related to Elijah

- *Breakthrough!* Interview with Elijah and Elisha
- Elijah (1 Kings, chapters 17–18)
- A Whisper (1 Kings, chapter 19)
- Elisha (1 Kings 19:19–21)
- No Shame (1 Kings, chapter 21)
- Saying Good-bye (2 Kings 2:1–15)

Elijah and Young Adolescents Today

- Elijah repeatedly stands up to opposition courageously, and his confidence in God gives him the strength and wit to do so. Young adolescents can likewise know that God gives them the strength needed to withstand peer pressure.
- Elijah is consistent in his message but adapts how he brings it to different people. For instance, he relates differently to the widow of Zarephath than he does to Queen Jezebel. He is truthful yet tolerant of others. Young adolescents are at the same time judgmental and loathe to judge. They can learn from Elijah that tolerance does not mean acceptance of all behavior.
- Elijah often encounters God in natural settings such as forests, mountains, caves, and deserts. Young adolescents can also sense God in the natural world.
- Elijah has a close, enduring relationship with God. His prayer reflects a range of attitudes such as praise, thanksgiving, doubt, and confidence. The young adolescent can see that a close relationship with God comes out of a prayer life that is honest and confident in God's loving call to us.

Highlighting God's Presence

"Don't worry," Elijah said to her. "Go on and prepare your meal. But first make a small loaf from what you have and bring it to me, and then prepare the rest for you and your son. For this is what the LORD, the God of Israel, says: 'The bowl will not run out of flour or the jar run out of oil before the day that I, the LORD, send rain'" (1 Kings 17:13-14).

"Go out and stand before me on top of the mountain," the LORD said to him. Then the LORD passed by and sent a furious wind that split the hills and shattered the rocks—but the LORD was not in the wind. The wind stopped blowing, then there was an earthquake—but the LORD was not in the earthquake. After the earthquake there was a fire—but the LORD was not in the fire. And after the fire there was a soft whisper of a voice.

When Elijah heard it, he covered his face with his cloak and went and stood at the entrance of the cave. A voice said to him, "Elijah, what are you doing here?"(1 Kings 19:11-13).

They kept talking as they walked on; then suddenly a chariot of fire pulled by horses of fire came between them and Elijah was taken up to heaven by a whirlwind (2 Kings 2:11).

Getting to Know the Story of Elijah

Elijah Action Figure Design Project

The story of Elijah shows us many heroic qualities in a biblical character. Some of these qualities can easily be translated into a product line for an action figure toy (with accessories).

Preparation

❑ Provide each participant with a Bible and the list of readings from "Scripture Passages Related to Elijah."

❑ Make sure each student has at least five sheets of copy paper and some markers or colored pencils.

1. Divide the class into seven groups and assign each of them one of the seven readings from "Scripture Passages Related to Elijah."

2. Ask students to reminisce about the dolls or action figures they have or had. Ask them to remind the group what kind of figures came with themed sets or accessories.

3. Instruct students to draw a design proposal for their version of "Elijah, the Prophet and Hero." From the Scripture passage they have read, have the young people create several accessories for Elijah (items that would be included with the toy figure) that would be part of the "Elijah Biblical Action Figure series." For each accessory, assign students to write the biblical citation that inspired their idea.

4. After all the project designs are finished, have the students present their action figures and accessories and tell the story from the Bible that inspired them, beginning with the first reading. Note which accessories are most common. Ask if these common accessories tell us something about Elijah.

Getting to Know Elijah

Calling Down the Fire

Preparation

❑ Gather candles, matches, and a metal container for extinguishing.

❑ Students will need bibles.

❑ Supply the classroom with a whiteboard, dry-erase markers, and eraser; a blackboard with chalk and eraser; or an easel with paper.

1. Have students read 1 Kings 18:18–40. Ask the students:
- Has anyone ever dared you to a contest or have you ever dared another person to do something?
- What made you want to take up the challenge?
- How does Elijah challenge the Baal priests? Why?
- When Elijah wins the contest, what does that say? (God is active in the world and more powerful than any other god.)
- Why is fire a symbol for God?

2. Tell the students that in our world we are constantly dared by the world to give up on God, to believe that God is not active in the world, and that we should give our hearts to other gods, such as possessions and activities that promise to fulfill our lives. Ask, "Who in the world today 'calls the fire down' to bring the light of God to our world?"

3. On the board draw a long horizontal line to represent the different intensity of fire. At one end put "a match" to represent the weakest kind of fire. At the other end put "lightning" or a "volcano" to represent an intense form of heat. Along the line put these other "fires": a bonfire, a blow torch, fireworks, and a forest fire.

4. After you have charted these types of fires, ask the students to think of prophetic people that "bring down the fire" in today's world. Depending on their strength and power, put their names along the chart.

5. Distribute an unlit candle to each student. For the closing prayer, light each candle and pray this prayer:

- O God of fire and light, when we are fearful of being alone or fearful for those close to us, help us to turn to you and to know your warmth and strength. We pray for those people who are sources of your light and your life for us. (Have each student name someone out loud.) O God, as you did in Elijah's time, let the fire fall on all your holy people again! Amen!

Have the students put the lit candles in a fireproof container. Make sure all the candles go out.

Going to the Cave: Listening for God

Preparation

❑ Each student needs a Bible, paper, and a pen or pencil.

1. Introduce the activity by sharing these thoughts:

- God speaks to people in all kinds of ways, but most people seem to struggle to hear God in their lives. Elijah encounters God in a most unexpected way in this account from 1 Kings.

Ask a student to read 1 Kings 19:1-8 aloud to the class and then ask the young people these questions:

○ What mountain is Elijah on and why is he in a cave there?

○ How does God come to him?

○ What is Elijah's reaction? Why do you think he reacts this way?

2. Focus on the cave in this story. First ask the students whether anyone has explored caves. Then ask these questions:

○ What are the qualities of caves? (mysterious, quiet, dark, hidden)

○ Why would a cave be a good place to listen for God? (It is quiet and forces us to listen in a deliberate way to our environment.)

3. Then focus on sounds with these questions:

○ What are some things that need to be said in a loud voice?

○ What are some things that need to be said in a quiet voice?

❍ What are some things God "says in a loud voice"?

❍ What are some things God "says in a soft voice"?

4. Give students some quiet time to pray by bringing them to a church or chapel or by creating some of the mystery of a cave in your own room with darkness, music, candles, and so on. Provide a half hour of time for students to experience this quiet. Then give them time to journal privately about the experience. If any young person wants to share thoughts about their prayer time, welcome them to do so.

Elijah

ELISHA

Preparing to Teach

Overview

Any young person who has followed one or more older siblings through school could think, "I have big shoes to fill." Elisha must have felt that way about following Elijah at times. Elisha, however, also calls on Elijah's strength to begin his ministry, so he "rides on his coattails" to some extent.

Elisha is a mighty prophet in his own right. He is able to keep a starving woman and her son going, raise that son from the dead, and otherwise do some of the same miracles as his predecessor. One of the charming stories about Elisha is his cure of Namaan, the Syrian commander. Namaan appears to almost prefer leprosy over bathing in the Jordan River, but he is persuaded to try it. The commander ends up taking home soil from Judah so that he can give offerings only to Elisha's God.

Because several of Elisha's stories have more character development, young people will enjoy getting a sense of this powerful prophet.

THIS CHAPTER AT A GLANCE

Getting to Know the Story of Elisha

- Remembering Elisha on *Good Morning Israel*

Scripture Passages Related to Elisha

- 1 Kings 19:19-21 (Elijah calls Elisha)*
- 2 Kings 2:1-13 (Elijah is taken up into heaven)
- 2 Kings 2:14 (Elisha does a miracle in Elijah's name)
- 2 Kings 4:1-7 (Elisha helps a starving widow and her son)*
- 2 Kings 4:8-37 (Elisha and the rich woman of Shunem)*
- 2 Kings 5:1-27 (Elisha cures Naaman)*
- 2 Kings 13:14-21 (Death of Elisha)

Asterisk (*) signifies key passages to cover.

Articles from *Breakthrough!* Related to Elisha

- *Breakthrough!* Interview with Elijah and Elisha
- Elisha (1 Kings 19:19–21)
- Saying Good-bye (2 Kings 2:1–15)
- Elisha the Rescuer (2 Kings 4:1–7)
- Seek Healing (2 Kings 5:1–14)
- Mercy, Not Revenge (2 Kings 6:8–23)
- Refugees (2 Kings 8:1–6)

Elisha and Young Adolescents Today

- Elisha is in farming before Elijah calls him to be his helper. God calls young people to listen for his call amid their ordinary activities.
- Elisha has a mentor in Elijah. Young people often have mentors or seek them out in relatives, coaches, and teachers.
- Elisha has a kind heart for the widow in trouble. Young people are very kind hearted when they hear of people in need.
- The rich woman whose son has died challenges Elisha to deal with the reality that her son has died and to fulfill his role as prophet. Young people are often challenged to be true to their own responsibilities.

Highlighting God's Presence

In grief, Elisha tore his cloak in two. Then he picked up Elijah's cloak that had fallen from him, and went back and stood on the bank of the Jordan. He struck the water with Elijah's cloak and said, "What is the LORD, the God of Elijah?" Then he struck the water again, and it divided, and he walked over to the other side (2 Kings 2:12–14).

He [Namaan] returned to Elisha with all his men and said, "Now I know that there is no god but the God of Israel" (2 Kings 5:15).

Getting to Know the Story of Elisha

In this chapter, the activity below both familiarizes the young people with the story of Elisha and also invites them to consider the spiritual meaning of his stories.

Remembering Elisha on *Good Morning Israel*

In this activity, students use a talk show format to interview people who encountered Elisha throughout his life.

Elisha

Preparation

☐ Every young person needs to have a Bible.

☐ Make several copies of resource Elisha-A, "Questions About Elisha," one for each talk show host, or make one copy and cut it up for the different hosts.

1. Divide the class into the following configurations and give them the following passages from 2 Kings to read:

- Four talk show hosts, one per segment below. These hosts should use the questions on resource Elisha-A, "Questions About Elisha," to prepare for the talk show. (Other questions may also be added.)
- Segment 1: The widow and her two sons (Direct these three people to read 2 Kings 4:1-7).
- Segment 2: The rich woman and her husband, Gehazi; before the son takes ill (Instruct these three people to read 2 Kings 4:8-17).
- Segment 3: The rich woman; her husband, Gehazi; and the son (Have these three people read 2 Kings 4:28-37).
- Segment 4: Namaan, the Israelite girl servant, two servants of Namaan, the king, and Gehazi (Tell these six people to read 2 Kings 5:1-27).
- Other young people can serve as the live audience or as a second interviewer.

2. Allow the students time to read the passages and to prepare for the talk show segments. Allow them to perform their talk shows in order to expose all the students to some key parts of Elisha's story.

3. In order to explore who Elisha is in greater depth, ask the young people these types of questions:

- The widow in 2 Kings, chapter 4 is in a vulnerable position. How is her own faith connected to the success of Elisha's miracle?
- How is the rich woman in the next story in almost the opposite position as the widow?
- How do she and Elisha both gift one another?
- How does the rich woman demand that Elisha live up to what he promised her?
- How do the widow, the rich woman, and Namaan need to trust in order to be blessed by Elisha?
- Does our own trust in God affect the way God is able to bless us? (Or help us recognize a blessing as we receive it?)

4. Close this activity with a prayer for trust.

Elisha

QUESTIONS ABOUT ELISHA

Notes to the talk show host: Elisha has recently died and you are hosting people who came in contact with him all week on your show, *Good Morning Israel.* These types of questions should get the conversation going:

Segment 1: The widow and her two sons 2 Kings 4:1-7

Welcome to the show.
Introductions
- Now if you don't mind my asking, how is it that your husband died? Is there a connection between your husband's death and his debts?
- Do you mind explaining to our audience exactly what was going to happen to your sons if you could not get the money?
- (To the sons) How were you feeling about that? How old are you?
- Did you really think that Elisha would be able to help you? Or was this a last resort?
- People say that Elisha was a sensitive man. Was that your experience? (Address first the mother and then the sons.)

Summary and signing off.

Notes to the talk show host: Elisha has recently died and you are hosting people who came in contact with him all week on your show, *Good Morning Israel.* These types of questions should get the conversation going

Segment 2: The rich woman and her husband, Gehazi, before the son takes ill (2 Kings 4:8-17)

Welcome to the show.
Introductions

- (To the rich woman and her husband) What was your first impression of Elisha? How is it that that you came to build a room for him on top of your house?
- Gehazi, can you tell our audience how Elisha was able to thank this woman for her kindness? What role did you play?
- (To the rich woman and then to her husband) What did you think when Elisha told you that you would have a son?

Summary and signing off

Notes to the talk show host: Elisha has recently died and you are hosting people who came in contact with him all week on your show, *Good Morning Israel.* These types of questions should get the conversation going:

Segment 3: The rich woman; her husband, Gehazi; and the son (2 Kings 4:28-37)

Welcome to the show.
Introductions.

Thanks to the visitors for returning for a second show.

- (To the husband) How did you first know that your son was in trouble?
- (To the woman) What did you do immediately when you realized that your son was dead?
- Gehazi, what happened when this woman came to Elisha? Were you able to help?
- (To the woman) Was Elisha able to do something for your son? What was it?

Summary and signing off

....

Notes to the talk show host: Elisha has recently died and you are hosting people who came in contact with him all week on your show, *Good Morning Israel.* These types of questions should get the conversation going:

Segment 4: Namaan, the Israelite girl servant, two servants of Namaan, the king of Israel, and Gehazi (2 Kings 5:1-27)

Welcome to the Show.
Introductions

- (To the Israelite serving girl) How is it that Commander Naaman came to know of Elisha in the first place?
- Commander Naaman, what role did the Syrian king play in your effort to be healed?
- King, what did you think when you received this letter from the king of Syria? Did you think you could help his commander?
- (To the servants) What happened when the commander arrived at the house of Elisha the prophet? What role did you play in the commander's healing?
- Namaan, what was your impression of Elisha's God? Did your experience of bathing in the river and being healed change your own beliefs?
- Gehazi, what made you turn away from your master, Elisha? What type of condition are you dealing with now?

Summary and signing off

....

HEZEKIAH

Preparing to Teach

Overview

King Hezekiah is a prophetic and courageous leader. When he comes to power, he immediately returns to the proper ways of worship and even invites people from Israel to come and share in a Passover celebration. Young adolescents can admire this type of "take charge" personality, especially when it is combined with integrity.

The proposed attack by the Assyrians forces Hezekiah to make an important decision on behalf of the city—rely on God, surrender, or fight. The Assyrians try to instill fear in the hearts of all residents of Jerusalem but God reassures the people through the prophet Isaiah. All young people have wrestled with fear—some with legitimate fear and others with fear that stems from self-doubt or insecurity.

The story of Hezekiah can inspire young people to turn to God when they are dealing with the fear of failure, instead of just succumbing to negative self-talk.

THIS CHAPTER AT A GLANCE

Getting to Know the Story of Hezekiah

- Drama at Court

Getting to Know Hezekiah

- Letting God Conquer Fear

Scripture Passages Related to Hezekiah

- 2 Kings 18:1–8 (The nature of Hezekiah's reign)*
- 2 Chronicles 29:3–36 (Hezekiah purifies and rededicates the Temple.)*
- 2 Chronicles 30:1–22 (Hezekiah invites the Israelites to the Passover celebration)
- 2 Kings 18:13–27 (Assyrian officials try to discourage the people of Jerusalem from believing in their God)*

- 2 Kings 9:1–7 (Hezekiah consults with Isaiah about the Assyrian threat)*
- 2 Kings 19:35–37 (God conquers the Assyrians)*
- 2 Kings 20:1–11 (Hezekiah almost dies but recovers)
- 2 Kings 20:20 (Hezekiah dies)

Asterisk (*) signifies key passages to cover.

Through! Articles from *Breakthrough!* Related to Hezekiah

- *Breakthrough!* Interview with Hezekiah
- One of the Good Guys (2 Kings 18:1–8)
- Pour Out Your Heart (2 Kings 19:14–19)

Hezekiah and Young Adolescents Today

- Hezekiah is such a successful ruler because he is focused on God. Young adolescents have experienced success from focusing on a task.
- Hezekiah turns around the religious climate of Jerusalem by taking the pagan gods out of the Temple, purifying it, rededicating it to God, and celebrating the Passover. Young people, by their example, also have power to lead their peers toward or away from God.
- It is difficult to frighten Hezekiah, but the Assyrians frightened him enough to ask for some reassurance from Isaiah. Young people struggle with anxiety when they face challenging tasks such as playing a difficult team, acting in public, or making an overture to a new friend. They also need encouragement.

Highlighting God's Presence

He [Hezekiah] was faithful to the Lord and never disobeyed him, but carefully kept all the commands that the Lord had given Moses. So the Lord was with him, and he was successful in everything he did (2 Kings 18:6–7).

"I, the Lord, the God of your ancestor David, have heard your prayer and seen your tears. I will heal you, and in three days you will go to the Temple" (2 Kings 20:5).

He [Hezekiah] said to them, "Be determined and confident, and don't be afraid of the Assyrian emperor or of the army he is leading. We have more power on our side than he has on his. He has human power, but we have the Lord our God to help us and to fight our battles" (2 Chronicles 32:7–8).

Getting to Know the Story of Hezekiah

Drama at Court

The story of Hezekiah is fairly dramatic, and because it has many characters, the story lends itself well to an oral reading.

Preparation

❏ Every young person needs a Bible of the same translation.

❏ You may want to move furniture in the room to stage the dramatic reading of the story or bring in some props.

❏ Read the selection carefully so you can show the students what they will be saying when it is read aloud.

❏ Assign young people the following roles:
- Narrator (more than one perhaps)
- Hezekiah
- Sennacherib
- three Assyrian officials
- Eliakim, Shebna, Joah
- Isaiah the prophet
- God

The rest of the group can be the people of Jerusalem.

Before you begin the reading, divide the speech by the Assyrian officials so that three young people can read it. The reading does not need to be acted out but the young people should be standing, and it would be good to assign a place for Isaiah to the side, a place for Jerusalem, and an area for the invading Assyrians. Begin the reading at 2 Kings 18:13 and continue through 2 Kings 19:37.

When the young people have finished the reading, review the important points from the story with them.

Getting to Know Hezekiah

Letting God Conquer Fear

In this activity, young people examine the tactics used by the Assyrians to psyche out the Jews and learn to look for God's voice instead.

Preparation

❑ Make copies of handout Hezekiah-A, "Negative Speak," for each young person.

❑ Provide each young person with a Bible and a pen or pencil.

1. Begin this activity by asking the young people to talk about sports psychology.

- What does it mean to get psyched for a game or to get psyched out?
- Why do some coaches ask their players to visually imagine a victory prior to a game or race?
- What is the effect of the cheering or jeering crowds on players' nerves?
- What are some other techniques people use to either boost their own confidence or to diminish the opponents' confidence?

2. After there has been some discussion of teams and sports, ask the young people to close their eyes for a few minutes and to think about the ways that they privately try to psyche themselves up with internal talking or that they tear themselves down internally.

3. Pass out handout Hezekiah-A, "Negative Speak," to the young people and ask them to look it over and see if they could put words into this dialogue about their present-day life or a present-day situation. Allow them to shift some of the words from 2 Chronicles if that enables them to create better meaning.

4. Invite some of the students to share what they have written. Ask them if this kind of language resembles either their internal self-talking or what they might hear from people on another team or from their fans. Make some of the following points:

- The encounter between the Assyrians and the people of Jerusalem is an example of one side, the Assyrians, using psychology to psyche out their opponents, the people of Jerusalem. (Ask a student to read 2 Chronicles 32:11–15 aloud from the Bible.)
- In the face of this very successful army, Hezekiah needs more reassurance that God will be with them, even though he does not lose faith in God. The prophet Isaiah is able to help him.
- Many of us can fall into the trap of talking negatively to ourselves. It might sound like this: "I am going to fail the test. I never have done well in history. Why would this be different?"
- Hezekiah's story shows us that God's voice reassures one who is faithful to him. The enemy's voice challenges and causes doubt. When we are going back and forth internally, we should stop when

we recognize that we are psyching ourselves out. At that point, we can follow Hezekiah's example and ask God for reassurance.

5. To close, consider teaching the young people some simple techniques to quiet themselves when they are in the heat of negative self-talk. Ask, "How can you allow God to take care of the fear?" Some examples include focusing on one's breath, saying a mantra like "Jesus" slowly, and so on.

NEGATIVE SPEAK

Fill in these blanks to create sentences that could relate to a modern-day situation—either your own or someone else's.

"_____ tells you that _____ will save you from our power but

_____ is deceiving you and will let you _____. He is the one who

_____ and then told (them) to

_____. Don't you know what (we) have done to

other _____ s? Did _____ ever save (them) from us? When

did _____ ever save (them) from us? Then what makes you think

that _____ can save you? Now don't let_____ deceive or

mislead you like that. Don't believe him! No _____ has ever been able to

save _____ from any _____. So certainly this _____

of yours cannot save you!" (2 Chronicles 32:11-15)

JOSIAH

Preparing to Teach

Overview

Josiah becomes king of the Israelites during a time when the people have turned away from God. Josiah faithfully follows God's law and tries to bring his people back to the ways of God by cleansing the Temple in Jerusalem and destroying everything that was used to worship other gods. Like Hezekiah, he is easy to admire for his reforms. One of the high points of Josiah's reign is the return to celebrating the ancient feast of Passover.

Josiah is also someone who does not mind consulting other wise people when he needs to make a decision. Young people need to know that it is not a sign of weakness to consult with other respected people when making a decision.

Though God recognizes Josiah's faithfulness, unfortunately God's anger toward his people does not go away.

THIS CHAPTER AT A GLANCE

Getting to Know the Story of Josiah

- A Eulogy for Josiah

Getting to Know Josiah

- Decisions, Decisions
- Life Is Fair—Sometimes

Scripture Passages Related to Josiah

- 2 Kings 21:23—22:2 (Josiah becomes king of Judah at the age of eight)
- 2 Kings 22:3-20 (Josiah consults with Huldah about a book found in the Temple)*
- 2 Kings 23:1-20 (Josiah cleanses the Temple and the land)*
- 2 Kings 23:21-23 (Josiah celebrates a great Passover feast)*
- 2 Kings 23:28-30 (Josiah dies)

Asterisk (*) signifies key passages to cover.

Articles from *Breakthrough!* Related to Josiah

- *Breakthrough!* Interview with Josiah
- An Amazing Woman (2 Kings, chapter 22)
- A Faith-Filled King (2 Kings 23:1-14)

Josiah and Young Adolescents Today

- Josiah becomes king at a young age. Young people are often asked to take on significant responsibilities.
- At his young age, Josiah turns away from the bad habits of his people and faithfully abides by God's laws. Without knowing it, young people often set a good example for adults as well as children.
- Josiah consults with the leading men and women of his region, and learns about the book of the law and the future of his people and himself. Young people seek out the advice of the adults who are important in their life as they move closer to making significant decisions.
- Unfortunately, all of Josiah's efforts to be faithful and live according to God's law do not alter God's anger toward his people. Life can seem to be unfair to young people sometimes, even though they play by the rules.

Highlighting God's Presence

Josiah did what was pleasing to the Lord; he followed the example of his ancestor King David, strictly obeying all the laws of God (2 Kings 22:2).

Getting to Know the Story of Josiah

A Eulogy for Josiah

Preparation

❏ Provide each young person with a pen or pencil and paper.

❏ Have at least six bibles on hand.

1. Divide the class into six small groups. Distribute the bibles, one per group, and assign one of the following passages to each group:
- 2 Kings 21:23—22:2
- 2 Chronicles 33:25—34:2
- 2 Kings 22:3-20
- 2 Kings 23:1-30

- 2 Chronicles 34:3-33
- 2 Chronicles 35:1-24

2. Tell the young people that each small group is going to write one part of a eulogy for Josiah based on what they read in the Bible. If they do not know what a eulogy is, explain that it is a short speech that looks back on the life of a person who has died and praises them.

3. Distribute the paper and pens or pencils. Ask the small groups to read the Scripture passage aloud to their group. Encourage everyone to read some portion of the text. When they are finished reading, each person is to write three sentences about Josiah on the piece of paper. Once they have finished completing their individual descriptions, the participants in the small groups should regather, share their responses, and choose the most important points that they want to make during their part of the eulogy.

4. Bring the large group back together. Using the order of readings in step 1, invite each small group to come forward and present their part of the eulogy.

5. To conclude, invite the group to answer these two questions:
- Why is it important for the Israelites to remember King Josiah in the books of the Kings and Chronicles?
- What do they want to remember about him after he died?

Getting to Know Josiah

Decisions, Decisions

In this activity, young people reflect on the role that they ask adults to play when they have to make decisions. They use role-playing as a further basis for discussion.

Preparation

❏ Copy and cut out the four roles listed in resource Josiah-A, "Dilemma Decisions." Fold them and put them in a bowl, jar, or hat. If you have a group of eight to twelve young people, one per group will be sufficient. You may need to give the same role to more than one group if the class is larger.

❏ Have a quarter-sheet of plain or lined white paper for every two or three students as well as a pen or pencil for each.

1. Explain what it means to play a role, if necessary. Note that two or three young people will be given a situation, and they will need to improvise the dialogue until they resolve the scene. Note that all the role-plays will involve someone their age who is approaching a challenging situation and at least one adult.

 2. To begin, ask four groups to present the role-plays from resource Josiah–A, "Dilemma Decisions." Discuss the way that the role-plays unfolded with the group.

3. Have the young people turn to one or two people near them to form a small group. Distribute the quarter-sheets of paper and pens or pencils to each group. Ask them to write about a decision they are facing or have faced and to name the adult they would go to for advice on what to do. (Let them know ahead of time that others will read about their decision and to keep in mind that the situations should not be embarrassing or too personal.) Direct the young people to fold their slips of paper at least two times. Collect the slips in the bowl, jar, or hat. Mix up the folded papers.

4. Choose one person per group to pick a folded sheet of paper. Have that person read the situation and pick the other people from their group who will be in the role-play. Assist the young person if he or she is having trouble identifying other possible roles in the situation. In turn, have the young people from the other groups act out their role-plays spontaneously. Repeat this step as time allows, encouraging all the young people to participate.

5. When the role-plays are completed, ask the young people to share the types of situations for which they seek adult help and why that advice is important to them. From the role-plays, ask the students to see if there are common characteristics displayed by the student "adults" that could teach adults how they could be most helpful to the young people in decision making.

6. Read 2 Kings 22:10–20 aloud. Note that Josiah, at twenty-six years of age, gets advice and information from his priest, Hilkiah, and the prophetess, Huldah. Ask the young people, Why did Josiah seek advice from both of them? How did he think they could help him?

Life Is Fair—Sometimes

Preparation

❑ Provide six pieces of newsprint.

❑ Have six markers, one for each group.

❑ Display additional sheets of newsprint around the room or at an easel.

❑ Have one green and one red marker available.

1. Select five young people to be "leaders" and identify them as such to the rest of the group. Then divide the rest of the class into groups of five. Distribute one piece of newsprint and one marker to each small group including the group of leaders.

2. Instruct each small group to write five rules for conduct during the class or session that everyone must obey. Each group's rules may be serious or fanciful. It is up to them. Tell the leaders and only the leaders that they are in charge of the class. Their rules can be as kind or harsh as they want them to be. They have one rule to start: they can overrule any rules that the others make. Let them know that in the next step.

3. Ask the groups to share their rules one at a time. The leaders group goes last. List their rules on newsprint in green marker. At any time, the leaders group can overrule a rule. When one of the leaders dismisses a rule, strike it out in red. If the other young people question why the leaders can do this, tell them that they have this authority because they are the leaders. Finish with the leaders' list of rules. If you find that any of the leaders' rules contradict rules that have already been stated, ask them to decide which rule will be kept. (You can either ask the leaders to make decisions in consensus or leave it up to them. Given the nature of their power, they may easily argue, which is another insight you may want to discuss if it arises.)

4. Review the completed list of rules. In the large group, get responses to the following questions:

   ❍ Which rules are the most fair? Why?

   ❍ Which rules are the least fair? Why?

   ❍ As we were creating this list of rules, was it a fair or unfair process? Why or why not?

   ❍ As we were creating this list, what did someone say or do when they thought a rule or rule change was unfair?

   ❍ What would you imagine life would be like with this particular group of leaders?

   ❍ What do you say or do when you feel like you are being treated unfairly?

   ❍ What are the characteristics of good leadership?

5. Read 2 Kings 22:10-20 aloud. Note that the prophecy of Huldah says that the Israelites will not escape God's anger, but Josiah will be spared because he has been faithful to God. What characteristics of good leadership does Josiah possess? Why is the prophecy fair to Josiah?

Dilemma Decisions

....

Dilemma 1: Your group of friends is splitting up. You and your best friend are trying to decide which group to stay friends with. Your favorite coach overhears you discussing this, and asks, "How can I help?"

....

Dilemma 2: The student next to you in math class cheats, but never gets caught. You saw this person cheating on the big math test, but the teacher caught the wrong person. You are trying to decide what you should do when your mom asks, "What's wrong?"

....

Dilemma 3: Your mom and dad are pressuring you into going to the Catholic high school instead of the public school where all your friends are going. Your youth minister asks, "So, where are you going to high school?" and you decide to talk to him or her about it.

....

Dilemma 4: You go to a party with friends, but when you get there, your classmates are drinking and smoking. You are uncomfortable with this, but aren't sure you want to leave your friends. You call your mom or dad, but aren't sure what to say.

....

EZRA AND NEHEMIAH

Preparing to Teach

Overview

The Books of Ezra and Nehemiah chronicle the restoration of Israel. In 587 BC, the Babylonians conquered Israel and held them in captivity until 538 BC, when they were in turn defeated by Persia. The Persians allowed the Israelites to return to their land, but by then their home had been reduced nearly to rubble. Both Ezra and Nehemiah participated in the rebuilding of Jerusalem, both physically and religiously.

Many young adolescents will initially find Ezra and Nehemiah's views to be too harsh and outdated, especially considering their stance on mixed marriages and Israel's exclusivity. Be sure to point out that the Catholic Church does not maintain these beliefs. At the same time, we must ask our students to put themselves in the shoes of these leaders who were watching their people's faith and culture deteriorate before their eyes. Emphasize the significant role these two devout Jews play in saving Israel's way of life during a precarious time.

THIS CHAPTER AT A GLANCE

Getting to Know Ezra and Nehemiah

- Down to the Essentials

Scripture Passages Related to Ezra and Nehemiah

- Ezra 1:1-10 (Ezra's time: Cyrus sends the Jews back to Jerusalem)
- Ezra 3:7-13 (Ezra's time: Jews begin to rebuild the Temple)
- Ezra 7:1-10 (Ezra's background)*
- Ezra 9:1—10:17 (Ezra leads people in denouncing mixed marriages)*
- Nehemiah, chapters 1-2 (Nehemiah returns to Judah to help rebuild Jerusalem)*
- Nehemiah 9:6-37 (The people recall God's works)
- Nehemiah 10:28-39 (The people of Jerusalem promise to reform)*
- Nehemiah, chapter 13 (Nehemiah reforms the people of Jerusalem)*

Asterisk (*) signifies key passages to cover.

Break Through! Articles from *Breakthrough!* Related to Ezra and Nehemiah

- Introduction to the Books of Ezra and Nehemiah
- *Breakthrough!* Interview with Ezra and Nehemiah
- Persian Correction (Ezra, chapter 1)
- Keep Trying! (Ezra, chapters 4–5)
- Yippee! (Ezra 6:1–12)
- Answers to Prayer (Ezra 7:27–28)
- Mixed Marriages (Ezra, chapters 9–10)
- Big Deal, a Wall (Nehemiah, chapters 2–3)
- Stupid! (Nehemiah 4:1–5)
- Nehemiah Works for Justice (Nehemiah 5:1–13)
- Creator God (Nehemiah 9:6–37)
- The Dedication (Nehemiah 12:27–43)

Ezra and Nehemiah and Young Adolescents Today

- Ezra speaks out firmly against mixed marriages. Some students may have parents who do not practice the same religion. It is important for them to see that the conditions the Jews were facing do not resemble those today.
- Being part of a particular crowd is important to adolescents and they often use this to define each other's identity. Appealing to this tendency is a good way to help them understand why mixed marriages are so threatening to Ezra and Nehemiah.
- These stories can help remind young people to be grateful for their gifts of home and freedom, which are sometimes taken for granted.

Highlighting God's Presence

In the first year that Cyrus of Persia was emperor, the LORD made what he had said through the prophet Jeremiah come true (Ezra 1:1).

Our God was with us and protected us from enemy attacks and from ambush as we traveled (Ezra 8:31).

Getting to Know Ezra and Nehemiah

Down to the Essentials

In this activity, young people collectively prioritize important elements of their life as a way of gaining insight into the efforts of Ezra and Nehemiah to re-establish the Jewish identity.

Preparation

❑ Make four to six copies of handout Ezra and Nehemiah-A, "Defining the Boundaries," (one per group).

❑ Each group of students needs to have a pair of scissors and a pen.

1. Divide the class into groups of four or five students each. Read the following passages aloud:
- Ezra 10:28-30
- Nehemiah 2:17-18
- Nehemiah 13:1-3

2. Then read the article "Mixed Marriages" (Ezra, chapters 9-10) in *Breakthrough!* Emphasize that Ezra and Nehemiah were protecting the Israelites' faith and way of life.

3. Make the following comments in your own words:
- The Israelites are in a time of crisis and they need to remember and to define who they are.
- When people feel vulnerable, they tend to sort out those who threaten their way of life from those who support it. This sorting requires decisions about identity, beliefs, and commitment to those beliefs.

4. Give each group a copy of handout Ezra and Nehemiah-A, "Defining the Boundaries." Read the directions and review each element with the young people. Remind them to argue constructively, respect one another's opinions, and note that most likely none of them will be completely happy with the outcome. They will have to come to a consensus about the priorities of their group.

5. Allow 15 to 20 minutes for debate and decision making, then announce that each group has entered a crisis and will lose the four lowest-placed elements. Give them 5 minutes to discuss how this will affect their lives. Afterward they will report their conclusions to the class.

6. Allow each group to briefly describe their experience to the class. Use the following questions to guide the conversation:
- What were the most important elements in your group's life? Why?
- Who was unhappy with the decision? Why?
- How did the loss of the bottom four elements affect your life?
- Does going through this process make you think differently about Ezra and Nehemiah's situation? Explain.
- How do Catholics define who they are?

Ezra and Nehemiah

DEFINING THE BOUNDARIES

Cut out each section below. In the space provided next to each element, number them in order of the importance they have to the people in your group, with 1 being most important and 8 being least important. Next to each, write how this particular element plays a role in your lives and why you chose to give it its particular level of importance.

....

____ Faith

....

____ National Citizenship

....

____ Wealth

....

____ Education

....

____ Romantic Interest

....

____ Friendships

....

____ Family

....

____ Culture (music, arts, and so on)

....

JUDITH

Preparing to Teach

Overview

The story of Judith is a historical novel about the triumph of the Israelites over the great armies of King Nebuchadnezzar of the Assyrians. This defeat comes about through the actions of a Jewish woman. Judith is able to personally defeat the great military leader because she is a devout and faithful follower of God.

As a widow, she has experienced very difficult times but did not lose her faith. She is a very smart woman who puts herself in a dangerous position in order to save her people. She prays before, during, and after her act of courage.

Judith teaches us many lessons. She shows us that knowing, praising, and thanking God is the most important thing in life. No other god—not gold, jewels, or a mighty man like the king—can take his place.

THIS CHAPTER AT A GLANCE

Getting to Know the Story of Judith

- Special Report: Judith Defeats the Assyrians

Getting to Know Judith

- Of Gods and God
- Prayer and Hard Times

Scripture Passages Related to Judith

- Judith, chapters 4-6 (Holofernes and Israel plan for battle)
- Judith 8:1-8 (Description of Judith, the widow)
- Judith 8:9-36 (Judith proposes her plan to defeat the Assyrians)*
- Judith, chapter 9 (Judith prays to God for assistance)*
- Judith 10:6-11:4 (Judith goes to the Assyrians and meets

Holofernes)*
- Judith 11:5—23 (Judith tells Holofernes her plan to destroy the Israelites)*
- Judith 12:1—13:11 (Judith puts her plan into action)*
- Judith 14:1—15:7 (The Israelites defeat the Assyrians)*
- Judith 15:8-13 (The Israelites praise Judith)*
- Judith 16:1-17 (Judith praises and thanks God)*

Asterisk (*) signifies key passages to cover.

Break Through! Articles from *Breakthrough!* Related to Judith

- *Breakthrough!* Interview with Judith
- Introduction to the Book of Judith
- Peace, Not Violence (Judith 13:1-10)

Judith and Young Adolescents Today

- Holofernes and the Assyrians trust the strength and numbers of their army. Judith and her people trust in God. Students need to trust in themselves and their relationships with God and others rather than in physical power and possessions.
- Judith takes a stand against the ancient "bully" Nebuchadnezzar. Students encounter bullies at school and in their neighborhoods regularly.
- Holofernes and the Assyrians believe that Nebuchadnezzar is their god and will lead them to victory. Students are faced with many different gods in their world, especially consumerism and sports.
- Judith bravely stands up for her people. Students are called on to stand up for their friends and family members.
- Judith does not believe in testing or putting conditions on God's friendship. Students face similar circumstances among their groups of friends.
- Judith is loyal to God, following his laws even when she is away from her own people. Students feel a strong sense of loyalty to their friends when they are close to each other and when they are apart.
- Judith prays to God for help before she faces the enemy. Students often call on God's assistance to aid them through tough times.
- The Assyrians judge Judith based on her beauty and overlook her intelligence. Students may feel that they are judged by others based on what they look like or can do rather than on who they are inside.
- Rather than creating a lie, Judith uses the truth to defeat the Assyrians. Students need to avoid the temptation to lie in order to get what they want and instead trust in the truth.

- Judith defeats the Assyrians through smart thinking rather than violence. Students can resolve conflict by thinking and talking through their problems rather than fighting.

Highlighting God's Presence

"If you follow my advice, God will do something great with you, and my LORD will not fail in his plan" (Judith 11:6; Judith to Holofernes).

Everyone in the city was utterly amazed. They bowed down and worshipped God, praying together. "Our God, you are worthy of great praise. Today you have triumphed over the enemies of your people" (Judith 13:17).

Getting to Know the Story of Judith

Special Report: Judith Defeats the Assyrians

Preparation

❑ Students will need bibles, paper, and pens or pencils.

1. Divide the large group into ten pairs or triads. Ensure that each small group has bibles, paper, and pens or pencils. Assign each group one of the readings under "Scripture Passages Related to Judith." (If the class is very small, combine consecutive readings and divide the students accordingly.)

2. Inform the students that they are going to be creating a radio or TV news program. The program will follow the breaking news about Judith and the defeat of the Assyrians. Designate an adult leader or peer minister as the emcee for the show.

3. Tell the students to read the Scriptures aloud in their small group, compose a headline for their story, and write the key elements of their story. Instruct each group to designate a reporter to represent it. Give the emcee all the headlines and the names of the reporters so that he or she can be prepared to introduce each story. Encourage the students to practice their presentations before the radio or TV show begins.

4. Gather the students into the large group. Provide the emcee with a chair or stool at the front of the group. Begin the radio or TV show by introducing the emcee. The emcee will give a short introduction to the main story of the day and announce the first headline and the reporters. The reporters can stand at their place and give their report. Continue until all the reports are completed.

5. Conclude by asking the group to identify the key actions in Judith's story. Highlight the fact that she prayed before, during, and after she killed Holofernes. Ask the group to name five things they learned from the story of Judith.

Getting to Know Judith

Of Gods and God

Preparation

❑ Provide the following items:
- Construction paper, multiple sheets of various colors
- Scissors, one for every four to five students
- Cellophane tape
- Glue sticks
- Markers, various colors
- One large (12-by-12-inch maximum) box, wrapped in gold paper
- One small table (round preferred), set at the front of the room—it may be covered with a formal tablecloth

❑ Using construction paper, make a "sculpture" of each of the following. Put these sculptures out of sight.
- A popular piece of electronics, e.g., Gameboy, Playstation
- Money
- A mother and father
- God (use images that would be relevant for your students)

1. Ask the students to think of something in their lives that is very, very important, for example, a particular friend, a sport, or a favorite game. This something should be more important to them than just about anything else.

2. With that "something" in mind, have them create a "sculpture" of that thing using construction paper and the other items you have provided. Require that the sculpture be at least one foot high or wide (This is necessary so that in later steps, everyone in the group will be able to see what it is.)

3. Asking for volunteers to go first, invite each person to come forward and put their sculpture on the table and to explain why and how it represents something so important to them. Affirm each student. At the conclusion of each presentation, tell the group that each sculpture is important. We want to find out which "somethings" are the most important to the entire group. Ask the rest of the group to rate each sculpture from 1 to 10, with 1 being not important to them and 10 being very important to them. Have the students raise their hands for each sculpture for a range of numbers. Keep a record of the responses. To the side, line up the sculptures in order of importance based on the vote total that they get.

4. After the last student sculpture is reviewed, put out the first of the four that were set aside and follow the same process as in step 3. Keep mother and father and God to present last.

5. Review the order of the sculptures based on importance. If the young people put God first, ask them why they have done so. If they do not put God first, request an explanation. Review the first several bullet points in "Judith and Young Adolescents Today" about Nebuchadnezzar being a god, and Judith and her relationship with God. Note that we sometimes place other things above God like our desires for great toys or cool friends. Ask these questions:

○ What can happen to a person's spiritual life if they put God at the end of their priority list?

○ Some Christians believe that they are putting God first but then do not act that way. Have you ever caught yourself doing the same thing?

○ Why is it hard to keep God as the most important thing in your life?

○ What are some ways that we can remind ourselves about God's place in our lives?

Prayer and Hard Times

Preparation

❑ Provide paper and pens or pencils.

❑ Bring newsprint and markers.

1. Read Judith, chapter 9, her prayer to God for assistance before she goes out to meet the Assyrians. Highlight that the Israelites are having hard times and that the Assyrians are preparing to fight and slaughter them.

2. Brainstorm examples with the students of tough times that a young adolescent might face. List them on the newsprint. Have them close their eyes, and as you name each one of the tough times, ask them to raise their hands if they have prayed to God when they were experiencing that tough time. Using a different color, highlight all of the examples where they prayed. Hopefully most, if not all of them, will be highlighted. Note that like Judith, they also pray to God during tough times.

3. Distribute paper and pens or pencils to the students. Invite the students to choose one of the tough times that they have experienced and write a prayer to God about it, putting themselves back into the situation for the sake of the prayer.

4. Without asking the students to read their prayers, ask them to share what they asked God for. They may ask for patience, kindness, or protection. Ask, "Why is it that we sometimes just ask God to be there with us?" Note that like Judith, we do not try to tell God what to do, but let God work as he chooses and as we need in our life, especially during tough times.

ESTHER

Preparing to Teach

Overview

The Book of Esther has two parts. The first, the Hebrew version of Esther found in chapters one through ten, does not contain direct references to God. The expanded Greek version, found in chapters A through F, has a strong focus on God and prayer. The book explains the origins of the Jewish festival of Purim and explores the nature of God's presence in the world. The story of Esther teaches us that God is always present and is ultimately in control. The overarching hero of the Book of Esther is the God of Israel.

Esther and her cousin, Mordecai, can mentor us in learning to pray with confidence and trust. When these two people encounter a challenge, they pray and then act. This is a good lesson for young people, who like many adults, can simply react rather than reflect, pray, and act.

Esther is also a book about virtue and vice. Modern-day Jewish festivities for Purim honor the courageous deeds of Esther and Mordecai, and rebuke the treacherous acts of Haman. Young people can appreciate Esther's bravery in confronting her husband. Life choices cultivate heroism; chance circumstances create a hero. Esther and Mordecai are heroes both by choice and chance.

THIS CHAPTER AT A GLANCE

Getting to Know the Story of Esther

- Divine Hide and Seek
- Alone, But Not Lonely

Getting to Know Esther

- Purim People: Heroes by Choice and Chance

Scripture Passages Related to Esther

- Esther, chapters A and 1 (Mordecai's rise; Queen Vashti's departure)

- Esther 2:1–18 (Esther becomes queen)
- Esther 2:19–23, chapters B and 3 (Haman and the king plot to kill the Jews)
- Esther, chapters 4 and C (Esther's prayerful plea)
- Esther, chapters 5 through 7 and D (Esther's banquet)
- Esther, chapters 8, E, and 9 (Esther and Mordecai save the Jews)
- Esther 9:20–32 (Commemorating the events)

Articles from *Breakthrough!* Related to Esther

- *Breakthrough!* Interview with Esther
- R-e-s-p-e-c-t (Esther, chapter 1)
- Supporting Immigrants (Esther, 2:10–11)
- The Final Solution (Esther, chapter 3)
- Let Nothing Disturb You (Esther C:23–25)
- The Courage of a Queen (Esther 4:9–17, D:1–16)
- Forgiving Our Enemies (Esther 5:9–14)
- Esther and Joseph (Esther 6:1–10)
- Saving the Jews (Esther 8:1–12)
- The Festival of Purim (Esther 9:20–31)

Esther and Young Adolescents Today

- Esther responds courageously to the needs of her people. Esther can inspire young people to step forward to help someone, despite the risks. See "The Courage of a Queen" in *Breakthrough!*
- Hatred against Jewish people affects Esther's life. Young people witness and experience various expressions of hatred in the world today.
- Difficult circumstances ultimately enable Esther to affect significant social change. Young people who are experiencing difficulties in their lives might ask themselves if God could be calling them to work toward changing things for the better. See "Esther and Joseph" in *Breakthrough!*
- Esther prays diligently when she is faced with challenges. Students can take heart and know that God will also listen to them when they are in trouble, helping them know what to do.

Highlighting God's Presence

Mordecai prayed to the LORD . . . : "O LORD, you are the LORD and King of all creation, and everything obeys your commands. If you wish to save Israel, no one can stop you" (Esther C:1–4).

She [Queen Esther] prayed to the LORD God of Israel, "My LORD and King, only you are God. I am all alone, and I have no one to turn to but you. Help me!" (Esther C:14).

But God changed the king's anger into tender concern (Esther D:8).

God, who governs all things, has turned that day of destruction into a day of celebration for his chosen people (Esther E:21).

Getting to Know the Story of Esther

Divine Hide and Seek

In this activity, students focus on the Hebrew part of the Book of Esther and search for God's presence in places where God's name is not explicitly mentioned.

Preparation

❏ Familiarize yourself with the Hebrew and Greek versions of the Book of Esther as explained in "Overview."

❏ Purim is celebrated today by wearing costumes, often to depict the players in this biblical drama. If you have a Sherlock Holmes hat, a magnifying glass, or some other detective costume, it might be fun to use such props for this activity of seeking out the hidden face of God in the Hebrew version of Esther.

1. Share the following background information with the students:

❍ More than two authors wrote the Book of Esther: one in the Hebrew language and one in Greek. For this exercise, you will be reading the Hebrew version. In the Jewish canon, the Book of Esther is the only book that does not mention the name of God directly.

❍ The name *Esther* comes from the Hebrew root *hester*, which means "hidden." The Jewish Bible explores the hidden face of God, *hester panim*, through the coincidences, twists of fate, and reversal of fortunes that are in Esther's story.

2. Give the students the following instructions:

❍ Read the Hebrew version of Esther as detectives in search of God's presence in the story. You can think of this search as a game of Hide and Seek, in which God wants you to find him but you need to search for him within the Book of Esther.

○ There is an expression, "A coincidence is a small miracle in which God chooses to remain anonymous." (Remind the students of miracles from Old Testament stories, such as the parting of the Red Sea.) Look in the story of Esther for small miracles—coincidences that reveal God's anonymous, hidden presence.

3. After the students have looked through Esther, ask them to pair off and talk about coincidences they find in their own lives. Ask them to discuss the question, "Could these coincidences have a connection to God?" Close by asking the students to think about the coincidences in their own lives, and invite them to act as detectives who try to discover God in these moments. Refer to Jesus' exhortation, "Ask, and you will receive; seek, and you will find; knock, and the door will be opened to you" (Luke 11:9).

Alone, But Not Lonely

In this activity, students look at the Greek portion of the Book of Esther and consider what it means that we are never really alone with God near us.

Preparation

❑ Familiarize yourself with the Greek portions of the Book of Esther: chapters A–F.

1. If you have not already done so, share the information about the Greek and Hebrew text that can be found in step 1 of the previous activity. Emphasize that the expanded Greek text uses God's name frequently, especially in prayer. The Greek part clearly identifies God in the orchestration of events in Esther's story. God's presence is just a prayer away!

2. Read Mordecai and Esther's prayer in chapter C aloud to the class. Ask: "What does it mean to trust God? How does praying make that trust stronger?" Refer to other prayers in the Bible in which people have trustingly affirmed God's presence in their lives. (Note the prayer attributed to King David in Psalm 34:1–9.)

3. Ask, "What is the difference between simply being alone and being lonely?" Discuss that there will be times in our lives in which we will be alone, but that God's ongoing presence can help us to not feel lonely, even in tough times. (If the students are familiar with the Andrew Lloyd Webber production of *Joseph and the Amazing Technicolor Dreamcoat,* they may also know a song from that production, "Close Every Door." In the song, Joseph lyrically expresses from his prison cell that we will never be lonely when we have a relationship with God. See appendix 1 for information about this production.)

4. Ask the students to reflect on an experience in which they were alone but did not feel lonely, and to write a prayer that captures those feelings. Close the exercise with the words of Saint Teresa of Ávila in the article, "Let Nothing Disturb You," from *Breakthrough!* near Esther C:23-25.

Getting to Know Esther

Purim People: Heroes by Choice and Chance

In this activity, students use Esther and Mordecai as role models to assess the virtues of heroes.

Preparation

❑ Make copies of handout Esther-A, "Purim People: Heroes by Choice and Chance," one for each student.

1. Distribute handout Esther-A, "Purim People: Heroes by Choice and Chance." Review the handout and explain that Purim commemorates a time of grief turned into joy because of the heroism of Esther and Mordecai. Ask the students to name heroic people and actions today and write their responses on the board.

2. As a large group, ask the students to suggest virtues that heroes have, and have them write these on their handouts. The letters of the word *Purim* are prompts to tie this activity to the biblical story. Start each line with a virtue that begins with that particular letter, but then fill the remaining space with many heroic virtues.

3. Close by discussing that our daily choices contribute to our character. Challenge the students with this question: "In an unpredicted or chance circumstance, can you be a hero?"

PURIM PEOPLE:
HEROES BY CHOICE AND CHANCE

Purim is a yearly Jewish celebration that marks the day in which Esther and Mordecai heroically saved their people from death. The name of the celebration, *Purim*, means "lots." Haman, the enemy of the Jews, drew "lots" (much like a game of chance using dice or a spinner) to decide the day of the death edict. Although Esther and Mordecai were somewhat surprised by their chance to be hero and heroine, they were good people who made that choice.

Today, we use the word *lots* to say that there are many of one thing or another, such as: "There are lots of pages in a Bible!" "There are lots of virtues that make people heroes." Facing unexpected difficulties with virtue creates heroes. Though the situation that creates a hero may be by *chance*, the characteristics that empower a hero are by *choice*.

What are the character traits that we find in heroes today? Think of all the qualities of a hero and begin your list by using the letters from the word *Purim*. Do not be limited to just those letters, though. You should be able to list LOTS of virtuous qualities! Is there a hero in you?!

P _____

_____

U _____

_____

R_____

_____

I _____

_____

M_____

_____

THE MACCABEES

Preparing to Teach

Overview

Though these two biblical books are named after the Maccabees and do tell their story, they also describe a larger struggle between the Greeks who want to impose Hellenism on the Jews and the Jews who want to remain faithful to their God and practices.

The books are named for Judas Maccabeus, who, along with his brothers, leads a successful revolt against the Greek overlords. The brothers then become successive leaders of Israel. Because God is with them, they are often able to win battles against armies much larger and better prepared than they are. Judas and his brothers are even able to reclaim the Temple and rededicate it after the Greeks have horribly defiled it.

In the books, we also find additional stories of the bravery shown by the Jews during this period in their history. Many Jews choose horrible deaths rather than show disrespect for their faith or God.

For young adolescents in the United States, the thought of someone imposing religious beliefs on them is unthinkable, but this is not so throughout the world. It is easy for American Catholics to take religious freedom for granted and to see their faith tradition and Church as "extra" rather than "central" to their lives. The stories in 1 and 2 Maccabees are an opportunity for young people to imagine what they would do if they were in an oppressive situation.

THIS CHAPTER AT A GLANCE

Getting to Know the Story of the Maccabees

- Flags and Banners for the Maccabees Era

Getting to Know the Maccabees

- Resistance or Compromise in the Maccabees' World

Scripture Passages Related to the Maccabees

- 1 Maccabees 1:1-9 (Background: History of Greek Dominance)
- 1 Maccabees 1:20-53 (Antiochus persecutes the Jews)*
- 1 Maccabees 2:15-25 (Mattathias refuses to submit to Greeks)*

The Maccabees

- 1 Maccabees 3:1–9 (2 Maccabees 8:1–7) (Judas leads victories against enemies)*
- 1 Maccabees 4:36–59 (2 Maccabees 10:1–8) (Purification and rededication of the Temple)*
- 1 Maccabees 9:1–31 (Judas dies; his brother Jonathon takes over)
- 2 Maccabees 2:19–24 (An introduction to 2 Maccabees)
- 2 Maccabees 3:1–40 (God thwarts the raiding of the Temple treasury and converts a perpetrator)
- 2 Maccabees 4:1–31 (Eleazar remains faithful unto death)
- 2 Maccabees 7:1–42 (Mother and sons tortured and die for their faith)*
- 2 Maccabees 10:1–8 (Judas and followers rededicate the Temple)*
- 2 Maccabees 12:38–45 (Judas encourages soldiers to pray for their deceased comrades)*

Asterisk (*) signifies key passages to cover.

Break Through! Articles from *Breakthrough!* Related to the Maccabees

- *Breakthrough!* Interview with the Maccabees
- Introduction to the First Book of Maccabees
- Where are the Maccabees? (Beginning of 1 Maccabees)
- Please and Thanks, God (2 Maccabees 1:24–29)
- Introduction to the Second Book of Maccabees
- Hanukkah (2 Maccabees 2:16–18)
- Praying for Enemies (2 Maccabees 3:29–40)
- Integrity (2 Maccabees 6:18–31)
- Eternal Life (2 Maccabees, chapter 7)
- God's Mercy Returns (2 Maccabees 8:1–7)
- Prayer for Protection (2 Maccabees 10:25–26)
- Praying for the Dead (2 Maccabees 12:39–45)

The Maccabees and Young Adolescents Today

- The Maccabees are five brothers underneath their father's leadership who take on the foreign occupants of Judea. This success story of the "underdog" is the stuff of movies, and young people can admire the brothers' courage and heroism. A key difference is that the Maccabees succeed because they rely on God.
- The Maccabees and other faithful families grow closer together and stronger in faith for struggling together through terrible times. Young adolescents often draw closer to their families in times of crisis.
- The Jewish faith in this era shows evidence that there is belief in the resurrection of the dead and appreciation of the value of praying for the dead. Young adolescents face death directly and indirectly. An important way of dealing with death is through the hope of eternal life for ourselves and those we love.

- Under Greek domination, the Jews must either stop their cultural and religious practices or accept the consequences, which may involve suffering. Young adolescents struggle to resist peer pressure alone. The Jewish families who resist the Greek domination are models of integrity for the young adolescent.

Highlighting God's Presence

When Judas's men saw the army coming against them, they asked, "How can our little group of men fight an army as big as that? Besides, we have not eaten all day, and we are tired!"

"It is not difficult," Judas answered, "for a small group to overpower a large one. It makes no difference to the LORD whether we are rescued by many people or by just a few. Victory in battle does not depend on who has the largest army; it is the LORD's power that determines the outcome. . . . When we attack, the LORD will crush our enemies, so don't be afraid of them" (1 Maccabees 3:17–19,22).

[The mother said to her son] "So I urge you, my child, to look at the sky and the earth. Consider everything you see there, and realize that God made it all from nothing, just as he made the human race. Don't be afraid of this butcher. Give up your life willingly and prove yourself worthy of your brothers, so that by God's mercy I may receive you back with them at the resurrection" (2 Maccabees 7:28–29).

If [Judas] had not believed that the dead would be raised, it would have been foolish and useless to pray for them. In his firm and devout conviction that all of God's faithful people would receive a wonderful reward, Judas made provision for a sin offering to set free from their sin those who had died (2 Maccabees 12:44–45).

Getting to Know the Story of the Maccabees

Flags and Banners for the Maccabees Era

In this activity, young people create twelve flags or banners that represent twelve readings from the first and second books of Maccabees.

Preparation

❏ Each student needs to have a Bible, markers, pens, copy paper, scissors, and a straightedge.

❏ Provide the list of readings from "Scripture Passages Related to the Maccabees" in a visible place.

1. Introduce the activity by saying that the military themes of these books call to mind flags and banners used as ways to memorialize key moments in the life of a nation.

2. Divide the class in half. The first half should read the first six selections from 1 Maccabees while the second half will read the second six listed for 2 Maccabees. Give students some quiet time to read through the chapters.

3. Distribute the pieces of copy paper, markers, scissors, and straightedges to each student.

4. Give the following instructions to the groups:

○ The first Maccabees group is to make a rectangle flag for each of their readings. (It would be easiest to subdivide the group and assign each of the six readings.) They can ask themselves, "What images and what patterns would convey the events that are in this particular reading?" On the back of the paper the student should summarize the reading and cite the Scripture passage being described.

○ The second Maccabees group is to make triangle flags for each of their readings with images that summarize what happens. (Subdivide the group into six smaller groups, one for each citation.)

5. Ask representatives to explain the twelve groups' flags and summarize the readings. Use these discussion questions:
• What impresses you about these stories?
• What disturbs you? Why?

Getting to Know the Maccabees

Resistance or Compromise in the Maccabees' World

In this activity, students debate and discuss the ways that people can respond to an oppressive situation. It would be good to know if any of your young people have, or have had, family members or friends in a combat zone. You may want to be careful in the debate and discussion not to create painful tension among your students about a topic that is very real for some of them.

Preparation

❑ Each student needs to have a Bible, the list of readings from "Scripture Passages Related to the Maccabees," paper, and a pen.

1. Introduce the activity in your own words:
• The story of the Maccabees raises a difficult issue for Christians. If

people are in a situation where their religion is being suppressed, they have several choices:

+ Fight for one's faith against overwhelming odds
+ Quietly appear to go along with the oppressor but secretly practice the faith
+ Quit practicing the religion

2. Divide the class into two groups. Assign one side to defend the "fight for one's faith" point of view and have the other side defend the "quiet, appearing to go along" point of view. Using the readings, have each side develop two arguments to support their side.

- 1 Maccabees 2:15-25 (Mattathias refuses to submit to Greeks)
- 1 Maccabees 3:1-9 (2 Maccabees 8:1-7) (Judas leads victories against enemies)
- 1 Maccabees 4:36-59 (Purification and rededication of the Temple)
- 2 Maccabees 4:1-31 (Eleazar remains faithful unto death)
- 2 Maccabees 7:1-42 (Mother and sons tortured and die for faith)

3. After each side has presented their position, have the students individually write a brief reflection describing how they would act in response to the Maccabean uprising if they were a Jew at that time. The reflection should be a first person account. Each student should either support the Maccabees or reject their plan to attack the overwhelmingly superior Greek forces.

4. Invite students to share some of what they have written. Ask these questions to further discussion with them:

- What is the relationship between believing in God and fighting a war?
- In 1 and 2 Maccabees, we see heroic families who suffer for their beliefs. What do you think motivates them to do this?
- Is there something or someone you would be willing to die or suffer greatly for? Who or what? Why? Why not? (This could be a private reflection.)
- Is there someone who has suffered for you or for someone you know? What motivated them to do so? (This could be a private reflection.)

5. Conclude the activity by prayerfully giving thanks for those courageous men and women in our communities who put their lives on the line for others.

Variations

- Invite a military chaplain and conscientious objector to the class to answer questions about the way that they live out their faith in relationship to the military.
- Put together a care package or a prayer package for some military personnel abroad.

JOB

Preparing to Teach

Overview

The Book of Job is a classic tale addressing the universal question, "Why do bad things happen to good people?" As young adolescents are reaching the developmental stage in which they acknowledge and struggle with injustices, they sooner or later tackle Job's question in one form or another.

The story offers excellent opportunities to explore how one's faith can be tested in troubling times. Though we are unsure when or by whom the Book of Job was written, many scholars suggest that much of it was recorded after the Israelites' captivity in Babylon. This timing could explain why this story of unjust punishment of the innocent would have so much meaning to the Israelites.

Young people may have a difficult time understanding why the story depicts God making a bet with Satan that includes the destruction of an innocent man's family and worldly goods. It is important to highlight the genre of this story, a folk tale. Also note that though the story may have some distant roots in a historical event, the Israelites used it as a means to address the question of divine retribution, the idea that God punishes those who sin during their earthly lives, not as an historical record of actual events. You may want to point out that the first line in the Book of Job has a similar tone not unlike the fairy tale beginning, "Once upon a time . . ."

The Israelites understood God as one who carried out justice in this world. Good was rewarded and evil was punished. They also believed that God sometimes punishes a person for the sins of that person's ancestors. Young adolescents are coming from a developmental stage that is not unlike this notion. They often perceive that those who follow the rules are rewarded and those who break the rules get punished. Though this may be true to some extent in grammar school, they're slowly learning that not all things in life follow this principle.

THIS CHAPTER AT A GLANCE

Getting to Know the Story of Job

- A Modern-Day Job

Getting to Know Job

- Finding Ourselves in Job's Shoes
- Where Can We Find Job Now?
- The Pillars of Our Lives

Scripture Passages Related to Job

- Job 1:1-5 (The goodness of Job)*
- Job 1:6-12 (God accepts Satan's bet)*
- Job 1:13-22 (Job loses everything)*
- Job 2:1-10 (Satan gives Job sores but Job remains faithful)*
- Job, chapters 3-28 (Job's friends debate the reasons for Job's suffering)
- Job, chapters 29-31 (Job pleads his cause and maintains his innocence)*
- Job, chapters 32-37 (Elihu's Speech)
- Job, chapters 38-41 (The Lord answers Job)*
- Job, chapter 42 (Job answers the Lord and has his life restored)

Asterisk (*) signifies key passages to cover.

Articles from *Breakthrough!* Related to Job

- *Breakthrough!* Interview with Job
- Introduction to the Book of Job
- The Fall from a Good Life (Job, chapter 1)
- Being There Is Enough (Job 2:11-13)
- Let Me Feel Peace (Job, chapter 3)
- The (Really, Really) Long Debate (Job, chapter 4)
- Honestly, God! (Job 7:7-21)
- Reward and Punishment (Job, chapter 21)
- Integrity (Job 27:1-6)
- Keepin' an Eye Out (Job 29:2-5)
- God's Wisdom (Job 40:1-5)
- God's Blessing for Job (Job, chapter 42)

Job and Young Adolescents Today

- Like Job, most young adolescents have experienced some kind of injustice, such as being accused of something that they did not do.
- As Job suffers the loss of his family and all his worldly goods, he has three friends who come and sit with him silently. Young people value the special friends who are there for them in time of great need.
- Like Job, some young adolescents may have already experienced a tragic event (such as the premature death of a family member) that has made them question God's reasoning and justice.
- Unfortunately in difficult times, young adolescents may feel that God holds a grudge against them and that they are not loved by God. They may question what they have done to deserve God's wrath.

- As many of your students become more aware of life's tragedies, they may question why God would allow these things to occur. Awareness of events such as the Holocaust or even the nightly news stories may bring this question to light.

Highlighting God's Presence

"Did you notice my servant, Job?" the LORD asked. "There is no one on earth as faithful and good as he is. He worships me and is careful not to do anything evil" (Job 1:8; God to Satan).

"Who are you to question my wisdom
   with your ignorant, empty words?
Now stand up straight
   and answer the questions I ask you.
Were you there when I made the world?
   If you know so much, tell me about it.
Who decided how large it would be?
   Who stretched the measuring line over it?
   Do you know all the answers?"

(Job 38: 2–5; God to Job)

Getting to Know the Story of Job

A Modern-Day Job

In this activity, the student will come up with a skit that will retell the story of Job in modern-day terms.

Preparation

❑ Each student should have a pen and some paper.

❑ Students need to have bibles.

❑ Provide poster board, markers, or other materials that could be used for props.

1. Have the students read the following abridged version of the Book of Job. If time is available, this highly emotional tale works well when read aloud. (Parts of it, especially those where Job laments his predicament, could benefit from a somewhat melodramatic reading. Although it's important to maintain respect for subject matter, the use of comical melodrama can make it entertaining and engaging, while still respectful.)

Use the following plan as you read the Book of Job aloud while the class follows along in their bibles.

- Job 1:1—3:10 (Job loses all)
- Job 4:1-11, 8:1-10, 11:1-9 (Job's friends debate the reasons for Job's misfortune)
- Job 13:1-4, 27:1-5 (Job replies to their arguments and maintains his innocence)
- Job 38:1-11, 39:1-4 (The Lord responds and puts Job in his place)
- Job 40:3-5, 42:1-6 (Job replies)
- Job 42:7-17 (Job is restored)

2. Divide the class into groups of five or six students each and assign each group a passage from Job. Direct them to come up with short skits that depict the story of a modern-day, junior high Job. Allow the students to ad lib a little with the story line, noting that this story addressed questions for people in a particular place and time, and that the students may have similar, but still different questions. Here is a list of possible passages and titles:

- Job 1:1-5 (The Junior High Job Who Has It All)
- Job 1:6-22 (God and Satan Make a Bet and Job Loses Everything— Even the Nintendo!)
- Job 2:11-13 (Job's Friends Come by His House to Comfort Him)
- Job, chapters 4, 8, and 11 (Job's Friends Argue About Why This Happened)
- Job, chapters 29 and 38 (Job Replies and God Puts Him in His Place)

3. After the skits have been performed, allow the students to discuss the notion that God rewards the good and punishes the evil in this world. At some point, explain why this idea seems absurd to us now. You can use the following questions as discussion starters:

- Are there events in life that can make you think that God blesses some but not others? Why or Why not?
- Does God punish people for the bad things that their great-grandparents did? Will God punish your grandchildren for the things that you do?
- If a baby is born with a disability or a serious illness, is God punishing that child? Explain your answer.
- Everybody has free will, the ability to freely choose to do right or wrong. How does this play a part in the suffering of other people?
- In 2004, a devastating tsunami hit Indonesia and other nearby countries killing over 200,000 people. What role, if any, do you think God plays in events like these?

Getting to Know Job

Finding Ourselves in Job's Shoes

In this activity the students reflect on the similarities between Job's suffering and their own.

Preparation

❑ Make a copy of handout Job-A, "The Suffering of Job," for each student.

❑ Students will each need a pen or pencil.

1. Read Job 7:1-7 aloud with the students. Emphasize the final line.

2. Comment that when people suffer they often feel that they will never be happy again, and yet this is almost never the case. You might offer an example from your own life, if appropriate.

3. Hand out and read aloud the questions on handout Job-A, "The Suffering of Job." Ask the students to reflect on their past experiences of suffering by answering the questions quietly in writing.

4. After students have completed the handout questions, have volunteers read their answers, as they are comfortable. Emphasize and praise their abilities to overcome adversity with perseverance and faith.

Where Can We Find Job Now?

Preparation

❑ Direct each student to bring a newspaper or news magazine.

❑ Make a copy of handout Job-B "Finding Job in Today's News," for each student.

❑ The students will need scissors, glue (or tape or a stapler), and a pen.

1. Have the students find a news article about a person who has been unjustly victimized—be it from crime or a natural disaster. Have them read and clip out the article.

2. Pass out handout Job-B, "Finding Job in Today's News," to the students. They should answer the questions about their article on the handout and then attach the article to it afterward.

3. After completing the assignment, take time for the students to summarize and comment on their articles on the back of the handout. Ask for volunteers to respond to some of the questions below to spark a discussion:

- ○ How would you react to this event?

- ○ Has anyone in the class been in a similar situation?

- ○ How could events like these affect our faith?

- ○ What do you think Job would do?

The Pillars of Our Lives

In this activity, the students reflect on the people to whom they turn in times of need.

Preparation

❑ Make a copy of handout Job-C, "Shapes of Support," for each student.

❑ Each student will need a pen or pencil.

1. Read Job 2:11–13 aloud with the students. Also read the article "Being There Is Enough" (Job 2:11–13) from *Breakthrough!* Discuss the importance of friends and family members who help each other in times of pain and sadness.

2. Offer your own personal story of a time when you needed someone to support you or when you supported someone else in a time of trouble.

3. Pass out handout Job-C, "Shapes of Support," for the students to complete *in private* and preferably at home. (Though this process can be an extremely valuable experience for young adolescents, it can also be very divisive and painful if their responses were expressed in public. By not appearing on a friend's list, some students could be very hurt. It would also be wise to explain to the students why this activity should be done privately. They'll know what you're talking about!)

THE SUFFERING OF JOB

Answer the following questions. Continue writing on the back if you need more room.

1. When the Book of Job was written, the Israelites believed that God rewarded the good and punished the evil in this world. But sometimes this did not make sense to them because they found that bad things sometimes happened to good people (like Job). Jesus is another example of an innocent person who suffers. Describe a time in your life when you thought that God was punishing you. Looking back, what do you think about that time now?

2. Some of Job's friends thought that he probably did something wrong, but was just not admitting it. Describe a time when you were accused of something that you did not do. How did you feel at the time? How did you react?

3. At one point Job complains to God, "I call out to you, O God, but you never answer" (Job 30:20). Many people have expressed this frustration at some point in their lives, yet it isn't necessarily a sign of someone who is losing their faith. The following passage was found etched into the wall of a Nazi concentration camp:

I believe in the sun,
even when it is not shining.

I believe in love,
even when I cannot feel it.

I believe in God,
even when he is silent.

In your life, when has God been the most silent?

4. It is interesting how much Job cries out to God and complains! God certainly puts Job in his place, yet he doesn't seem to be bothered by Job's anger. When and why have you been angry at God? Did you feel as comfortable as Job in expressing it? Why or why not?

FINDING JOB IN TODAY'S NEWS

Title of Article:

_____

_____

Answer the following questions about the article.

    1. How does the victim's story resemble Job's story? Describe similarities and differences.

    2. What might be some of the emotions that the victims are experiencing?

    3. How would you feel in this particular circumstance?

    4. Is there anything about the story that leads you to think that the victims in the article might feel as if they have been abandoned or punished by God?

    5. What could someone do that might remind the victims that God still loves and cares for them despite this tragedy?

SHAPES OF SUPPORT

Like Job we all need friends and family members to whom we can turn in our times of pain and sorrow. Fortunately our support comes in all shapes and sizes! Use these fill-in-the-blank statements to think about the people to whom you turn in times of need. If you can think of more than one person to put in the blank, write them both down! Remember all the people in your support system: parents, friends, teachers, siblings, trusted adults, doctors, other family members, and so on. Who else?

LADY WISDOM

Preparing to Teach

Overview

The Wisdom books address everyday practical problems, virtuous living, and the deeper questions of life. These books include Job, Proverbs, Ecclesiastes, Sirach, Song of Songs, and Wisdom of Solomon. Though Lady Wisdom is not an actual person, the biblical writers sometimes use this personification to characterize God's wisdom.

Lady Wisdom is an image the Old Testament writers sometimes use to portray the Spirit of God. Rather than presenting wisdom in the abstract, these sages occasionally give it the flesh of a woman in their descriptions, maybe because they associate the creative nature of God's Spirit with a woman's role in birthing new life.

Though they might not be quick to admit it, young people are hungry for true wisdom. With the relatively recent arrival of the Internet into our homes, young people of the early twenty-first century have access to more information than ever before in history. Unfortunately they probably also have less exposure to true wisdom than ever before. T. S. Elliot once posed the question, "Where is the wisdom we have lost in knowledge?" In our present age of information, access to wisdom is vital.

THIS CHAPTER AT A GLANCE

Getting to Know the Story of Lady Wisdom

- Proverbial Billboards

Getting to Know Lady Wisdom

- Wisdom Journal
- Wisdom Wordplay
- The Masks of Lady Wisdom

Scripture Passages Related to Lady Wisdom

- Proverbs 1:20–33 (Wisdom reprimands those who ignore her)*
- Proverbs, chapter 8 (Wisdom calls people to herself)*
- Wisdom 6:12–21 (Wisdom is valuable)*
- Wisdom 8:2–20 (Solomon declares his love for Wisdom)

- Sirach 24:23-31 (Wisdom recounts her relationship to Israel)
Asterisk (*) signifies key passages to cover.

Articles from *Breakthrough!* Related to Lady Wisdom

- *Breakthrough!* Interview with Lady Wisdom
- God's Wisdom (Job 40:1-5)
- Parental Wisdom (Proverbs 1:8-9)
- Two Ways (Proverbs 4:24-27)
- Wisdom in the World (Proverbs 8:15-16)
- Prudence (Proverbs 14:15-17)
- A Great Gift! (Song of Songs 6:1-9)
- The Gift of Wisdom (Wisdom 7:22—8:1)
- Don't Judge a Book . . . (Sirach 11:2-6)

Lady Wisdom and Young Adolescents Today

- The Wisdom literature of the Old Testament is one way that a civilization passed on their wisdom to the young people of their culture. Many have suggested that in modern western civilization, we seem to have more or less abandoned rituals and methods of imparting wisdom and replaced them with furthering our understanding of science.
- The Wisdom literature defines and imparts wisdom. Young people might sometimes mistake the difference between wisdom and intelligence.
- Wisdom literature attempts to define the life of the wise person as opposed to the life of the foolish person. In an overwhelmingly consumer culture such as ours, true wisdom might often appear foolish to young people. Young people look not only to the Scriptures but also to adults to share wisdom with them and guide them.

Highlighting God's Presence

Then out of the storm the LORD spoke to Job.
"Who are you to question my wisdom
with your ignorant empty words?"

(Job 38:1)

It is the LORD who gives wisdom; from him comes knowledge and understanding (Proverbs 2:6).

All of us should eat and drink and enjoy what we have worked for. It is God's gift (Ecclesiastes 3:13).

Wisdom once rescued an innocent and holy people from a nation of oppressors (Wisdom 10:15).

The LORD himself created Wisdom;
    he saw her and recognized her value,
    and so he filled everything he made with Wisdom.
He gave some measure of Wisdom to everyone,
    but poured her out on those who love him.

(Sirach 1:9-10)

Getting to Know the Story of Lady Wisdom

Proverbial Billboards

In this activity, students choose a proverb and then make a billboard to communicate it.

Preparation

❑ Provide five or six poster boards, one for each small group.

❑ Provide pencils and markers for each small group.

❑ Each small group needs to have a Bible.

    1. Define the word *wisdom*. A wise person (a person with the quality of wisdom) understands the right way to live a good life. Explain that the Bible has numerous parts specifically devoted to encouraging us to live a life pleasing to God. Explain that it is no coincidence that living a life pleasing to God would also make the world a peaceful and happy place to live.

    2. Define the word *proverb*. A proverb is a short saying that expresses a type of truth or a grain of wisdom. Explain that proverbs are not confined to the Bible, but can be found in almost every religion and culture. You might want to remind students about the proverbs found in fortune cookies, often attributed to Confucius; the wisdom found in the *Old Farmer's Almanac;* or even the sayings of Benjamin Franklin.

    3. Divide your class into groups of four or five students each and give each group their supplies. Assign each group one of the chapters between Proverbs, chapters 10 and 22. Their task is to read it and decide on one short passage that could best be applied to people their age.

4. Have the students make a "billboard" with that passage written on it along with a picture that portrays a current scene in which this wisdom is being applied by people their age.

5. Afterward each group should present their billboard to the class and explain why they chose that particular passage and what it has to say to their peers today.

Getting to Know Lady Wisdom

Wisdom Journal

In this activity, young people begin a "wisdom journal" that they can work on throughout the year and into the future.

Preparation

❑ Instruct students to have a journal, a notebook, or a section set aside in their binders for this long-term activity.

❑ Hang a sheet of butcher paper on the wall (optional).

❑ Provide one set of colored markers (optional).

1. Explain to the students that the Wisdom Books of the Bible are not the only place to meet Lady Wisdom. There are many other places in the Scriptures where we can find her. Not only can we meet her in the Bible, but in our daily lives as well.

2. Present the following points in your own words:
- As we know from the Book of Sirach, "(God) gave some measure of Wisdom to everyone" (Sirach 1:9–10), and from the Book of Proverbs, "Listen! Wisdom is calling out in the streets and marketplaces, calling loudly at the city gates and wherever people come together" (Wisdom 1:20), we can safely assume that God's wisdom is available to us in many ways. The Bible isn't the only place to meet Lady Wisdom!

3. Direct the students to begin keeping a wisdom journal. This journal (which they would maintain over a long period of time) would consist of short entries of wise sayings, Bible passages, their own meaningful and learning experiences, and so on—any wisdom that resonates deep within their own lives. Be sure to encourage selectivity though, as adolescents might want to quickly judge something or someone as wise before any real discernment takes place.

4. Throughout the school year, occasionally remind them to update their journal every time they "meet" Lady Wisdom. If it is possible, post a sheet of butcher paper on the wall and allow them to share the wisdom they have found with each other.

Wisdom Wordplay

Preparation

❑ Give each student a copy of handout Lady Wisdom-A, "Proverbs from A to Z."

❑ Make sure each student has a pen or a pencil.

1. Read Proverbs 31:10–31 with the students.

2. Share the following information with the students:

○ This is not only a beautiful passage about a woman who is a wonderful wife, but also an interesting piece of writing. If one were to read this in its original Hebrew, she or he would realize that each verse begins with the succeeding twenty-two letters of the Hebrew alphabet. This literary device is called acrostic text.

3. Pass out the copies of handout Lady Wisdom-A, "Proverbs from A to Z," to each student. Read through the directions with the students and give them some examples to help them begin creating their own proverbs. Give them some time to work on them.

4. When the young people have completed their work, have them share some of their thoughts with their peers. If the young people feel comfortable, post their handouts around the classroom.

The Masks of Lady Wisdom

In this activity, students make a collage of modern people who impart wisdom.

Preparation

❑ Each student should have access to a poster board, glue , and magazines they can cut pictures from at home.

❑ The teacher may want to prepare an example of the project beforehand (optional).

1. Read Proverbs 8:1–4 to the students.

2. In your own words, say the following:
• The Bible seems to say that Lady Wisdom is calling us all the time. But what does she look like today? With whose voice does she speak? What mask does Lady Wisdom wear today?

3. Assign the students a project in which they have to find the "masks" that Lady Wisdom uses today. Have the students cut out and paste on poster boards a collage of pictures of contemporary people they think offer great wisdom. These people could be famous or not, dead or alive, but have been around in the past one hundred years at least. It could be their family members, religious leaders, teachers, musicians, politicians, and so on. Along with their pictures, instruct the students to print a short quotation from each one.

4. When the young people bring their assignments to class, have them display their work on their chair or desk so that everyone can walk around and look at them. Ask the group, Are there any people that are in quite a few posters?

PROVERBS FROM A TO Z

Write down proverbs, enough to fill twenty-six lines. The proverbs should address the problems and questions of people like you. Craft your proverbs carefully so that each line will begin with the appropriate letter. (A longer proverb might take up several letters because it would have several lines such as in the Book of Proverbs.)

A _____

B _____

C _____

D _____

E _____

F _____

G _____

H _____

I _____

J _____

K _____

L _____

M _____

N _____

O _____

P _____

Q _____

R _____

S _____

T _____

U _____

V _____

W _____

X _____

Y _____

Z _____

ISAIAH

Preparing to Teach

Overview

Isaiah is one of the major prophets in the Old Testament. It might be more accurate to say that when we are talking about the book of the prophet Isaiah, we are really talking about the "books" of the prophets Isaiah. This is because the biblical scholars hear the voices of three distinct authors who, while writing over a course of two centuries, still maintained a certain continuity of style and message.

The first thirty-nine chapters of the Book of Isaiah deal with the impending fall of Judah to the Babylonians. The prophet catalogues the people's failings (primarily idolatry and injustice to the poor) and describes how, as a result of these sins, their enemies will capture Judah and deport her citizens to exile in Babylonia. In addition, however, Isaiah offers two powerful images of hope. First, he announces the coming of a special chosen king, "The Anointed One" (Messiah), who will emerge from the lineage of David to restore Judah to her covenant relationship with God in a new and more fulfilled way. Second, despite the impending demise of the faithless people of God, who will be banished into exile, a remnant will remain faithful to God and will be the seed of a restored Judah when they return.

The "Second Isaiah," whose writings are contained in chapters 40-55, describes the return of the exiles to Judah some seventy years after they were first taken to Babylon. These chapters are also called "The Book of Consolation," so encouraging and hopeful are they for those about to return home. Christians see a foreshadowing of Jesus in this section's "Servant of God" and of the role he would play in salvation history.

"Third Isaiah" makes up chapters 56-66 of the Book of Isaiah and describes the life of the Jerusalem community in the postexilic period. "Third Isaiah" expresses the same concern for the people's misbehavior that First Isaiah does, for it seems that the people have learned nothing from their ancestor's fickle treatment of the Covenant.

In the three different voices of Isaiah, young people can find a familiar pattern. They can see that God is not happy with the sins of the people and that he must punish them. Yet, though he needs to punish them, God also looks forward to the day when the punishment is over and he can relate with them in the loving way that he wants. Sometimes young adolescents misinterpret strict rules or consequences (such as grounding) as a sign that their parents or teachers do not love them. In fact, parents and teachers often inwardly cringe as they need to spell out the consequences. They would much rather have peaceful and positive relationships with them.

Young people will find many beautiful signs of hope in Isaiah. Encourage them to copy down passages that especially touch them.

THIS CHAPTER AT A GLANCE

Getting to Know the Story of Isaiah

- Dear Holy One of Israel: Isaiah's Diary

Getting to Know Isaiah

- Playing on God's Team with "Coach Isaiah"
- "The People Who Walked in Darkness Have Seen a Great Light"

Scripture Passages Related to Isaiah

- Isaiah 2:1-5 (Isaiah predicts future peace to Jerusalem)
- Isaiah 6:1-8 (God calls Isaiah)*
- Isaiah 7:10-14 (Isaiah makes a prediction of Immanuel to Ahaz the king)*
- Isaiah 37:1-38 (Isaiah reassures Hezekiah the king)
- Isaiah 40:1-11 (God gives his people comfort)*
- Isaiah 42:1-4 (Isaiah introduces a special servant of God)*
- Isaiah 44:1-3 (God consoles Israel)
- Isaiah 49:1-6 (Israel is a light to the nations)*
- Isaiah 52:13—53:12 (The Suffering Servant)*
- Isaiah 58:6-12 (The type of fasting God wants)
- Isaiah 65:17-25 (Isaiah predicts a new heaven, a new earth, and a new Jerusalem)*

Asterisk (*) signifies key passages to cover.

Articles from *Breakthrough!* Related to Isaiah

- *Breakthrough!* Interview with Isaiah
- Prophets and Prophecy (Isaiah, chapter 6)
- Advent (Isaiah 7:10-14)
- Names of God (Isaiah 9:6)
- Keeping God No. 1 (Isaiah 28:22-29)
- Holiness and Healthiness (Isaiah, chapter 35)
- Second Chance (Isaiah, chapter 38)

Isaiah and Young Adolescents Today

- Isaiah is sent to warn Israel about the consequences of her sins but also to give her reason to hope that she will emerge from this time more faithful to God. Young adolescents hear much about the possible negative consequences of their behavior but they also need to hear hope about their future.

- Isaiah predicts the coming of a special anointed king, the Messiah, who will renew God's people in their covenant identity. Young adolescents are looking for role models, women and men who embody the qualities a student wishes to possess. They also seek to feel special, set apart, "anointed."

- Isaiah describes a lowly faithful few, a "remnant" (literally, "the leftovers") who will remain close to God despite the people's despair in the beginning of the Exile period. Most young adolescents at times feel like a "leftover," overlooked or not taken seriously by others. Through Isaiah's words, the young person can see how God has an important purpose for everyone even when it seems like they are disposable or don't count.

Highlighting God's Presence

In the year that King Uzziah died, I saw the Lord. He was sitting on his throne, high and exalted, and his robe filled the whole Temple. Around him flaming creatures were standing, each of which had six wings. Each creature covered its face with two wings, and its body with two, and used the other two for flying. They were calling out to each other:

"Holy, holy, holy!
The Lord Almighty is holy!
His glory fills the world."

(Isaiah 6:1–3)

Then I heard the L ORD say, "Whom shall I send? Who will be our messenger?"

I answered, "I will go! Send me!"

(Isaiah 6:8)

"Comfort my people," says our God. "Comfort them!
Encourage the people of Jerusalem.
Tell them they have suffered long enough
and their sins are now forgiven.
I have punished them in full for all their sins."

(Isaiah 40:1-2)

"Israel," the L ORD who created you says,
"Do not be afraid—I will save you.
I have called you by name—you are mine.
When you pass through deep waters,
I will be with you;
your troubles will not overwhelm you.
When you pass through fire, you will not be burned;
the hard trials that come will not hurt you.
For I am the L ORD your God,
the holy God of Israel, who saves you."

(Isaiah 43:1-3)

The L ORD says, "I am making a new earth and new heavens. The events of the past will be completely forgotten. Be glad and rejoice forever in what I create. The new Jerusalem I make will be full of joy, and her people will be happy. I myself will be filled with joy because of Jerusalem and her people" (Isaiah 65:17-19).

Getting to Know the Story of Isaiah

Dear Holy One of Israel: Isaiah's Diary

In this activity, young people "write" Isaiah's diary, using passages from the prophet's book for inspiration.

Preparation

❏ Each student needs to have a Bible, a pen, and some blank sheets of copy paper. Provide staplers and markers if necessary.

❏ List the following Scripture passages on the board or in another visible place:
  • Isaiah 6:1-8
  • Isaiah 7:3-14

- Isaiah 8:1–3
- Isaiah 8:11–21
- Isaiah 21:1–10
- Isaiah 30:8–14
- Isaiah 37:1–5

1. Introduce the activity by sharing this information in your own words:

- The Book of Isaiah contains primarily his prophetic messages. Still, there are some interesting sections that describe how the prophet lives and how he interacts with God and people. To better understand Isaiah, you will create a diary or journal recording and reflecting on some key events in the life of this prophet.

2. Distribute sheets of blank copy paper to each student. Give the young people the following directions:

○ Fold two sheets of blank paper in half from the top down.

○ Staple them in the middle to make a booklet. Leave room on the front page for the cover illustrations.

○ Read the scriptural selections about Isaiah's life. For each passage, put yourself in the shoes of Isaiah and journal about what you, as Isaiah, would have recorded, along with your feelings and your interpretations of it.

○ For each entry, give a date and year for the event (the events will have occurred around 740 BC, but remind your students that the people of that time would not have been using the calendar system we use today) and address each entry to God. Isaiah's title for God is "Dear Holy One of Israel."

3. After students finish their versions of Isaiah's journal, distribute markers so that they can design the covers. After you collect the journals, read some of the entries out loud. Use these entries to discuss the nature of prophets. Ask these questions:

○ What was the life of the prophet like?

○ Are there still prophets today? Why or why not?

○ If there are prophets today, who are they?

○ Do today's prophets resemble Isaiah in any way?

Getting to Know Isaiah

Playing on God's Team with "Coach Isaiah"

In this activity, young people look to the modern role of a coach to help them understand the work and approach of the prophets.

Preparation

❑ Each student needs to have a Bible, a pen, and loose-leaf paper.

❑ Bring in the sports pages of a local newspaper (several days' worth) and copies of sports magazines.

❑ Provide poster board, markers, scissors, and glue for each young person.

1. Begin the activity by asking the young people to describe the characteristics of a good coach, using the following questions. Have them brainstorm ideas and then list them on the board.
- How do these qualities make a coach stand out?
- How is winning and losing related to having a good coach?
- How should a good coach react to a losing team or player? Why?
- How should a good coach react to a winning team or player? Why?

2. Share these thoughts with the students in your own words:
- The role of the prophet can be compared to the role of a sports coach. Both individuals try to motivate their charges to "play up to their ability" by using a combination of warnings and encouragement.
- The language of sports and the language of faith overlap at times. Saint Paul uses the image of the runner and a race to talk about following Christ and finishing the race as salvation. A pinch hitter in baseball is like a "savior figure" for the team. Football players sometimes make "Hail Mary passes," and so on.

3. Discuss these questions:
- From what you know of good coaches, do you think that Isaiah is a good coach in his role as prophet?
- What lessons from coaching would you advise a modern-day prophet to take to heart when interacting with people?

4. Using the piece of poster board and letters and images clipped from sports magazines, ask the students to make posters that feature five "coaching guidelines" that Isaiah could adapt to help the people of Judah be faithful to God.

"The People Who Walked in Darkness Have Seen a Great Light"

Young people explore the symbolism of light and darkness in Isaiah through a short prayer experience.

Preparation

❑ Each student needs to have a Bible, a pen, and paper.

❑ Provide readings for seven readers and a taper or votive candle for each participant.

❑ Meet in a room that can be darkened.

1. Introduce this prayer experience by sharing this thought:

   ○ The images of light and darkness are used often in the Book of the prophet Isaiah. Examining this metaphor can remind us of the real power of the Spirit in a world struggling to be illuminated with God's love.

2. Dim the lights. Gather the young people into a circle. Assign the readings from Isaiah to seven of the young people present. In addition, distribute candles to each student.
   - Isaiah 5:20,30
   - Isaiah 9:2
   - Isaiah 29:18–19
   - Isaiah 30:25–26
   - Isaiah 49:6,9
   - Isaiah 60:1–3
   - Isaiah 60:19–22

3. Call the students' attention to the fact that even one small match will illuminate the room and dispel the darkness. As each student reads one of the Isaiah quotes out loud, light his or her candle. When the readings are complete, the readers should then light the candles of the remaining participants. Ask the students to prayerfully discuss these questions:
   - What does it mean to be "in darkness"? to be "in light"?
   - What "light" does Isaiah say God promises people? What will its effect be on people?

Conclude the prayer time by asking the young people to share any prayers of petition in which they would like to call down God's light. Instead of having students respond with "Lord, hear our prayer," you may use the response, "God of Light, hear our prayer."

JEREMIAH

Preparing to Teach

Overview

Jeremiah is a fascinating biblical character who gives us an intimate view of the life of a prophet. The Book of Jeremiah contains the prophetic messages he delivers and describes the effects they have on the people of Judah. The book also reveals his own personal struggles to carry out his vocation in the face of both inner and outside turmoil.

Jeremiah is a passionate, challenging, and relentless prophet whose life reveals that God wants conversion of hearts. God desires to give us the spirit of conversion so that we can know him and relate to him in ways that would be impossible by ourselves. He wants us to see our future in the light of mercy.

The young adolescent will identify with Jeremiah's struggles to do the right thing in the face of peer pressure. Hearing Jeremiah's intense feelings and struggle in his prayer to do the right thing can be a great consolation to a young adolescent who wants to be close to God yet is aware of new feelings that seem "unspiritual."

Jeremiah's awareness of his ultimate dependency on God and of God's desire to deepen a relationship with him can be a helpful example to young adolescents. They often struggle to stand their ground when they feel misunderstood due to the many changes at work at this time in their lives. Jeremiah's prophecy reveals God as the Faithful One who is always available and is always calling us back to himself so that people can begin again with faith, hope, and love in God, others, and ourselves.

THIS CHAPTER AT A GLANCE

Getting to Know the Story of Jeremiah

- Jeremiah Book Covers

Getting to Know Jeremiah

- God's Call to Jeremiah and Our Call Today
- God's Covenant Broken and Renewed

Scripture Passages Related to Jeremiah

- Jeremiah 1:1-10 (God calls Jeremiah)*
- Jeremiah 2:1—3:5, 4:1-31 (God's problem with Israel)*
- Jeremiah 8:18—9:16 (Jeremiah's Song of Sorrow)
- Jeremiah 13:1-11 (Jeremiah and the mysterious linen shorts)
- Jeremiah 15:10-21, 18:18-23, 20:7-18 (Jeremiah argues with God)*
- Jeremiah 18:1-12 (Jeremiah goes to a potter's house)
- Jeremiah 31:1-14,31-40 (God tells Jeremiah of the New Covenant)*
- Jeremiah 37:1—38:13 (Jeremiah is imprisoned)

Asterisk (*) signifies key passages to cover.

Jeremiah

Break Through! Articles from *Breakthrough!* Related to Jeremiah

- *Breakthrough!* Interview with Jeremiah
- Introduction to the Book of Jeremiah
- Who, me? (Jeremiah 1:4-10)
- Help! Rescue me! (Jeremiah 2:26-27)
- Why? (Jeremiah 12:1-4)
- Why me, O Lord? (Jeremiah 15:10-21)
- Single for God (Jeremiah 16:1-4)
- My Place of Safety (Jeremiah 17:14-18)
- I'm Sick of It! (Jeremiah 20:7-18)
- Turning Point (Jeremiah 27:21-22)
- Putting Your Heart in It (Jeremiah 31:31-33)
- Down and Out (Jeremiah 38:1-13)
- Stories After the Fall (Jeremiah, chapter 40)
- Egypt (Jeremiah 43:1-6)

Jeremiah and Young Adolescents Today

- Jeremiah struggles with God's call to be a prophet at a young age. Young adolescents can find it difficult to believe that God calls them to serve him in a special way.
- Jeremiah's desire to speak truthfully and lovingly about what he has seen happening to his people reminds young adolescents to speak to others with honesty and love.
- Jeremiah's frustrated cry to God about being a prophet shows the young person how important honesty is in prayer.
- Jeremiah's dramatic and symbolic presentation of his message shows young people that communication consists of more than words. Actions and gestures can be powerful ways to share God's word with others.
- Jeremiah's life and martyrdom in Egypt shows young adolescents that speaking up for God can result in suffering and rejection. Young adolescents may find this reality difficult to accept.

Highlighting God's Presence in Jeremiah's Story

The Lord said to me, "I chose you before I gave you life, and before you were born I selected you to be a prophet to the nations (Isaiah 1:4).

Listen, I am giving you the words you must speak . . . to build and to plant" (Jeremiah 1:9-10).

The Lord says . . . "I alone know the plans I have for you, plans to bring you prosperity and not disaster, plans to bring about the future you hope for" (Jeremiah 29:10-12).

The Lord says, "The time is coming when I make a new covenant with the people of Israel and with the people of Judah. . . . The new covenant that I will make with the people of Israel will be this: I will put my law within them and write it on their hearts. I will be their God, and they will be my people" (Jeremiah 31:31,33).

Getting to Know the Story of Jeremiah

Jeremiah Book Covers

In this activity, students work as designers who will design and illustrate a mock book series that follows the story of Jeremiah.

Follow the directions for "Character Book Covers" in appendix 2, "Tools for Teaching," on page 325. You may want to use the readings from "Scripture Passages Related to Jeremiah" to divide the class into groups of eight students.

Getting to Know Jeremiah

God's Call to Jeremiah and Our Call Today

Preparation

❑ Each student needs a Bible, paper, and a pen or pencil.

❑ Obtain a copy of the movie *Mother Teresa, Woman of Compassion,* by William Paul McKay and Tom Ivy (AIM International Television, 2002, 50 minutes, NR). See appendix 1, " Additional Resources," for more information.

❑ Bring a VHS player and a television.

❑ Optional: Invite adults from the faith community to present to the students their call or vocation to serve God's people.

1. Ask the students to reflect on the idea of a calling from God.
- Have you ever heard of someone receiving a calling from God? If so, how did they receive it?
- What did God call them to do?
- Do you think that God has a calling for everyone?
- What is the word for having a calling? (a vocation)

2. Have the students read God's call to Jeremiah in chapter 1:1–9. Have students reflect on these questions:
- What is Jeremiah's response? Why?
- What is the sign that Jeremiah will be God's spokesperson?
- What will Jeremiah do as God's prophet?
- Does God still call people today to speak on his behalf? Do people respond like Jeremiah? Why or why not?

3. Make this point with the students:
- God calls all people to serve one another out of love, in their own way. We are most truly ourselves when we give ourselves to others.

4. Show part of the movie *Mother Teresa: Woman of Compassion,* especially the part where she describes experiencing a "call within a call" to serve the poorest of the poor in Calcutta, India.
    After showing parts of the film, ask the students these questions:
- Who speaks for God today? (Examples: bishops and servants of the poor)
- What are they telling us? (to trust God with our hearts, to live simply, to take care of the poor, to not be afraid of loving like Christ, to forgive others)
- What is the sign that they have been chosen to speak for God? (They are humble, prayerful, and respectful of the Church; they see the world through the eyes of the poor; and they are hopeful, creative, persistent, patient, kind.)

5. Bring in some speakers who can talk about their own sense of call. In a subsequent class period, have the students compare and contrast the sense of call among the presenters.

God's Covenant Broken and Renewed

Preparation

❑ Students need a Bible, paper, and a pen or pencil.

❑ Optional: Each student will need two wooden dowels (each ¾-inch in diameter by 12 inches long), an 8.5-by-14-inch (legal-size) sheet of copy paper, some tape, and some markers. (Such dowels can be found in home improvement centers such as Home Depot or in craft stores.)

1. Tell the students this old joke:

• Two elderly men, Bob and Jerry, who have been friends for years, were talking about their favorite topic: baseball. Bob says to Jerry, "I wonder if there is baseball in heaven?" Jerry says, "Let's promise that whichever one of us dies first will come back and tell the other." So months go by and Bob dies first. Jerry wonders if his friend will be able to keep his promise.

   One day Jerry is sitting on a bench in a park and Bob appears to him. "Bob, is that you?" asks Jerry. "Yep, it sure is!" says Bob. "So," says Jerry, "is there baseball in heaven?" "Well, Jerry, on that, I've got some bad news and I've got some good news." "What's the good news?" asks Jerry. "Yes, there is incredible baseball here. All the greats are here," says Bob. "Well, what's the bad news?" asks the bewildered Jerry. Bob answers, "You're starting pitcher tonight."

2. Make the connection between the joke and your study of Jeremiah with the following thoughts:

• Jeremiah's message is a combination of things that the people of Judah do not want to hear as well as things they are glad to hear: bad news and good news. From Jeremiah they will learn that because they are not faithful to God, they will be punished. They will be sent into exile. But, ultimately God will bring them home and will make a new covenant with them. God will promise to be even more involved in their lives. Christians understand that this new covenant is God becoming human in Jesus.

3. Divide the students into groups and have the students review the readings from Jeremiah (listed in "Scripture Passages Related to Jeremiah") and look for Jeremiah's "bad news, good news" approach to the situation in Judah at his time. Have them make a two-column chart on their paper, one column titled "Bad News" and one column titled "Good News." Challenge them to try and find three entries for each side.

4. Use these questions to discuss the "bad news, good news" dynamic:

• How can something that is broken be made stronger after the break? (Have the students brainstorm examples like bones, tree limbs that are grafted and tightly bond, some epoxies or other glues that are stronger than the original material.)

- How can covenant relationships be made stronger after they are broken? (For example, If the stronger member, God, absorbs the break and renews the strength of the bond with the other. Friendships that go through tough periods are sometimes stronger afterward.)
- What are some ways covenants are made and then recommitted in our culture? (Marriage vows are renewed, we celebrate special days with our families, we ask forgiveness, we share in the sacraments.)

5. At the bottom of the columns, have the students write a reflection on the question, How is your life a combination of "Bad News" and "Good News from God"?

6. Have the students find Jeremiah 29:11–14. Then provide a sheet of paper for the students to construct a biblical-type scroll out of the two dowels and the sheet of 8.5-by-14-inch paper. Use tape to attach the paper to the dowels. On the paper, have the students copy Jeremiah's "Letter to the Captives" (Jeremiah 29:11–14), addressing it to someone they know (or to themselves) who needs to be reminded of God's good plans for them.

Jeremiah

EZEKIEL

Preparing to Teach

Overview

Ezekiel is a complex prophetic character of the Exile for whom actions really do speak louder than words. He has two main messages for the people. The first is a call to repentance for their sinfulness lest they be destroyed by Babylon. The second is a message of hope for the Jews when they find themselves taken captive to Babylon after their defeat at the hands of their enemies. Like the people of Judah, young people need to be accountable for their actions yet not become too discouraged if they make some mistakes.

In addition to performing striking dramatic gestures as part of his ministry, Ezekiel is also given a series of fantastical prophetic visions that he conveys to the people of Judah about their future as God's people. Given such a wide range of prophetic inspiration, Ezekiel's message continues to echo down through the ages and to speak to people of faith today.

Though the symbolism of the Book of Ezekiel is baffling at times, the dramatic nature of his ministry and the intensity of his visions can appeal to the image-rich experience of many young adolescents. In some ways, Ezekiel's medium of prophetic message is more inviting to the young adolescent of today than other prophetic styles simply because it is so similar in presentation to the media-driven environment in which our students live.

THIS CHAPTER AT A GLANCE

Getting to Know the Story of Ezekiel

- The Wild, Wild World of Ezekiel Comic Book

Getting to Know Ezekiel

- These Bones: From Death to Life

Scripture Passages Relating to Ezekiel

- Ezekiel 1:1–28 (Ezekiel sees God's throne)*
- Ezekiel 2:1–10 (God calls Ezekiel)
- Ezekiel 3:1–15 (Ezekiel eats a scroll and receives the spirit)*

- Ezekiel 4:1-17 (Ezekiel acts out the Babylonian siege of Jerusalem)
- Ezekiel 5:1-3, 11-12 (Ezekiel acts out another prophecy)*
- Ezekiel 12:1-16 (Ezekiel acts out the flight of those exiled)
- Ezekiel 16:59-63 (God will renew the covenant)
- Ezekiel 18:1-4,14-24 (Punishment for sins will not fall on children)*
- Ezekiel 24:15-27 (The death of the prophet's wife)
- Ezekiel 34:11-31 (God as the good shepherd)*
- Ezekiel 36:22-36 (God will give the people a new heart and mind)*
- Ezekiel 37:1-14 (Vision of the dry bones)*

Asterisk (*) signifies key passages to cover.

Break Through! Articles from *Breakthrough!* Related to Ezekiel

- *Breakthrough!* Interview with Ezekiel
- Introduction to the Book of Ezekiel
- Only God Is God (Ezekiel, chapters 2-3)
- I.M.s from God? (Ezekiel 4:1—5:4)
- God Is . . . (Ezekiel 10:4)
- The Dreaded Ms. G (Ezekiel 20:33-44)
- Then and Now (Ezekiel 22:1-12)
- Losing Someone Special (Ezekiel 24:15-27)
- Wrong Secrets (Ezekiel 33:7-9)
- Praying with New Life (Ezekiel, chapter 37)
- God, the Builder (Ezekiel 41:15-21)

Ezekiel and Young Adolescents Today

- Ezekiel's strong, strange prophetic experiences can fascinate the young adolescent. It can remind the young adolescent of the mystery of God in the midst of their ordinary lives.
- Ezekiel's twin messages of repentance for the present and hope for the future reminds us that while actions do have consequences, with God's mercy, there is always a second chance. This realization is especially important for young adolescents to hear as they are painfully aware of how incomplete they are and are quite sensitive to their failures.

Highlighting God's Presence

While the voice was speaking, God's spirit entered me and raised me to my feet, and I heard the voice continue, "Mortal man, I am sending you to the people of Israel. They have rebelled and turned against me and are still rebels just as their ancestors were. They are stubborn and do not respect me, so I am sending you to tell them what I, the Sovereign Lord, am saying to them. Whether those rebels listen to you or not, they will know that a prophet has been among them" (Ezekiel 2:2-5).

"I will give you a new heart and a new mind. I will take away your stubborn heart of stone and give you an obedient heart. I will put my spirit in you and will see to it that you follow my laws and keep all the commands I have given you" (Ezekiel 36:26-27).

He [the LORD and his spirit] said to me, "Mortal man, can these bones come back to life?"

I replied, "Sovereign LORD, only you can answer that!"

He said, "Prophesy to the bones. Tell these dry bones to listen to the word of the LORD. Tell them that I, the Sovereign LORD, am saying to them: I am going to put breath into you and bring you back to life. Then you will know that I am the LORD" (Ezekiel 37:3-6).

Getting to Know the Story of Ezekiel

The Wild, Wild World of Ezekiel Comic Book

In this activity, students familiarize themselves with Ezekiel's story by doing comic strips.

Preparation

❑ Each student needs to have a Bible and pens.

❑ Make copies of the handout Tools-A, "The Comics," from appendix 2, "Tools for Teaching." Each young person should have four frames or two copies of the handout to work with.

❑ Copy the readings from "Scripture Passages Related to Ezekiel" onto the board.

1. The stories of Ezekiel are very visual and students can portray them in a variety of ways in a comic book setting. Students can work in groups or individually to produce a summary of the prophet's work.

2. Divide the class into groups to produce a comic book version of Ezekiel. Pass out copies of handout Tools-A, "The Comics." Have the students summarize the scriptural passages somewhere on the drawings.

3. Photocopy the finished products from different groups for everyone to read.

4. After students have reviewed some of the Ezekiel comics in full, have them write their impressions of the prophet's message on a separate sheet of paper. They should answer these questions:

- What was most challenging about his message? Why?
- What was most hopeful in his message? Why?

Getting to Know Ezekiel

These Bones: From Death to Life

Preparation

❑ Each student needs to have a Bible, paper, and a pen.

❑ Obtain a copy of the film *The Lord of The Rings: The Return of the King* that you can play on your DVD or VHS player. (The extended version of the film works better because it has a strong image of bones. Cue the film to "Paths through the Dead" if the majority of your students have already watched the film. An earlier scene, "Aragorn Takes the Paths of the Dead," helps to provide some context for the later one. Both scenes are close to the halfway point of the movie.)

1. Have the students read Ezekiel 37:1–14. Discuss the meaning of this biblical scene in the context of Ezekiel (God will restore his people; he will give them his spirit.) Note that the image of the dry bones coming back to life is a powerful image of renewal.

2. Show the scene "Paths through the Dead" from *The Lord of the Rings: The Return of the King.* In this scene, Aragorn, the eventual King of Middle-earth, goes to seek assistance from a ghostly army that has been cursed to a state between life and death because the soldiers broke a vow to a former king. Aragorn goes to seek their assistance and offers them a way to remove the curse.

3. Discuss these questions with the students:
- What are the similarities between the scene that Ezekiel encounters and the one found by Aragorn and his companions?
- How do the bones take shape in each account?
- How do Aragorn and Ezekiel offer new life to the bones? How does the new life differ?

4. Give students this private in-class writing assignment that you will not read. Their short essay should answer these questions:
- What is one area in your life that is dry or dead?
- What is God doing in your life to help you feel more alive in that part of your life?

HOSEA

Preparing to Teach

Overview

Warning! Had the Book of Hosea been a modern movie, it most likely would have received at least a PG-13 rating! Explaining this extremely interesting book will require some tact and possibly some patience, especially with young adolescents.

Hosea is from the southern kingdom, but during the eighth century BC, becomes a prophet to the northern kingdom. His fellow Israelites are being overwhelmed by the Assyrian Empire and their pagan practices. Their religious rituals include sexual acts with prostitutes in the Canaanite temples where they worship the fertility god, Baal. Hosea wants the Israelites to realize how their involvement in these and other pagan rituals make them unfaithful to the Lord. The young people may know that Israel continuously falls into idolatry; they may just not know what that idolatry involves.

Following God's direction, Hosea marries a prostitute named Gomer and remains devoted to her despite her continued infidelity. Hosea uses his marriage as a metaphor for God's relationship with the Israelites. Hosea, like God, is a faithful spouse, while Gomer, like Israel in her worship of false gods, is unfaithful and adulterous. Young people can easily relate to the difference between having a friend who is constant and trustworthy and one who is hard to depend on.

This powerful and passionate book is fascinating to young adolescents, not only because of its somewhat lurid symbolism but also because of Hosea's single-minded devotion to God despite what the rest of the Israelites are doing.

This book is also refreshing because these readers will find God portrayed as one who wants to love and forgive his children, even when they go astray. At the same time, your students also may need to be challenged with the image of God as the loving parent who confronts his kids and allows them to suffer the consequences of their behavior. Hosea is a prophet of both justice and mercy.

Getting to Know the Story of Hosea

- Hosea's Complaints

Getting to Know Hosea

- Hosea's Way of Knowing God

Scripture Passages Related to Hosea

- Hosea 1:1-9 (Hosea obeys God's request to get married and have children)*
- Hosea 1:10—3:5 (Consequences for an unfaithful wife)*
- Hosea, chapter 3 (Hosea and God are both faithful)
- Hosea, chapters 4-10 (Israel's condemnation and punishment)
- Hosea, chapter 11 (God's tender love for his children)*
- Hosea 12:1—14:3 (The consequences of Israel's infidelity)
- Hosea 14:4-9 (The Lord promises new life to those who return to him)*

Asterisk (*) signifies key passages to cover.

Articles from *Breakthrough!* Related to Hosea

Break Through!

- *Breakthrough!* Interview with Hosea
- Introduction to the Book of Hosea

Hosea and Young Adolescents Today

- Like Hosea, adolescents place a lot of importance on loyalty and fidelity.
- Hosea does something that most adolescents find very difficult: he goes against the crowd. Hosea makes a great role model as the lonely voice of virtue in a mass of immorality.
- Hosea complains about the insincerity of the Israelites. Young teenagers are very sensitive about hypocrisy. They do not like it when people's words say one thing, but their actions say something else—and especially when those people are adults!
- Many of today's youth ministers and teachers are finding that despite their seemingly sincere expressions of faith in God, many adolescents are sexually active. Studying the Book of Hosea is an opportunity to explore the gap between their beliefs and their actions.

- Hosea's main complaint with the Israelites concerns idolatry. In today's world, teenagers can discover idolatry in many shapes and forms including wealth, pleasure, popularity, power, and so on.

Highlighting God's Presence

Israel, I will make you my wife;
> I will be true and faithful;
> I will show you constant love and mercy
> and make you mine forever.

(Hosea 2:19)

"Yet I was the one who taught Israel to walk.
I took my people up in my arms,
> but they did not acknowledge that I took care of them.
I drew them to me with affection and love.
> I picked them up and held them to my cheek;
> I bent down to them and fed them."

(Hosea 11:3–4; the Lord speaking)

The LORD says,
"I will bring my people back to me.
I will love them with all my heart;
> no longer am I angry with them."

(Hosea 14:4)

Getting to Know the Story of Hosea

Hosea's Complaints

In this activity, the students will explore Hosea's complaints to the Israelites and come up with modern parallels in our society. Then they will express both of these artistically.

Preparation

❑ Provide a set of markers and one poster board for every four or five students.

❑ Students need to have bibles.

1. Give the students some background information on Hosea using the information in the overview of this chapter and the introduction to Hosea in *Breakthrough!* Then read Hosea, chapters 1–3 aloud with the class.

2. Divide the class into groups of four or five students each. Tell them that their job is to read their assigned passage, decide what the Israelites are doing wrong, and come up with a similar problem in our culture. Below are some passages you can assign, as well as some suggested modern-day parallels you might offer the students who need some help making the modern connection.

- Hosea 4:1–3 (Modern-day parallels: murder, adultery, theft, and so on)
- Hosea 5:4–7 (Modern-day parallels: wealth, pleasure, popularity, power, and so on)
- Hosea 7:3–16 (Modern-day parallels: selling out to save yourself, having no principles, lacking trust, disloyalty, and so on)
- Hosea 8:1–14 (Modern-day parallels: corrupt politicians, decisions based on national self-interest or fear instead of doing what is right, building "palaces" instead of God's kingdom, and so on)
- Hosea 12:7–11 (Modern-day parallels: dishonest businesses, exploitation of workers, and so on)

3. After their reading and discussion, have the students artistically display this modern-day parallel on their poster board. On one half of the poster, they should portray the problems of the Israelites, and on the other half, the similar problems in our society.

4. Have the students present their posters to the rest of the class. Direct them to explain both the complaints against the Israelites and the modern-day parallels.

Getting to Know Hosea

Hosea's Way of Knowing God

This activity will provide the opportunity for the students to prayerfully converse with God in a guided meditation.

Preparation

❏ Each student should have a sheet of paper and a pen or pencil.

1. Read Hosea 6:4–6 aloud with the class. Make the following points in your own words:

- Hosea is upset with the Israelites because while they say they worship the Lord, their love tends to disappear "as quickly as morning mist" (Hosea 6:4). They are failing to live out this love. They do not practice what they preach.
- In verse 6, Hosea says that their sacrifices and burnt offerings are meaningless unless they are backed up with love and knowledge of God.

- Just because you know a person's name doesn't mean you know *her or him*. For Hosea, "knowing God" also means more than believing that God exists. Hosea wants us to know God like we know the members of our family or our best friends. For when we truly know God, we will know what is good, and will live accordingly.

2. Prepare the students to listen and respond to the meditation you are about to read. Students should have some distance between them and keep distractions to a minimum. Establish silence in the room. (Turning the lights out can be helpful. Having students put their heads down works too.) In order to avoid sleeping students, try not to do this activity immediately after a meal. The students should have paper and a pen available.

3. After the students have quieted down, explain that they will be listening to a meditation that will include some questions for them to consider. Let them know that at any time, they are free to pick up their pens and write. They can write the entire experience, answer just the questions, or write nothing at all. Begin with the sign of the cross and about a minute of silence. Then read the meditation. Read slowly and allow 20 or more seconds of silent reflection when you see the ellipses (. . .)

- I want you to imagine you are sitting on top of a mountain that is overlooking a vast city. Darkness is falling, the sun has just set, and you notice the lights coming on in the city. . . . Watch them come on until the whole city seems like a lake of lights. . . . You are sitting here all alone, gazing at this beautiful spectacle. . . . What are you feeling? . . .

- After a while you hear footsteps behind you and you know they are the footsteps of a holy man who lives in these parts, a hermit. He comes up to you and stands by your side. He looks at you gently and says just one sentence to you: "If you go down to the city tonight, you will find God." Having said this, he turns around and walks away. No explanations. No time for questions. . . .

- You believe that this man knows what he is talking about. What do you feel now? Do you feel like doing what he said and going into the city? Or would you rather stay where you are? . . .

- Whatever you actually feel like doing, imagine that you go down to the city in search of God. . . . What do you feel as you go down? . . .

- You have come to the outskirts of the city and you have to decide where to go to search for God and find him . . . Where do you decide to go? Use your heart to choose the place. Don't be guided by where you think you "ought" to go. Just go where your heart tells you to go. . . .

○ What happens to you when you arrive at this place? . . . What do you find there? . . . What do you do there? . . . What happens to you? . . . Do you find God? . . . How do you recognize God? . . . What is it like to find God there?

○ Then you come to the realization that God has something to give you—a gift. It is a gift that is unique and it is given especially to you, but not only for you. It is a gift that is meant to be shared with everyone. Where do you go to find it? . . . Are there other people there or are you alone? . . . Does someone give you the gift or do you just find it? . . . How does it feel when you find the gift? . . .

○ Now you realize that it is time to go. Thank God for your gift and take it as you leave the city. As you walk back up the mountain, you encounter the holy man again. What do you tell him about your journey? . . . The holy man tells you that many others have made the same journey into the city, and though their experiences were different, they too were given gifts to share. Then he tells you that God wants you to know something. He says, "When you were young, God loved you and called you his child. Even when you turned away from him, God still carried you in his arms. When you forgot about God, he picked you up and held you to his cheek. When you were needy, he bent down to care for you" . . . (Adapted from Hosea 11:1–4).

○ Then the holy man begins to walk away, but then stops and turns around. He tells you to take some time to get to know God and he reminds you that God is with you always. What else does the holy man do or say now? . . .

○ You bid the holy man good-bye and you return to the top of the mountain to watch the lights of the city. . . .

(Adapted from Anthony de Mello, *Sadhana, A Way to God*, pp. 85–86)

Tell the students to take a moment or two, and when they are ready, they can open their eyes.

4. Afterward, ask for volunteers to share something about their experiences. Go through the different parts of the meditation and inquire about their particular reactions to the different situations. Be sure to respect their privacy and avoid pushing for responses.

Amos

Preparing to Teach

Overview

God calls Amos, a native of Tekoa in Judah, to speak his prophetic word to the people of Israel. Amos is likely quite a sight in the affluent capital city of Bethel because he is a herdsman. Amos is a candid, blunt-speaking character who tries to shake the people out of their complacency with the injustice they are allowing to grow in their midst. People who are straightforward are attractive to young people because "what you see is what you get."

Amos is very courageous to deliver his message, which is to say that the affluent inhabitants of Bethel are not paying attention to the poor or to God's Covenant. He is not well received and is told to go home. When young people stand up for values that conflict with those of their friends, they may feel somewhat like Amos—unwelcome and bothersome. They too need Amos's courage that comes from God.

Amos's unsubtle and often exaggerated means of expression are his desperate attempts to give "spiritual CPR" to God's people in the northern kingdom. They have so much but they are about to lose it all.

THIS CHAPTER AT A GLANCE

Getting to Know the Story of Amos

- Front Page News: Amos's Message to Bethel

Getting to Know Amos

- Continuing the Work of Amos Today

Scripture Passages Related to Amos

- Amos 2:4–5 (Amos predicts God's judgment against Judah)
- Amos 2:6–8,13–16 (Amos predicts God's judgment on Israel)*
- Amos 5:1–7 (Amos calls people to turn away from false gods)
- Amos 5:10–15,18–20 (Because of Israel's sin, Amos describes a coming disaster, "the day of the Lord")*
- Amos 6:3–8 (Amos's special warning to complacent rich people)
- Amos 7:1–9 (Amos's visions from God)

- Amos 7:10–17 (Amos and Amaziah the priest argue)
- Amos 8:4–14 (Amos condemns the unjust practices against the poor and predicts Israel's doom)*
- Amos 9:11–15 (Amos predicts a future restoration of Israel)*

Asterisk (*) signifies key passages to cover.

Break Through! ## Articles from *Breakthrough!* Related to Amos

- *Breakthrough!* Interview with Amos
- Introduction to the Book of Amos

Amos and Young Adolescents Today

- Amos is direct and blunt in his message of "repent or die" to the people of the northern kingdom. The young adolescent can identify with the clear, no-nonsense way Amos communicates God's disdain for hypocrisy and God's commitment to justice. The vulnerability of this stage of life makes the young adolescent particularly sensitive to how honestly and justly people, including themselves, are being treated.
- Amos is a migrant worker, an outsider to the community he is sent to work with. The young adolescent will identify with the feelings of being an outsider at times and not being welcomed into a group. At the same time the student can remember that inviting "the outsider" in is important to the life of our families and communities.

Highlighting God's Presence

The Lord says, "The people of Israel have sinned again and again, and for this I will certainly punish them. They sell into slavery honest people who cannot pay their debts, the poor who cannot repay even the price of a pair of sandals. They trample down the weak and helpless and push the poor out of the way" (Amos 2:6–7).

The Lord says, "A day is coming when I will restore the kingdom of David, which is like a house fallen into ruins. I will repair its walls and restore it. I will rebuild it and make it as it was long ago" (Amos 9:11).

Getting to Know the Story of Amos

Front Page News: Amos's Message to Bethel

In this activity, students use the stories about Amos to create a newspaper front page.

Preparation

❏ Each student needs to have a Bible and a copy of the list of readings from "Scripture Passages Related to Amos," a pen or pencil, and paper.

❏ If you can, provide computer access with a newsletter-publishing program that would allow the final product to be done in class.

Use the activity, "A Newspaper Account" on page 323 of appendix 2, "Tools for Teaching," to familiarize the students with the story of Amos. Introduce the activity with the following comments:

○ Amos certainly knew how to stir things up! He goes to the religious capital of the northern kingdom, Bethel, during the affluent reign of Jeroboam II to present his bold message of "Repent or else!" He is sure to get everyone's attention (whether they want to give it to him or not!). If there were newspapers (or "news-scrolls") then he certainly would be front page news.

○ Create a front page for the *Israel Times,* special edition on Amos. Headline: "'Day of the Lord Coming' Predicts Prophet!"

After completing this project ask the students to compare their newspaper about Amos with a current daily newspaper. Ask: "Does the news of Amos's world resemble the news in our world? If so, how?"

Getting to Know Amos

Continuing the Work of Amos Today

Preparation

❏ Students need to have a Bible, a pen, and paper.

❏ Provide materials from the following groups: Bread for the World, Habitat for Humanity, Casa Juan Diego Catholic Worker House, Maryknoll, Amnesty International, Heifer International, National Right to Life, and Catholic Relief Services. See the Saint Mary's Press Web site for links to these organizations.

❏ Bring in several copies of the daily newspaper.

1. Ask a student to read Amos 3:7–8, 7:10–15 aloud to the class. Discuss the following questions:
• What is the mission of a prophet?
• How does Amaziah see Amos and what does he want him to do?
• Why is Amos a prophet also for those of us who live today?

2. Make the following observations in your own words:

- God speaks through the words of Amos still today. God's call is still "comforting the afflicted and afflicting the comfortable," which means that God helps people grow spiritually, depending on people's situations in the world. For those who are suffering or are afflicted in some way, God comforts. When people are comfortable and unwilling to help others, God challenges them. Prophets bother those who are comfortable so that they can live God's way, and so that God's Kingdom may come.

- Where in the world or in our own community do we comfort the afflicted and afflict the comfortable? (Use the newspaper as well as any other situations that the students are aware of.)

- Who is defending the weak today? (List names or groups.) What struggles do they face to defend the weak?

3. Assign students the task of learning about various organizations that today comfort the afflicted, afflict the comfortable, or both. (Provide the students with literature about these organizations, give a presentation about them yourself, or have the students go online to learn more about them.) These are some organizations you may consider. See appendix 1, "Additional Resources," for more information about these organizations.

- Amnesty International
- Bread for the World
- Casa Juan Diego Catholic Worker House (Houston, Texas)
- Catholic Relief Services
- Habitat for Humanity
- Heifer International
- Maryknoll
- National Right to Life

(Speakers from any of these agencies would be worth your class time. Your diocese can help with other possibilities.)

4. After the young people have learned more about the organizations, ask what the similarities are between standing up for justice in Amos's time and our time?

Variation

In addition to these agencies, local experiences of food banks and clothing banks provide opportunities for direct service. Encourage your students to write letters to any of the agencies you decide to study and work with. It will help them stay connected to solutions for faith, hope, and love in the world. And, for a more imaginative twist, have them write them to "Amos," telling him how they are keeping the prophetic spirit alive in the twenty-first century.

MARY OF NAZARETH

Preparing to Teach

Overview

"I am the Lord's servant," said Mary, "may it happen to me as you have said." Without hesitation, Mary willingly says yes to the angel Gabriel, and helps fulfill God's promise to send a savior. Young adolescents will read the stories about Mary with new eyes when they realize that they are about the same age that she was when she became pregnant with Jesus by the Holy Spirit.

Mary's willing participation in the birth of Jesus indicates that she is Jesus' first disciple. She is a humble servant chosen by God who gives birth in the modest setting of a stable. There was nothing about Mary or the birth of Jesus that can be considered "lofty," yet this event changes salvation history. Students will be able to relate to the ordinary circumstances by which Mary lives her life. Mary is very approachable as the "Mother of God" and the most important saint. Young people, especially girls, should know that they can find a special friend in Mary.

Mary allows the Holy Spirit to overshadow her and work within her. Young adolescents, especially those who are preparing for Confirmation, will identify with the role of the Spirit in Mary's life and in their lives as well.

We see very human moments in Mary's story. Mary is a typical expectant mother when she excitedly visits Elizabeth with the news of her pregnancy. Good news such as this must be shared, and so students in turn need to share the Good News of the Gospel with others. Mary composes a beautiful hymn or prayer in response to this blessing God has bestowed upon her. When adolescents experience emotional highs, they often express them in artistic ways.

Another very human moment in Mary's life occurs when Jesus becomes separated from his parents while in the Temple. Mary and Joseph are concerned, and Mary later scolds Jesus for his lack of consideration. Jesus responds by telling his mother that his intentions were deliberate because he was doing his Father's work. Similar conflicts of opinion occur as young adolescents negotiate their freedom with their own parents.

Before she becomes a mother figure for young adolescents, she can first be one of them, a young woman in the world, trying to figure it all out. Later, having been one of them, she becomes a compassionate ear for people struggling at this age.

Getting to Know the Story of Mary of Nazareth

- Mary Remembers

Getting to Know Mary

- The Annunciation
- A Marian Prayer Service

Mary of Nazareth

Scripture Passages Related to Mary of Nazareth

- Isaiah 7:14 (Prophecy concerning Mary)
- Luke 1:26-38 (The Annunciation)*
- Luke 1:39-45 (Mary visits Elizabeth)*
- Luke 1:46-56 (The Magnificat)*
- Matthew 1:18-25, Luke 2:4-20 (The birth of Jesus)*
- Luke 2:22-38 (Jesus is presented in the Temple)
- Luke 2:39-40 (The Holy Family returns to Nazareth)
- Luke 2:41-52 (Jesus remains in the Temple to teach)
- John 2:1-12 (The wedding in Cana)*
- Matthew 12:46-50 (Mary seeks Jesus when he is teaching)
- John 19:25-27 (Mary is present at the cross)*
- Acts 1:12-14 (Mary prays with the disciples in Jerusalem)

Asterisk (*) signifies key passages to cover.

Articles from *Breakthrough!* Related to Mary of Nazareth

- *Breakthrough!* Interview with Mary of Nazareth
- "Born of the Virgin Mary" (Luke 1:26-38)
- Hail Mary! (Luke 1:41-42)
- Mary as the First Disciple (John 2:1-12)
- Making Something Out of Nothing (Titus 2:11-14)
- Evil Wages War (Revelation, chapter 12)

Mary of Nazareth and Young Adolescents Today

- Mary is an ordinary girl in many ways, yet God chooses her to be part of an extraordinary event, giving birth to Jesus, the Son of God. Young adolescents, especially those who receive

228

Confirmation, are called to carry on the work of the early Church of which Mary was a part.

- Mary willingly says yes to God without hesitation. In Mary we find a perfect role model for discipleship. Students can use her example as a spiritual model for faith development.
- Mary is a young woman when God calls her to accept her role in salvation history. These young people are of the same age.
- Filled with excitement, Mary visits her cousin Elizabeth, intending to share her good news. When noteworthy events happen in the lives of students, they willingly share their excitement with friends and relatives.
- Mary composes a song of devotion to God. Students enjoy poetry and music as expressions of self.
- Mary expresses concern and worry over losing Jesus in the Temple. Students express a desire for independence that at times conflicts with their parents' desires to care for them. Students along with their parents may have experienced a similar emotional situation when being separated or lost.
- Mary requests her son's help at the wedding feast at Cana. Jesus complies with her wishes. Like Mary, we can seek the help of Jesus knowing we will never be turned down.
- Mary supports her son at the foot of the cross. Like Mary, young people support those they love when they are going through difficult times.

Mary of Nazareth

Highlighting God's Presence

Well then, the LORD himself will give you a sign: a young woman who is pregnant will have a son and will name him "Immanuel" (Isaiah 7:14).

(See the Annunciation reading, Luke 1:26-35,37-38.)

Joseph went from the town of Nazareth in Galilee to the town of Bethlehem in Judea, the birthplace of King David. Joseph went there because he was a descendant of David. He went to register with Mary, who was promised in marriage to him. She was pregnant, and while they were in Bethlehem, the time came for her to have her baby. She gave birth to her first son, wrapped him in cloths and laid him in a manger—there was no room for them to stay in the inn (Luke 2:4-7).

When the parents brought the child Jesus into the Temple to do for him what the Law required, Simeon took the child in his arms and gave thanks to God. . . . Simeon blessed them and said to Mary, his mother, "This child is chosen by God for the destruction and the salvation of many in Israel. He will be a sign from God which many people will speak against and so reveal their secret thoughts. And sorrow, like a sharp sword, will break your own heart" (Luke 2:27-28,34-35).

Getting to Know the Story of Mary of Nazareth

Mary Remembers

In this activity three students will portray Mary in various stages of her life.

Preparation

 ❏ Make a copy of resource Mary-A, "In Mary's Voice," and select three students to read the three monologues. They should take the readings home to practice ahead of time.

1. Introduce the activity with the following words:

○ Today you will come to know Mary, the Mother of Jesus, as she remembers significant events in her life and that of her son's life. We will begin with her visit to Elizabeth, then hear about her life as Jesus is moving into adulthood, and finally have insight into her thoughts at the foot of the cross.

2. Have the three students give their performances. After each reading, ask the young people to share their initial reactions to the reading. Did the reading complement or challenge their perceptions of Mary?

3. Conclude with a discussion on what the students gained from the presentation.
• Did Mary come alive for them?
• What would they have added or changed in the script?
• Can they relate to the emotions Mary felt in the portrayal presented?

Variation

Choose another scene from Mary's life and ask students to write an internal reflection about the Annunciation or the wedding at Cana.

Getting to Know Mary of Nazareth

The Annunciation

Preparation

❏ Bring in two or more images of the Annunciation. See the Saint Mary's Press Web site for several suggestions. In addition, you can do a simple image search online with the key word "Annunciation." An interesting painting to use is Henry O. Tanner's 1898 painting *The Annunciation.*

❑ Put individual letters of the alphabet in a box or container, using pieces of paper or selected pieces from a Scrabble game. You will need at least one letter for each young person.

1. Display the images of the Annunciation. Explain the following points in your own words:
- At the time of the angel's visit, Mary was probably thirteen or fourteen years old. As was the custom at the time, a marriage had been arranged for her, and she was betrothed, or engaged, to Joseph. Because she was not living with Joseph and was presumed to be a virgin, becoming pregnant would be extremely shameful.

2. Ask a volunteer to read aloud Luke 1:26–38. Note that Luke's Gospel is the only one that tells Mary's story from her perspective.

3. Elicit the girls' opinions about which of the displayed images is most appealing, and which is most accurate according to the Bible passage. Ask the young people to imagine being in Mary's place when the angel appeared to her. Ask or adapt the following questions for discussion or reflection:
- What kind of girl do you think Mary was before the angel appeared? If she were living today, what kind of peer group would she be in?
- Do you think you would have liked her as a friend or an acquaintance?
- What feelings do you think Mary had when the angel appeared with the astounding news? What would your first reaction have been?
- Mary questioned the heavenly visitor. What questions would you have had for the angel?
- Mary's situation as an unwed mother was problematic during her time. What support systems would she have had? What problems do girls in her situation face today?
- What do you think of Mary's response: "Here am I, the servant of the LORD: let it be with me according to your word" (Luke 1:38). Was it a passive, "Okay, I don't have much choice" yes, or an active, courageous, "I can and will do this" yes?
- After the angel departed and Mary was alone, what would she have thought and felt? Who would she have turned to, or what would she have done? What would you have thought, felt, shared with others, or done?

4. Encourage the students to reflect on their own sense of Mary's Annunciation by writing a poem about Mary. Pass the container of

Mary of Nazareth

alphabet letters that you prepared before the activity, and direct the young people each to pick one letter. Instruct the students each to write a ten- to twelve-line poem about Mary, with each line beginning with the letter that they picked. Compile the completed poems into a book, and make copies to share.

(Adapted from an activity of the same title in Janet Claussen, *Biblical Women: Exploring Their Stories with Girls*, pp. 89–90.)

A Marian Prayer Service

In this activity, students will use the framework provided to write a Marian prayer service.

Preparation

❑ Each student will need a Bible.

❑ Make copies of handout Mary-A, "Planning a Marian Prayer Service," for each student.

❑ Write the following framework on the blackboard:
- Call to Worship
- Opening Prayer
- First Reading
- Psalm
- Second Reading
- Gospel
- Prayer of the Faithful
- Closing Prayer

1. Divide the class into seven groups and assign each group one of the above parts of the prayer service, omitting the psalm.

2. Pass out handout Mary–A, "Planning a Marian Prayer Service," to each student. Go over each aspect of the prayer service with the whole class and answer any questions they may have. Students may want to include in their prayer service the use of appropriate hymns. Ask students for suggestions or have them look through the parish Hymnal for songs.

Variation

Conclude the activity by using the writings to hold a Marian prayer service for the school or parish community.

In Mary's Voice

The Visit

Elizabeth was pregnant. It was her first child, and she was over thirty-five. A first child at that age could result in a difficult birth.

I wanted to go and visit her, and help her as her time to deliver drew near.

I hadn't seen Elizabeth for about two years. I didn't remember her well—she was closer to my mother's age, and Elizabeth and I had little in common. With my own mother gone, I wished to take her place in being of help to our kinfolk.

It was with mixed feelings that I began my journey to Elizabeth's home. I wanted to help . . . I missed my mother so deeply. I didn't really know Elizabeth. I was pregnant myself, through this very unusual gift from God. . . . Joseph had seen my pregnancy and couldn't understand it. I didn't know what to do. God finally told Joseph about it in a dream and we were reconciled, but the confusion was still upsetting me. What did God want of me with this child? I was physically very tired. These thoughts churned in my head and my heart. I had a lot of time to think about these things on the long journey, which seemed even longer because of my confusion.

"Mary." I heard my name called at what seemed a great distance. I was absorbed in the moment and the sound of my name was an unwanted intrusion. "Mary?" It was a question—it echoed the question in my mind: "Who am I?"

I turned and saw a woman heavy with child. She was radiant with life. Her face, ruddy with health, smiled with the tenderest of feelings. I stood up, and couldn't help smiling back. Was this lovely woman, so alive, so charming, my "old" cousin Elizabeth? She extended her hands to me, and I moved toward her. We stood there, two women, each ripe with hidden life inside of us.

Suddenly she was holding me. The small extension of my body bumped against the large protrusion of hers. We laughed. Without warning, I found myself sobbing. Tears everywhere, pouring out of me. "Mary," she said again, and the sound of Elizabeth's voice rang through my spirit and gentled it.

She eased me down and we sat on the hill together, her arm around me, holding me firmly but gently.

"You honor me, Mary," she said. "You are blessed among all women in the world. Just now when our bodies touched, awkwardly, the child I carry knew of the mystery you hold within you. He danced, alive with joy, at the presence of the precious burden you carry."

"You and this child, Mary, are for all time—for the glory of our God and the glory of God's people."

This woman, my cousin, knew. She understood the mysterious working of God in me. As I sat there in the warmth of her strong arms, the tensions and fears drained from me. I could talk. She listened. How wonderful a gift.

"My whole being glories in the wonder of our God. I am so small . . . and God has touched me so mightily. God saw my weakness—I am but a girl—and has called me to give to the world a gift through which all peoples for all times will remember me. God is saving all people, my cousin! God is fulfilling the Covenant, and will continue to do so!"

(This reading comes from a longer reading titled "The Visit," in *Mary Remembers: Cherished Memories of Jesus,* by Velma McDonough [Mystic, CT: Twenty-Third Publications, 1987], pages 13–15. Copyright © 1987 by Velma McDonough. Used with permission.)

Letting Go

I was worried about my son. I shared this with Joseph, and he told me that my worries didn't help Jesus and only made me upset. But I still worried.

Jesus was off to Jerusalem by himself. Only seventeen years old. He wanted to learn from the rabbis. His search for knowledge about the Scriptures was insatiable. I knew this, and I knew also that he had learned all he could from the local teachers. But it was the first time he had gone off on his own.

He planned to stay with some relatives in the city. Once he was there, I knew he would have a warm place to stay and get good meals.

But I was afraid of the journey. There had been so much talk here in the village about bandits who attacked travelers. I wanted Jesus to wait until the feast days when Joseph would be going to the holy city with the other men. But that would have been two months off, and he couldn't wait.

Jesus was such a loner. Sometimes it worried me. He did things other boys his age would never think of doing. He was wonderful to Joseph and me, and he was very comfortable with friends his own age. But he was so deep, so reflective. Those days I just didn't know what he was thinking about. And he didn't share it with me.

I guess I shouldn't have been surprised. I had been that way myself. I remember my mother complaining about me in the same way after I had returned from the temple school. I would go off by myself for hours at a time. I thought deep thoughts too, and told no one. I shouldn't have complained when my son did the same.

Still, I worried about him. It would be so long until I got word that he had arrived safely. And I wouldn't know what he was doing, or how he was, except once a month when the caravan came with news.

Now he was a man. He needed to stretch his mind and put even physical distance between us. He had to become his own person and he had to do it by himself. I had to let go.

I allowed myself a few silent tears as I experienced this separation, so painful for me as mother; so necessary for Jesus as a son. I reflected that the only pain greater than this would be the separation of death.

From now on our relationship would have to be different. How would it be? Only he could tell me. And maybe he couldn't either. That was frightening. Again, I was asked to wait . . .

"Behold Your Son"

I knew it firsthand.

When I was on the hill of Calvary watching my son die, he gasped for air. He, the light, the one who had brought fire from heaven, was being consumed by fever and thirst. He gasped again and again, struggling to breathe.

I don't know how I got through those hours. . . . It was awful. I kept trying to breathe for him.

It would have been so easy just not to breathe. I said to myself, "Mary, if you don't breathe you'll die too." It was exactly what I wanted at that moment. To die with him. My son. He was my very life.

But somehow I just couldn't. He had told me to care for John, and had asked John to care for me. John was the only one of Jesus' close friends to be there with us.

So I couldn't die. Jesus wanted me to live and take care of John and the others.

How hard it was for me to hear Jesus say, "Mother, behold your son." Jesus was my only son. I wanted him and only him. I didn't want him to die and to have some other son replace him. I wanted my son to live, to grow old with me, not to die at an early age.

And what a waste! Pilate had sent the order, but the religious leaders of our people killed my son.

Yes, there was anger mixed with my tears and sadness. And perhaps it was the anger that moved me out of the despair of wanting to die. It enabled me to say, "Yes, my son. You will die. I must stand here and watch. And I will do as you ask. I will be mother to John, and to the others. It is your last request to me. And it was so hard for you to get the breath to say it."

More new work for me to do. I felt too old to start something new again, and I didn't know what that work would be. I realized I was waiting again. I prayed, "O, my God, you would think I would have learned to wait by this time. I do it better now than years ago, but it is still so hard."

As I was thinking this, I heard him say, "It is finished."

(This reading comes from a longer reading titled "Behold Your Son," in *Mary Remembers: Cherished Memories of Jesus,* by Velma McDonough [Mystic, CT: Twenty-Third Publications, 1987] pages 55-56. Copyright © 1987, by Velma McDonough. Used with permission.)

PLANNING A MARIAN PRAYER SERVICE

Call to Worship. A call to worship is like an introduction to a prayer service. The leaders must introduce the reason why people are gathering to pray. Write a paragraph that answers these questions.

- Why are we honoring Mary?
- What is special about her?

Opening Prayer. An opening prayer helps the people to gather themselves and to focus on the intent of the prayer service. In this case, the opening prayer will invite people to slow down the pace of the day and focus on Mary. After brainstorming several ideas, put down several sentences that ask God to calm us and to reflect on Mary.

First Reading. The first reading will relate to the focus of the prayer service. In this case, students will copy the words of the Scripture passage found in Luke 1:26-38. The group should also write a short homily (one paragraph) about the importance of the Annunciation. (Trust is a concern for people today and an important aspect of the reading.)

Psalm or Reflection. This part of the prayer service comes from the Book of Psalms or can be another type of reflection related in this case to Mary. You may want to read Luke 1:46-55, Mary's *Magnificat,* or play a song about Mary.

Second Reading. The second reading will also relate to the focus of the prayer service. Copy the words of the Scripture passage found in Luke 2:4-7,15-19 and then write a short homily (one paragraph) on the birth of our Lord, reflecting on the simple events surrounding this humble birth.

Gospel. The Gospel reading always comes from the books of Matthew, Mark, Luke, or John. For this prayer service, copy John 2:1-11, the story of the wedding feast at Cana, and write a short homily focusing on the way Mary was concerned with the needs of others.

Prayer of the Faithful. In this part of the prayer service, we lift up the prayers of the people gathered. Write prayer intentions for the following needs.

- Church leaders
- World leaders and issues
- The poor, suffering, and oppressed
- The school and parish community

Instead of the traditional response of "Lord, hear our prayer," you may choose to create a response such as "Mary, full of grace, pray for us."

Closing Prayer. In the closing prayer, the leader helps us to conclude our prayer time and sends us out into the world to live as better followers of Jesus. Brainstorm together the most important concepts of the prayer service and ways that they can translate into everyday life. Then, compose a short prayer of several sentences that reflects these ideas. In this case, the prayer might speak of Mary's discipleship and ask her help to live like her.

JOHN THE BAPTIST

Preparing to Teach

Overview

John the Baptist's strong relationship with Jesus and his purpose in life kept him focused on his mission to "make a straight path for the Lord to travel!" John is a good role model for students who find it difficult to stay focused on important things in their own lives.

John the Baptist set himself apart from others by his dress and his countercultural attitude. Young adolescents are at a stage in their lives when they are searching for identity. Some young adolescents can identify with John's choices in being different from others in dress and attitude. It is important to help them understand that being different is fine as long as one's life is centered on God. This affirmation can ease the burden they might experience from being negatively labeled by their peers.

John the Baptist spoke the truth even though he was imprisoned for it and eventually put to death. Students need to be encouraged to stand up for what is honest and righteous. They can achieve this courage by building a relationship with the Holy Spirit, who offers numerous gifts that empower. You might ask students to share experiences they have had of courage and telling the truth.

Although John the Baptist had the potential to brag and become pompous due to his notoriety, he remained humble. Students at times will experience accolades due to winning sports awards, academic honors, and various talent contests. They need to be reminded that there is greatness in humility. You may want to discuss their feelings about winning, losing, competition, and popularity.

THIS CHAPTER AT A GLANCE

Getting to Know the Story of John the Baptist

- John the Baptist Bible Search

Getting to Know John the Baptist

- John the Baptist in the Desert
- John the Baptist's Message of Repentance

Scripture Passages Related to John the Baptist

- Luke 1:5-25 (The announcement of John's birth)
- Luke 1:57-66 (The birth of John the Baptist)
- Luke 1:67-80 (Zechariah's prophecy)
- John 1:29-34 (John calls Jesus "the Lamb of God")
- John 3:22-30 (John's relationship to Jesus)
- John 1:35-43 (John directs his disciples to Jesus)
- Matthew 3:1-12, Mark 1:1-8, Luke 3:1-18, John 1:19-28 (The preaching of John the Baptist)*
- Matthew 3:13-17, Mark 1:9-11, Luke 3:21-22 (The baptism of Jesus)*
- Matthew 11:1-19, Luke 7:18-35 (The messengers from John)*
- Matthew 14:1-12, Mark 6:14-29, Luke 9:7-9 (The death of John)*

Asterisk (*) signifies key passages to cover

Break Through!

John the Baptist

Articles from *Breakthrough!* Related to John the Baptist

- *Breakthrough!* Interview with John the Baptist
- Announcing God's Kingdom! (Matthew 3:1-12)
- The Blind Can See (Matthew 11:1-6)
- Foreshadowing (Matthew 14:1-12)
- Advent (Luke 3:1-18)
- It's Always Something (Luke 7:31-35)

John the Baptist and Young Adolescents Today

- The parents of John the Baptist, Zechariah and Elizabeth, pray for a child and receive one. God also answers the students' prayers.
- John's name is chosen in a surprising manner, very different from the customary way. Some students have unusual circumstances under which their names were chosen.
- John the Baptist was born of elderly parents. Some students have older parents or guardians that care for them.
- John lived in the desert and dressed differently than others. Certain students can relate to being different from their peers either in mannerisms or dress.
- Although John the Baptist was different, he had a following (many believed he was the Messiah). Adolescents strive to be popular with their peers.

- John the Baptist was bold in his approach to preaching the truth. Students can relate to times in their lives when they have had to take a stand, although difficult, for what is right.
- John the Baptist was a cousin to Jesus. Students enjoy relationships with their relatives (especially cousins who are close in age).
- Although John the Baptist was popular in his day, he gave all the glory to Jesus. Students may have experienced situations in their lives when they have had to relinquish glory and fame to siblings or friends that achieved recognition for outstanding performance in a given talent.
- King Herod had John killed because of the pressure he felt from his guests. Students experience peer pressure that at times leads to inappropriate behavior.

Highlighting God's Presence

"Don't be afraid, Zechariah! God has heard your prayer, and your wife Elizabeth will bear you a son. You are to name him John" (Luke 1:13).

"And don't think you can escape punishment by saying that Abraham is your ancestor. I tell you that God can take these rocks and make descendants for Abraham" (Matthew 3:9; John speaking to the Pharisees and Sadducees).

"I baptize you with water, but someone is coming who is much greater than I am. I am not good enough even to untie his sandals. He will baptize you with the Holy Spirit and fire" (Luke 3:16; John speaking of Jesus).

"You are my own dear Son. I am pleased with you." (Luke 3:22; God the Father to Jesus from heaven).

"There is the Lamb of God, who takes away the sin of the world" (John 1:29; John referring to Jesus).

Getting to Know the Story of John the Baptist

John the Baptist Bible Search

In this activity, students will research the facts behind the birth of John the Baptist.

Preparation

❑ Make copies of handout John the Baptist-A, "Bible Search," for every young person.

 1. Begin the study of John the Baptist by researching the facts behind his birth using handout John the Baptist-A, "Bible Search." When students have completed the handout, use these answers to help assess their search:

1. priestly
2. children
3. old
4. burn incense
5. angel
6. Gabriel

7. Son
8. Holy Spirit
9. Speak
10. John
11. Speak
12. Fear
13. "What is this child going to be?"

Getting to Know John the Baptist

John the Baptist in the Desert

In this activity students will identify the desert as a special place for John the Baptist to communicate with God. They will then come to either discover or identify their own special place to find God and communicate with him.

1. Allow students quiet time to read about John the Baptist's preaching in the desert by having them refer to the following citations: Matthew 3:1-12, Mark 1:1-8, Luke 3:1-18, John 1:19-28.

2. Discuss the readings with the students.

3. Have students write about or draw a place they like to go to communicate with God. If they are writing about a special place, encourage them to use descriptive language along with an expression of feelings. If they are drawing their special place, encourage them to be detail oriented.

4. Invite students to talk about places where they can communicate with God, as they are comfortable. Conclude the discussion by reminding them that a church building is not the only place one can feel close to God.

John the Baptist's Message of Repentance

In this activity, students identify John's message of repentance and create a relevant message for today's young generation.

Preparation

❑ Young people need to have bibles and a pencil or pen.

❑ Make copies of handout John the Baptist-B, "A Message of Repentance," for each of your students.

1. Read Matthew 3:2, Mark 1:4, and Luke 3:10-14 aloud to the class.

2. Discuss what temptations the students have in their present lives. If they are reluctant to share, give them the following questions to think about quietly for a minute: Where do you find you are continually making the same bad choices (cheating, lying, stealing)? Where do you have areas of weakness?

3. Give each of your students handout John the Baptist-B, "A Message of Repentance." Have students create a contemporary message of repentance on the skateboard deck provided. Post their handouts on the wall.

 John the Baptist

4. When they have completed their messages, discuss the messages they have written, inviting students to share their reactions to the statements on the wall.

BIBLE SEARCH

Fill in the blanks by referring to the following scriptural citation: Luke 1:5-25,57-66.

Elizabeth and Zechariah were husband and wife They were both from _____

families. Elizabeth could not have _____ , and both were very

_____.

    Zechariah's job as a priest was to _____ at the altar.

An _____ named _____ appeared to him standing

at the right side of the altar with an important message. Elizabeth will bear a

_____ who will be filled with the _____ from birth. Because

Zechariah didn't believe the message, he was unable to _____ .

The baby was named _____ . At the moment Zechariah wrote the

child's name on a writing pad, he was able to _____ again. The

neighbors present were filled with _____ . Everyone who heard the

news of this birth asked _____ ?

A Message of Repentance

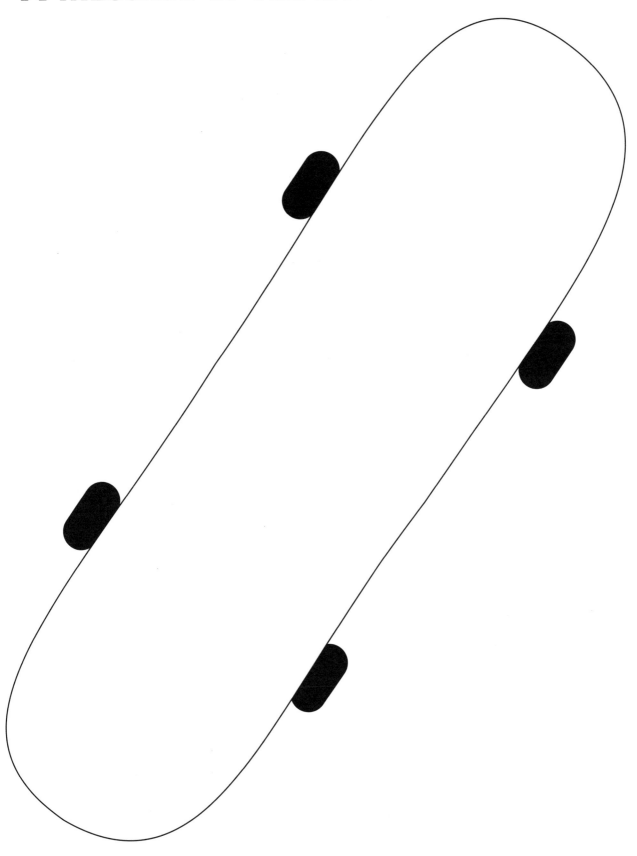

PETER

Preparing to Teach

Overview

A homilist once called Peter a "spiritual yo-yo." He asks to walk on water; he sinks as his faith fails. He pledges never to betray Jesus; he denies him three times. He asks Jesus not to wash his feet; then he wants his whole body to be washed. Although Jesus calls him "the rock," he is a very human rock, the type of person upon whom a Church can be built.

The young adolescent experiences life very intensely. Very up and enthusiastic one day, she could be the bluest blue the next day. Brimming with self-confidence on Monday, he could be highly critical of himself on Tuesday. Peter is a good apostle for young adolescents not only because his energy resembles theirs but also because we can read enough about him to see him grow and change while Jesus is alive and then again after his Resurrection. Young adolescents can express a beautiful eagerness about their faith, one that should be affirmed and encouraged by adults. As they grow in faith, however, they will balance their enthusiasm with the adult responsibilities of faith seen in Peter in the early Church.

Peter is the type of apostle who can give us great hope. Jesus looks at his great faith rather than his human shortcomings and gives him chance after chance. It is easier for us to be faithful if we believe that God has his eye on our goodness rather than our failings.

THIS CHAPTER AT A GLANCE

Getting to Know the Story of Peter

* Wanted: Leader of New Christian Movement

Getting to Know Peter

* Peter Declares His Faith
* Dear Peter
* The Papal Coat of Arms

Scripture Passages Related to Peter

- John 1:35-42 (Call to be a disciple)*
- Matthew 16:13-20 (Peter names Jesus the Messiah)*
- 2 Peter 1:16-21 (The Transfiguration)
- Matthew 26:69-75 (Peter denies Jesus)*
- John 21:15-19 (Jesus talks with Peter after the Resurrection)*
- Acts 2:14-42 (Peter's message about Jesus)*
- Acts 3:1-10 (Peter heals lame beggar)
- Acts 4:1-22 (Peter and John before the council)
- Acts 10:34-48 (The Gentiles receive the Holy Spirit)*
- Acts 12:6-18 (God frees Peter from prison)
- 1 Peter, chapters 1-5 (Encouraging letter addressed to Christians in northern Asia Minor)
- 2 Peter, chapters 1-3 (Letter addressing false teachers)

Asterisk (*) signifies key passages to cover.

Articles from *Breakthrough!* Related to Peter

- *Breakthrough!* Interview with Peter
- Jesus Rules! (Matthew 14:22-33)
- Peter the Rock (Matthew 16:13-20)
- Forgive, Forgive, Then Forgive Again! (Matthew 18:21-35)
- What's Your Answer? (Mark 8:27-30)
- Dazzled by Glory (Mark 9:2-8)
- I Messed Up Again, Jesus (Mark 14:32-72)
- What's Your Name? (John 1:42)
- Apostolic Succession (John 21:15-19)
- You Can't Buy Miracles (Acts 8:9-25)
- The Power of Prayer (Acts 12:1-19)
- Introduction to the First Letter of Peter
- Introduction to the Second Letter of Peter

Peter

Peter and Young Adolescents Today

- Jesus calls Peter to be a disciple. Jesus calls every Christian to be a witness to their faith.
- Jesus asks Peter to declare his loyalty and faithfulness to him. Jesus asks the same of us.
- Peter has an impulsive nature. Students can identify with Peter's tendency to act prior to thoughtful reflection and reasoning.
- Peter is an eager apostle. Many young adolescents are also eager and enthusiastic.
- Peter betrays Jesus when he denies knowing Jesus three times. Students have occasions in their lives when their loyalty to friends is tested.

- Jesus calls Peter to a leadership role. Students are called to various positions of leadership such as student council or peer mediation.
- In the beginning of their relationship, Peter has difficulty trusting Jesus. Learning to trust Jesus requires great faith. Students can find this to be a challenging aspect to their spiritual development.
- Peter is strong-willed. Young adolescents are experiencing life between childhood and adulthood. They will sometimes be willful at this stage in their lives.
- On Pentecost the Holy Spirit descended upon the Apostles. Some students will soon share this experience on their day of Confirmation.

Highlighting God's Presence

Then Peter spoke up, "Lord, if it is really you, order me to come out on the water to you."

"Come!" answered Jesus. So Peter got out of the boat and started walking on the water to Jesus. But when he noticed the strong wind, he was afraid and started to sink down in the water. "Save me, Lord!" he cried.

At once Jesus reached out and grabbed hold of him and said, "What little faith you have! Why did you doubt?" (Matthew 14:28-31).

Jesus went to the territory near the town of Caesarea Philippi, where he asked his disciples "Who do people say the Son of Man is?"

. . . Simon Peter answered, "You are the Messiah, the Son of the living God."

"Good for you, Simon son of John!" answered Jesus. "For this truth did not come to you from any human being, but it was given to you directly by my Father in heaven. And so I tell you, Peter: you are a rock, and on this rock foundation I will build my church, and not even death will ever be able to overcome it. I will give you the keys of the Kingdom of heaven; what you prohibit on earth will be prohibited in heaven, and what you permit on earth will be permitted in heaven" (Matthew 16:13,16-19).

A third time Jesus said, "Simon son of John, do you love me?"

Peter became sad because Jesus asked him the third time, "Do you love me?" and so he said to him, "Lord, you know everything; you know that I love you!"

Jesus said to him, "Take care of my sheep" (John 21:17).

Peter

Getting to Know the Story of Peter

Wanted: Leader of New Christian Movement

Preparation

❑ Bring in several employment ads from the local newspaper.

❑ Each student will need a Bible.

1. Pass out some of the employment advertisements that you have brought in and discuss some of the psychology of advertising, such as, what is included in each ad and how it is written to attract possible applicants to seek employment with the employer.

2. Divide the key passages listed in the "Scripture Passages Related to Peter" section of this chapter among your students.

3. Tell the class that they will be writing an employment ad for the local paper advertising for a leader of a new Christian movement. Remind them that the ad must include a listing of the qualifications the applicant should have for the position, suggested present and past work experience, and salary specifications. Write the ad as if you are looking for an applicant that would fit Peter's profile. Each student should emphasize the qualities that Peter demonstrates in their own passage.

4. Invite the students to share their ads and how their ads were influenced by their assigned stories. Consider making one single advertisement as a class that captures the main qualities that Peter displays in the different entries.

5. After finishing the assignment, you may want to extend the activity by having students write a résumé for Peter assuming he is applying for the position. Include Peter's past work experience, his education, his positive qualities, and his personal experiences with Jesus.

Getting to Know Peter

Peter Declares His Faith

In this activity, students use the Scripture passage of Matthew 16:13–20 to write a short script that highlights Peter's profession of faith.

Preparation

❏ Each student will need a Bible.

1. Have students read Matthew 16:13-20 quietly to themselves. Then put the class into groups of four.

2. Tell the students that their groups are to write a script involving Jesus, two disciples, and Peter that is based on this passage. They are to use the actual words found in the verses to develop the lines for the script. They should also include acting gestures and movement in parentheses.

3. When the students have finished the assignment, ask for volunteers to act out the scripts.

4. Have the students compare and contrast the skits. Ask, "What stands out for you in this passage?" Discuss their insights. Conclude with an in-class or homework assignment in which you have the students write a paragraph or two answering the same question Jesus asked Peter (Who do you say I am?). Ask them also to use nouns that would describe the role that Jesus plays in their life. (Some examples might be savior, friend, physician, teacher, healer, comforter, brother, and so on).

Dear Peter

The purpose of this activity is to familiarize the students with the First and Second Books of Peter, which are his letters addressing the early Christian community.

Preparation

❏ Each student will need a Bible.

❏ Divide the class into two groups and assign one group the First Book of Peter to read and the second group the Second Book of Peter to read. Assign this for homework just prior to the day you will be doing the following activity.

1. Ask all the students to write a letter to Peter addressing the concerns they have about world issues in this day and age as if writing to an advice columnist. (See the introductions to the First and Second Letters from Peter in *Breakthrough!* Have the students read over the "factoids" to learn about who most likely wrote these letters.)

2. Collect the letters from the first Peter and second Peter groups and shuffle them separately. Randomly, hand out first Peter letters to students in the second Peter group and vice versa, or ask the groups to randomly exchange the letters with each other. Direct each student to write an answer to the Dear Peter letter as if they are Peter or someone writing in his name, using insight from the First and Second Books of Peter, respectively.

3. Conclude the lesson by discussing the relevance of the letters' message for the world today. Ask, "If you were an advice columnist and received such a letter, how would your response resemble your response 'from Peter' and how would it differ?"

The Papal Coat of Arms

This activity highlights Peter's role as first Pope by using artistic expression in designing a coat of arms for Peter.

Preparations

❑ Reproduce enough copies of handout Peter-A, "Peter and the Papal Coat of Arms," for each student.

❑ Bring in several papal coats of arms, if possible. The Vatican Web site offers some helpful background about these that can be found by doing a search for "coat of arms."

1. Tell the students that for the past eight centuries, popes have had their own personal coat of arms, with each papal shield being unique. Symbols are chosen to represent important aspects of the pope's life. If you have any examples to share, pass them around or put them in a visible place.

2. Have students use handout Peter-A, "Peter and the Papal Coat of Arms," to design a coat of arms for Peter using information they have gained by reading the Scripture passages about his life. Explain that the shield on the handout is divided into three sections, using a different symbol for each section.

3. When students have finished their artwork, you may want to have them discuss why they chose certain symbols and then hang the artwork for display.

PETER AND THE PAPAL COAT OF ARMS

MARY MAGDALENE

Preparing to Teach

Overview

Of his disciples, Mary Magdalene holds a special importance because she is the one who first spreads the wonderful news of his Resurrection.

The Scriptures tell us that Jesus heals Mary Magdalene of seven demons. Unfortunately, many artists have traditionally focused on this negative sinful state. Although the Scriptures portray Mary Magdalene as a faithful follower and a "repentant believer," the emphasis on Mary as "sinner" can overshadow her role in the Gospels. Ironically, only one Evangelist mentions the demonic possession and healing and yet all four Evangelists tell of the risen Christ appearing to Mary.

The story of Mary Magdalene can help students see that a personal relationship with Jesus can change lives. First, Mary is someone that Jesus heals but she becomes one of his most significant disciples, willing to stand by him at the cross and be with him even in death at the tomb.

Young adolescents may want to take note that Mary Magdalene is at first one in need of Jesus' healing touch. Not all disciples come to Jesus whole and ready to follow! It is her conversion experience that leads her to be such a faithful follower. Young people have to feel that it is okay that they go to Jesus in need and that they do not need to be someone other than who they are to be Jesus' follower.

THIS CHAPTER AT A GLANCE

Getting to Know the Story of Mary Magdalene

- Interviewing Mary Magdalene

Getting to Know Mary Magdalene

- At the Foot of the Cross
- Apostle of the Resurrection

Scripture Passages Related to Mary Magdalene

- Luke 8:1-3 (Women who accompanied Jesus)*
- Matthew 27:45-56, Mark 15:33-41, John 19:16-27 (Mary Magdalene is present at the death of Jesus)*
- Matthew 27:57-61, Mark 15:42-47 (Mary Magdalene is present at the burial of Jesus)*
- Matthew 28:1-10, Mark 16:1-8, Luke 24:1-12, John 20:1-10 (Mary Magdalene visits the tomb of Jesus)*
- Mark 16:9-11, John 20:11-18 (Jesus appears to Mary Magdalene)*

Asterisk (*) signifies key passages to cover.

Articles from *Breakthrough!* Related to Mary Magdalene

- *Breakthrough!* Interview with Mary Magdalene
- A Model Friend (Mark 16:1-11)

Mary Magdalene and Young Adolescents Today

Mary Magdalene

- Mary Magdalene is perceived to be a sinner. Sin is a weakness in the human condition that we all share.
- Many people throughout Christian history have portrayed Mary Magdalene in her sinful state rather than as a devoted disciple. The media often portrays young people as troublemakers rather than focusing on their positive qualities.
- Mary Magdalene is a courageous and devoted follower of Jesus. She follows him on the road to Calvary and stands at the foot of the cross. Young adolescents at times need to be courageous to stand by friends or family in unjust situations.
- Jesus reveals himself to Mary after the Resurrection. Though students may not receive such a personal revelation, they too experience God's power and grace.

Highlighting God's Presence

At about three o'clock Jesus cried out with a loud shout, "*Eli, Eli, lema sabachthani?*" which means, "My God, my God, why did you abandon me?"

. . . Jesus again gave a loud cry and breathed his last.

. . . There were many women there, looking on from a distance, who had followed Jesus from Galilee and helped him. Among them were Mary Magdalene, Mary the mother of James and Joseph, and the wife of Zebedee (Matthew 27:46,50,55-56).

Then she (Mary) turned around and saw Jesus standing there; but she did not know that it was Jesus. "Woman, why are you crying?" Jesus asked her. "Who is it that you are looking for?"

She thought he was the gardener, so she said to him, "If you took him away, sir, tell me where you have put him, and I will go and get him."

Jesus said to her, "Mary!" She turned toward him and said in Hebrew, "Rabboni!" (This means "Teacher.")

"Do not hold on to me," Jesus told her, "because I have not yet gone back up to the Father. But go to my brothers and tell them that I am returning to him who is my Father and their Father, my God and their God."

So Mary Magdalene went and told the disciples that she had seen the Lord and related to them what he had told her (John 20:14-18).

Getting to Know the Story of Mary Magdalene

Interviewing Mary Magdalene

In this activity, the young people put themselves in the place of Mary Magdalene in an interview, answering questions about her experiences with Jesus. Although *Breakthrough!* also offers an interview with Mary, the following activity invites students to explore Mary's experiences at a deeper level.

Break Through!

Mary Magdalene

Preparation

❑ Make enough copies of handout Mary Magdalene-A, "An Interview with Mary Magdalene," for each person in the class.

❑ Each student needs to have a Bible.

1. Pass out handout Mary Magdalene-A, "An Interview with Mary Magdalene," to the young people and have them read the Scripture passages on the handout to themselves. Then ask them to answer the questions with accuracy regarding the biblical text but with some imagination to flesh out missing pieces in the story.

2. When students have had sufficient time to work on the handout, ask for two or more volunteers to present their interview to the class. Invite other young people to share how they imagined that Mary Magdalene experienced some of the events.

3. Conclude the activity by asking the class the following questions:

o When you first learned that we were studying about Mary Magdalene, did you have an image of who she was?

o After exploring the Scripture passage pertaining to Mary Magdalene, has your image or impression of her changed? If so, how?

Variation

Because of Christians' emphasis on Mary the sinner, invite a conversation about the power of the media to affect the way their audience sees people. Ask, "Does the media tend to portray young people as 'sinners' more than it shows the goodness of teens?"

Getting to Know Mary Magdalene

At the Foot of the Cross

In this activity, students reflect on the kind of courage that Mary Magdalene shows at the foot of the cross.

1. Read the following scriptural quote to the students: "Standing close to Jesus' cross were his mother, his mother's sister, Mary the wife of Clopas, and Mary Magdalene" (John 19:25).

2. Emphasize that Mary Magdalene displays extreme courage, empathy, and loyalty as she watches Jesus being put to death. Give the students this in-class assignment:

- Write about someone you know personally or have learned about that has displayed the same type of courage that Mary Magdalene does at the foot of Jesus's cross. Cite specific reasons why you have chosen to write about this person. In other words, tell that person's story of courage, empathy, and loyalty.

Apostle of the Resurrection

By comparing Mary Magdalene to one of the Apostles, students decide if her title "Apostle of the Resurrection" is valid.

Preparation

❑ Make enough copies of handout Mary Magdalene-B, "Mary Magdalene: Apostle of the Resurrection?" for each student in the class.

❑ Each student will need a Bible.

1. Read John 20:11–18 to the students.

2. Tell the students that some consider Mary Magdalene the "Apostle of the Resurrection." The *Catechism of the Catholic Church* defines *apostle* in this way: "Apostle is a term meaning one who is *sent* as Jesus was sent by the Father, and as he sent his chosen disciples to preach the Gospel to the whole world. He called the Twelve to become his Apostles, chosen witnesses of his Resurrection and the foundation on which the Church is built." (p. 866)

3. Pass out handout Mary Magdalene-B, "Mary Magdalene: Apostle of the Resurrection?" to the students and go over the directions. Give the essay as a homework assignment.

4. In a following class period, discuss what the young people have written about Mary Magdalene and the second Apostle. Have students share their comparisons in class. Conclude by bringing the activity to the present time and ask, "Although we were not eyewitnesses to Jesus' ministry, is there a way we could be considered apostles of the Resurrection?"

Mary Magdalene

AN INTERVIEW WITH MARY MAGDALENE

Read the following Scripture passages and then answer the interview questions as if you were Mary Magdalene.

- Luke 8:1–3
- Matthew 27:45–56
- Mark 15:42–47
- John 20:1–18

What was it like to be a close friend of Jesus?

There is talk that Jesus drove seven demons from you. Tell us about it.

Were you present at the Crucifixion? What went on?

You were the first person to see the risen Lord. Is that true? Give us the details.

Some consider you an "Apostle of the Resurrection." Why is that?

MARY MAGDALENE: APOSTLE OF THE RESURRECTION?

Write a short essay comparing Mary Magdalene to one of the Apostles. Support any comparison you make with a Gospel and verses about the Apostle.

The *Catechism of the Catholic Church* defines *apostle* in this way: "Apostle is a term meaning one who is *sent* as Jesus was sent by the Father, and as he sent his chosen disciples to preach the Gospel to the whole world. He called the Twelve to become his Apostles, chosen witnesses of his Resurrection and the foundation on which the Church is built (857)" (p. 866).

Consider These Topics for both Mary Magdalene and the Apostle

- How is this person an Apostle of Jesus? (Provide the book and verses that support this for both Mary Magdalene and the other Apostle.)
- Name a miracle of Jesus that Mary and the other Apostle either witnesses or experiences.
- What impact does Jesus have on this person's life? Is there a change in attitude, a life-altering experience?
- Is this person present during most of Jesus' ministry? What significant events does he or she witness?
- Is this person devoted to Jesus?

After doing this initial work, conclude your essay by answering this question:
- Is the title "Apostle of the Resurrection" an appropriate one for Mary Magdalene? Why or why not?

MARY AND MARTHA

Preparing to Teach

Overview

"Jesus loved Martha and her sister and Lazarus" (John 11:5). These words show us the relationship Jesus has with Martha and Mary as well as with their brother, Lazarus. Although very different from one another in personality, Martha and Mary both love Jesus very much. Martha expresses her love through the hospitality of a meal. Mary expresses her love by paying careful attention to Jesus. Young people may be learning that some friends appreciate having things *done for* them while other friends just want to *be with* them.

Jesus' message to Martha helps us keep our priorities in check. We are reminded that if our spiritual life is not in order then we will not be effective in carrying out our Christian responsibilities to love and serve one another. While it is cooking that distracts Martha from the company of Jesus, it may be work, softball, or video games that can distract young people from spending time with Jesus.

Despite her busyness, Martha expresses great faith in Jesus when she meets him after her brother has died. "Yes, Lord!" she answered. "I do believe that you are the Messiah, the Son of God, who was to come into the world" (John 11:27).

Close to the time of his death, both Mary and Martha are with Jesus, Lazarus, and some disciples. Martha serves the meal while Mary perfumes and wipes Jesus' feet. Both of these sisters actively serve and love Jesus. Young people can see that Christians can love God in their own unique ways.

THIS CHAPTER AT A GLANCE

Getting to Know the Story of Mary and Martha

- Mary or Martha?

Getting to Know Mary and Martha

- A Party with Jesus

Scripture Passages Related to Mary and Martha

- Luke 10:38-42 (Jesus visits with Mary and Martha)*
- John 11:1-44 (Lazarus dies and is brought back to life)*
- John 12:1-8 (Jesus is anointed at Bethany)*

Asterisk (*) signifies key passages to cover.

Mary and Martha and Young Adolescents Today

- Certain students can relate to the character of Martha, who is a "doer," a person who is willing to get her hands dirty when a job needs to be done. Other students can relate to the character of Mary, who is more reflective, one who is focused on the "bigger picture" and not the here and now.
- Jesus knew that Martha was "worried and troubled over so many things" (Luke 10:41). Young adolescents also carry much stress. Jesus asks Martha to focus on him instead. Students need to as well.
- Mary is drawn toward spiritual matters more so than practical ones. Martha does not understand her. Students who are quiet can relate to this interior focus and to the lack of understanding in others.
- Martha and Mary are very close to and protective of their brother, Lazarus. Siblings share these same family dynamics.
- Martha and Mary welcome people into their home. Students enjoy having friends over.

Highlighting God's Presence

As Jesus and his disciples went on their way, he came to a village where a woman named Martha welcomed him in her home. She had a sister named Mary, who sat down at the feet of the Lord and listened to his teaching. Martha was upset over all the work she had to do, so she came and said, "Lord, don't you care that my sister has left me to do all the work by myself? Tell her to come and help me!"

The Lord answered her, "Martha, Martha! You are worried and troubled over so many things, but just one is needed. Mary has chosen the right thing, and it will not be taken away from her" (Luke 10:38-42).

When Martha heard that Jesus was coming, she went out to meet him, but Mary stayed in the house. Martha said to Jesus, "If you had been here, Lord, my brother would not have died! But I know that even now God will give you whatever you ask him for."

"Your brother will rise to life," Jesus told her.

"I know," she replied, "that he will rise to life on the last day." Jesus said to her, "I am the resurrection and the life. Those who believe in me will live, even though they die; and those who live and believe in me will never die. Do you believe this?"

"Yes, Lord!" she answered. "I do believe that you are the Messiah, the Son of God, who was to come into the world" (John 11:20-27).

Getting to Know the Story of Mary and Martha

Mary or Martha?

In this activity, students use the Scriptures to identify characteristics and events that pertain to either Martha or Mary.

Preparation

❑ Make enough copies of handout Mary and Martha-A, "Is This Mary or Martha?" for each student in the class.

❑ Each student will need to have a Bible.

1. List the following Scripture passages on the board: Luke 10:38-42; John 11:1-44, 12:1-8.

2. Tell the students to read quietly through the Scriptural passages in order to prepare for the handout on Mary and Martha.

3. Once students have finished reading about Mary and Martha, pass out handout Mary and Martha-A, "Is This Mary or Martha?" to the students. Have them answer the handout from memory.

4. Conclude the lesson by having the students check their own answers for accuracy. Ask the students to write the biblical citation that indicates where the answer can be found and put it next to the space.

5. Ask the students to verbally summarize what they think about each character's personality.
- What are the differences between Mary and Martha?
- Is there a Mary and Martha in each of us?

Mary and Martha

Getting to Know Mary and Martha

A Party with Jesus

In this activity, students plan an evening get-together with Jesus.

Preparation

❑ Each young person will need to have a Bible.

❑ If young people do not have these items with them, provide letter-size white or colored paper and markers, crayons, or colored pencils.

1. Assign students to quietly reread these passages: Luke 10:38–42 and John 12:1–8.

2. When students have had sufficient time to read the Scripture assignment, pass out the supplies, and explain the activity:

○ Design an invitation to a dinner party that Martha and Mary will host. The invitation should have a theme such as "meet Jesus," or "learn Scripture from the Master." Be creative and original yet base your theme on the Scripture passages you have just read. The design of the invitation should reflect the theme of the party.

○ Include the following information:
   - Who is invited
   - Where it is being held (Martha and Mary's house in Bethany)
   - When it is being held
   - You may want to add other information, such as whether to bring a dish to share or if there is going to be any entertainment.

3. Allow sufficient time for the young people to complete their invitations. Ask students to share the ideas presented in the invitations. Discuss the hospitality that Martha and Mary display toward Jesus and others.
- Take a minute and analyze your own level of hospitality toward others.
- Do you exclude certain people when making social plans?
- Are you and your friends involved in working for others whether through Church or on your own?

4. Conclude with a conversation about the relationship between hospitality and ministry in a Catholic parish or school. How might we ourselves make our institution a more hospitable place?

Mary and Martha

Is This Mary or Martha?

Read each sentence and decide if it describes Mary or Martha. Write your choice on the line that follows.

1. When Jesus comes to visit, she sits at his feet and listens to his teaching.

   _____

2. She is upset over all the work she has to do at home.

   _____

3. The Lord tells her that she is worried and troubled over many things.

   _____

4. Jesus says she has chosen the right way.

   _____

5. When she hears that Jesus is coming to see Lazarus, she goes out first to meet him.

   _____

6. When Jesus comes to see Martha and Mary about Lazarus's death, she first stays inside.

   _____

7. She says this to Jesus: "I do believe that you are the Messiah, the Son of God, who was to come into the world" (John 11:27).

   _____

8. She helps to serve dinner to Jesus when he arrives in Bethany six days before the Passover.

   _____

9. She takes a pint of very expensive perfume and pours it on Jesus' feet and wipes them with her hair.

   _____

10. Jesus says to Judas Iscariot, "Leave her alone! Let her keep what she has for the day of my burial" (John 12:7). Who was he referring to?

    _____

JAMES

Preparing to Teach

Overview

Jesus gives James and his brother John the title "Sons of Thunder." This title conjures up visions of men who can make things happen by their impressive presence. James, the fisherman, is one of the first disciples chosen to follow Jesus and become a "fisher of men."

James is present at some significant events in Jesus' life, including the Transfiguration. Young people can relate to having the opportunity to attend a brother or sister's wedding, the birth of a younger sibling, or an event like a friend's bat mitzvah.

Like James, Jesus chooses us to be his disciples. Feeling special, however, can sometimes lead to pompous behavior. For example, James and John ask Jesus if they can sit at his right and left hands in his Kingdom. Jesus replies that it is not up to him but to God to grant this request. Jesus calls us to serve one another, not to be served. This dialogue about discipleship between Jesus and James and John reminds us of what this role really means.

Young people see Christianity lived out in very different ways in their community, Church, and country. They probably have witnessed powerful Christian people as well as disciples who serve the poor in humble ways. They can see that James and John's request is inconsistent with their experience of Jesus.

THIS CHAPTER AT A GLANCE

Getting to Know the Story of James

- Son of Thunder

Scripture Passages Related to James

- Matthew 4:18–22 (Jesus calls several fishermen)*
- Mark 5:35–43 (Healing the daughter of Jairus)
- Mark 10:35–45 (The request of James and John)*
- Mark 14:32–42 (Jesus prays in Gethsemane)*
- Luke 9:28–36 (The Transfiguration)

- Luke 9:51-56 (Jesus rebukes James and John)

Asterisk (*) signifies key passages to cover.

Articles from *Breakthrough!* Related to James

- *Breakthrough!* Interview with James
- Dazzled by Glory (Mark 9:2-8)
- Me First! (Mark 10:35-45)
- I Messed Up Again, Jesus (Mark 14:32-72)

James and Young Adolescents Today

- Jesus calls James to bring the Gospel message to others. Jesus also calls us to the role of evangelization.
- James is "out of line" in asking to sit at the right hand of Jesus. When adolescents experience success without hard work and dedication, they can feel pompous just as James did. Jesus reminds us that God our Father is in charge.
- In the garden of Gethsemane Jesus asks his disciples to keep watch. James is among this group. Not one Apostle is able to meet his request. Adolescents experience times when good friends let them down.
- James and John are ready to use retribution in dealing with a village in Samaria that rejects Jesus. Jesus does not let them; in fact, he rebukes them for suggesting it. Loyal friends will defend one another when threatened. Jesus' response will help the students understand Jesus' position on retaliation and violence.

James

Highlighting God's Presence

He [Jesus] went on and saw two other brothers, James and John, the sons of Zebedee. They were in their boat with their father Zebedee, getting their nets ready. Jesus called them, and at once they left the boat and their father, and went with him (Matthew 4:21-22).

Six days later Jesus took with him Peter and the brothers James and John and led them up a high mountain where they were alone. As they looked on, a change came over Jesus: his face was shining like the sun, and his clothes were dazzling white. Then the three disciples saw Moses and Elijah talking with Jesus.

. . . While he was talking, a shining cloud came over them, and a voice from the cloud said, "This is my own dear Son, with whom I am pleased—listen to him!" (Matthew 17:1-3,5).

Getting to Know the Story of James

Son of Thunder

This guided meditation uses the Scriptures and imagery to lead students through a process where they personally meet Jesus and the Apostle James. It is inspired by Matthew 4:18-22, Luke 9:28-36, and Mark 14:32-42.

Preparation

❏ If there is a way to make your room more comfortable, do so. You might also want to take the students to another location for this exercise.

❏ Bring in instrumental music, if desired.

❏ Decide which sections of the meditation you want to use, or if you want to use all of them.

1. Have students choose a comfortable position. Ask them to close their eyes. Soft instrumental music can be used to establish the mood. Read the following script slowly, pausing where indicated.

❍ Imagine you are walking along the beach, it is morning, and the sun is glistening on the horizon. . . . You have promised James and John that you will help them repair the worn nets that they use for fishing. As you look in the distance you see a third person standing beside their father, Zebedee. You squint to block the sun from your eyes but you do not recognize this man's face. As you walk closer you sense excitement in the air as James calls you by name. He introduces you to his new friend. He tells you he is leaving his father to follow Jesus. Then Jesus turns and asks you to join him. He tells you that along with James and John, you will be "fishers of men." Take a moment now to respond to Jesus. . . . I will give you a moment of quiet time so you can talk together. . . .

❍ It is afternoon; Jesus has invited you on a hike along with Peter, James, and John. You are not sure where the hike will lead, but you like an adventure and you are sure this will be one. Life has not been the same for you since you decided to follow Jesus. As you ascend a high mountain, Jesus takes on an appearance that startles you. His face is shining like the sun and his clothes are dazzling white. You see Moses and Elijah talking with Jesus. A voice from the cloud says, "This is my own dear Son, with whom I am pleased—listen to him!" (Matthew 17:5). You look at James, John, and Peter as they throw themselves down on the ground. You sense the fear in their hearts and you understand the significance of this event. This Jesus is not just any man but the Son of God! You want to help your friends overcome their fear so you lift them up and tell them this. . . .

I will give you a moment of quiet time so you can talk with them.

○ It is evening in the garden of Gethsemane. You are with Peter, James, and John. Jesus asks you to keep watch because the high priests are looking to arrest him. You feel great sorrow as you sense the anguish in Jesus' face. The moon is out but it seems much darker than it should be. As you wait for Jesus to return, you feel your eyes getting heavy and you can hardly stay awake. You notice that Peter, James, and John have fallen asleep. You think to yourself, how could they do this to Jesus! Upon returning Jesus mentions to Peter how disappointed he is with you, that you couldn't stay awake for just one hour. You want to explain to Jesus how you really feel and what his friendship means to you, so you turn to him and say the following . . . I will give you a moment of quiet time so you can talk with Jesus.

○ When you are ready, return to the present time and place. . . . Open your eyes and come back to the group.

2. After you have finished reading the meditation, have students pair off and walk together, sharing with each other what they thought and how they felt during the meditation.

James

266

JOHN

Preparing to Teach

Overview

What would it be like to be the closest friend of Jesus the Christ? According to the Scriptures and scholars, John is likely the "one who Jesus loved." Interestingly, John also shares characteristics with young adolescents. John's youthful eagerness to please, combined with his (at times) awkward desire to "show off" a bit so as to be noticed, are signs of a growing passionate spirit we see in young adolescents. Like John, young adolescents all want to be picked, to be chosen, to be special to someone special. With this in mind, John's experience can resonate with them.

While the Apostle John initially shares many of the characteristics of a younger person, he really grows and matures as he spends time with Jesus. Jesus allows him to witness some important miracles. He is deeply moved by Jesus' Last Supper, Passion, and death, even to the point of standing with Jesus' mother, Mary, at the foot of the cross. He is one of the first Apostles to experience the risen Jesus.

John's faith is both simple and deep. His love for Jesus matures over time as does his own sense of leadership in the Church, as his mission with Peter demonstrates. Students should know that it does take some time for a person to get to know Jesus. The Apostle John gives us some insight into that process.

THIS CHAPTER AT A GLANCE

Getting to Know the Story of John

- John the Apostle Comic Book

Getting to Know John

- A John the Apostle CD
- A Relay Race to the Tomb

Scripture Passages Related to John

- Matthew 4:18–22, Mark 1:16–20, Luke 5:1–11 (Jesus calls James and John, sons of Zebedee)

- Matthew 17:1-13, Mark 9:2-13, Luke 9:28-36 (The Transfiguration)
- Matthew 26:36-48, Mark 14:32-42, Luke 22:39-46 (Gethsemane)
- Luke 9:51-55 (Jesus scolds John)
- John 21:1-24 (Jesus appears to the seven disciples)

It has been customary to identify John with the "Beloved Disciple" in the Gospel of John. Several of these Scripture references are included below as well.

- John13:23-29 ("The one whom Jesus loved" during the Last Supper)
- John 19:25-27 (Jesus entrusts Mary to "the one he loved")

References to John outside the Gospel

- Acts 4:1-22 (With Peter, John is arrested and brought before Jewish leaders)
- Galatians 2:9 (John is one of the leaders in Jerusalem)

Articles from *Breakthrough!* Related to John

- *Breakthrough!* Interview with John
- Dazzled by Glory (Mark 9:2-8)
- Me First! (Mark 10:35-45)
- I Messed Up Again, Jesus (Mark 14:32-72)
- Introduction to the Book of John
- You Can't Buy Miracles (Acts 8:9-25)
- Introduction to the First, Second, and Third Letters of John

John and Young Adolescents Today

- John is the younger brother to James in the Zebedee family and one of the youngest Apostles. The students' place in the family affects their experience of their family.
- John is with Jesus at some of the highest points of Jesus' mission and at some of his lowest points. Students share peak experiences and difficult moments with family and friends as well.
- John develops a deep friendship with Jesus and Peter, both older than he. Students are developing relationships with older students and adults.
- John travels with Jesus and Peter to encounter different kinds of people. Students are beginning to notice the variety of people in the world.
- John works alongside his brother and father. Students have family projects or interests they all share.
- John is willing to step out in faith and work with others on the mission with Jesus. Students have been parts of teams and know what it takes to make a project work.

John

- Many scholars believe that the Apostle John is the same person as "the one whom Jesus loved" (John 13:22). Young adolescents value "best" friends but are still learning what it means to be a friend. Exploring the friendship between Jesus and John can shed light on the young people's current friendships as well as on their relationship with Jesus.

Highlighting God's Presence

About a week after he had said these things, Jesus took Peter, John, and James with him and went up a hill to pray. While he was praying, his face changed its appearance, and his clothes became dazzling white.

. . . A cloud appeared and covered them with its shadow; and the disciples were afraid as the cloud came over them. A voice said from the cloud, "This is my Son, whom I have chosen—listen to him!" (Luke 9:28-29,34-35).

Getting to Know the Story of John

John the Apostle Comic Book

In this activity, students learn about the stories of John the Apostle through creating comic strips and sharing them with one another.

Preparation

❑ Review the activity "The Comic Book Approach," on page 325 in appendix 2, "Tools for Teaching."

❑ Make copies of handout Tools-A, "The Comics," so that each young person has two or three copies of the handout.

❑ Provide markers or crayons.

❑ Choose enough stories from John's life so that his story line is complete and there is some variety of stories among the group. Consider choosing the stories listed under "Scripture Passages Related to John."

❑ Make sure each student has a Bible.

After giving your students a general introduction to the Apostle John, assign your chosen passages to the students. Ask them to read their stories quietly to themselves first. Walk around and answer any questions about the stories that they have.

From this point forward, follow the directions in "The Comic Book Approach" for the rest of the activity.

Getting to Know John

A John the Apostle CD

In this activity, students create a CD cover and select songs for a CD that reflect the Apostle John's story and growth in faith.

Preparation

❑ If the students are not very familiar with John the Apostle's story, select some or all of the stories under "Scripture Passages Related to John" to read with the students. This activity is best done when the students are familiar with the stories.

❑ Have markers and crayons on hand. The squares on handout Tools-A, "The Comics," also work well for the front and back of a CD jewel case. Otherwise, provide paper.

❑ You may want to have some CD covers on hand so that students can get ideas for their designs.

1. Ask students to create a CD cover to describe John's life of faith. Tell students to include the following items:
- The title of the CD
- Twelve modern songs that describe the key events in his faith life
- Some design on the cover

2. After the young people have finished their designs, give them time to share their ideas. Consider voting on a "Top Ten" list from the songs suggested. Ask, "How would you describe John the Apostle after thinking more about his life and faith journey?"

Variation

You can also ask students to create a CD cover for themselves with a title and songs to represent their faith lives. You can then ask the students to compare their own CD cover with John's.

A Relay Race to the Tomb

In this activity, students participate in a "biblical relay race" and use this image of a relay to discuss the nature of teamwork.

Preparation

❏ Find a place where you can hold a relay race for your class. If this will be in the classroom, desks should be moved out of the way. This would best be undertaken outside, in a gymnasium, or in an auditorium. Put two desks covered with cloths 5 to 10 feet apart. Place a start line to correspond with each desk about 20 or 30 feet away from the desk.

1. Read aloud John 20:2-10, the account of Peter and John running to the tomb of the Resurrected Jesus. Highlight that when Peter and John ran to the tomb, John waited for Peter to enter the grave first. They both see the shroud material folded up and then run back to tell others.

2. Create two teams, each having an even number of students. (Prepare to join in if necessary.) Explain that the class will re-enact this story through a relay race. Ask each team to arrange themselves into pairs to represent "Peter and John." When you say "go," a pair from each team must run up to the desk (which represents the tomb), kneel down and look under the cloth, and then run back to tag the next pair, who will do the same thing. The team whose last pair comes back first is the winning team.

3. After the race, create parallels between the race, John the Apostle, and the young people's lives.
- You may have run fast for the sake of your team or because you did not want to appear slow, but imagine that you were running because your best friend, who you thought had died, was really alive! Imagine how fast you would need to run.
- How do the Apostles resemble a team?
- How do disciples working together share a team element?
- What can your experiences of good and bad teamwork teach you about what it means to be a Christian?

THOMAS

Preparing to Teach

Overview

Thomas the Apostle is often called "doubting Thomas" because of his skeptical response to the news of Jesus' Resurrection. But Thomas also shows great faith. When he encounters the Risen Jesus, he declares, "My Lord and my God" (John 20:28).

But who was Thomas? His name appears in each of the different Gospels' lists of the Apostles, but it is only in John's Gospel that we learn something about him. We hear him declare a loyalty to Jesus unto death (John 11:16), pose a question at the Last Supper in regards to where Jesus is ultimately going with his life (John 14:5), and profess doubt that Jesus has risen (John 20:24-25). With Jesus' help, Thomas's faith is renewed in the presence of the glorified Christ (John 20:26-28). What can we take from such a slim biography to apply to a young adolescent? Perhaps a clue can be drawn from the meaning of Thomas's name.

Thomas's name, we are reminded several times in John's Gospel, means "twin." While we do not have any information about Thomas having a biological twin, he appears to have two sides to him. Thomas is filled at times with eagerness but at other times he is skeptical. He resembles an adolescent who at one moment is thoroughly energized by the possibilities of a developing faith life but in the next is completely disengaged from it. Thomas's dual attitudes toward faith may resonate with not only our students' faith lives, but our own faith lives as well.

THIS CHAPTER AT A GLANCE

Getting to Know the Story of Thomas

- Seeing Thomas in Ourselves

Getting to Know Thomas
- I Am the Way . . .

Scripture Passages Related to Thomas

- John 11:1-16 (Thomas encourages disciples to accompany Jesus to Jerusalem)
- John 14:1-14 (Thomas asks Jesus a question at the Last Supper)
- John 20:19-25 (Thomas doubts Jesus' Resurrection)*
- John 20:26-29 (Thomas makes an act of faith in Jesus)*
- John 21:1-14 (Thomas witnesses Jesus' appearance at the Sea of Galilee)

Asterisk (*) signifies key passages to cover.

Thomas and Young Adolescents Today

- Thomas is eager to stand with Jesus as his friend and he encourages others to do so. Young adolescents also express their loyalty to friends.
- At the Last Supper, Thomas listens closely to Jesus' words but does not understand what he says. Adolescents often struggle with difficult questions about faith.
- Thomas misses the first Resurrection encounter with Jesus. He does not appear to be happy about it. We can help the young adolescent reflect on similar experiences of being left out or "in the wrong place at the wrong time" in light of what the Lord does for Thomas.
- Thomas's declaration of faith in Jesus comes out of his sheer wonder and joy at finding his friend alive. Adolescents also feel a divine wonder during moments in their lives.

Highlighting God's Presence

Thomas said to [Jesus], "Lord, we do not know where you are going; so how can we know the way to get there?"

Jesus answered him, "I am the way, the truth and the life; no one goes to the Father except by me. Now that you have known me," he said to them, "you will know my Father also, and from now on you do know him and you have seen him" (John 14:5-7).

Then [Jesus] said to Thomas, "Put your finger here, and look at my hands; then reach out your hand and put it into my side. Stop your doubting, and believe!"

Thomas answered him, "My Lord and my God!" (John 20:27-28).

Getting to Know the Story of Thomas

Seeing Thomas in Ourselves

In this activity, students examine the different ways that Thomas responds to Jesus and the Apostles in the Gospels and then reflect on ways that their own faith resembles Thomas's faith.

Preparation

❑ Students need Bibles and pens or pencils.

❑ Make enough copies of handout Thomas-A, "It Sounds Familiar," so that each student can have one.

1. Point out that Thomas's name appears only four times in the Gospels. Ask students to read each passage in "Scripture Passages Related to Thomas" aloud to the class. Note that while Thomas appears infrequently, he is present at key moments. You might have your students read his lines exactly the way he may have said them—with eagerness, confusion, doubt, wonder.

2. Pass out handout Thomas-A, "It Sounds Familiar," to the students. In each quadrant, have the students write examples when they approach their own faith with these same attitudes. Ask the students, "In what ways does Thomas resembles all of us?"

Getting to Know Thomas

I Am the Way . . .

In this activity, students attempt to portray visually some of what Jesus shares with Thomas and the other Apostles at the Last Supper.

Preparation

❑ Provide poster board, card stock, or some sort of paper for students to draw on.

❑ Have markers, colored pencils, and watercolors on hand.

❑ If your students are technologically savvy and you have access to computers, you can invite them to use Microsoft PowerPoint or Windows Paint. Some of the possibilities on the computer might highlight the mystical quality of Jesus' words.

1. Read John 14:1-7 aloud to the class. Examine the passage verse by verse with the students because there is quite a bit of material in this short passage. (If the students express confusion, you can share that Thomas and Philip were perplexed as well!) Ask questions such as "What does it mean for Jesus to say that he is the way and the truth and the life?"

2. Ask students to take any of the phrases from these verses and to present them in some way visually. Both the words and other images should be in the visual presentation. Ask them to imagine that they are conveying the meaning of the words rather than just the words themselves.

3. Invite students to group together by the verses they choose and compare their portrayal. Then have the students share their work with the whole class.

Thomas

IT SOUNDS FAMILIAR

People can go through ups and downs in faith or have a mixture of feelings and experiences around their faith. For each description, list some times you have experienced that feeling about your faith. You could also list questions or describe events to fill in the boxes.

Eagerness	Confusion
Doubt	Wonder

MATTHEW

Preparing to Teach

Overview

When we first read about Matthew in the Gospels, he is a tax collector. By the end of the Gospel narratives, he is one of the twelve men chosen by Jesus to be an Apostle. To go from tax collector to Apostle is quite a transition! When Matthew meets Jesus, his life is transformed. Jesus has that kind of effect on people.

In Jesus' day, tax collectors were considered dishonest and were seldom invited to social events where people would dine together. Jesus, however, eats dinner at Matthew's house with the tax collector and other outcasts.

What is it about Matthew that makes Jesus call him to his role as Apostle and subsequent Evangelist? In Matthew, Jesus sees a heart willing to change. And what does Matthew see in Jesus? He sees a man who treats him with dignity. He recognizes that Jesus is special and likely marvels at his own conversion.

Young adolescents can sometimes feel like outcasts, perhaps because they do not think that they are popular, are self-conscious about their appearance, or do not succeed in the same way that their peers do. They need to know that Jesus does not see them as outcasts but rather sees their hearts like he does with Matthew. While the rest of the world sees a despicable, cheating person in Matthew, Jesus sees an Apostle. Praying to Jesus in times of low self-esteem is important! Jesus can give us a better vision of ourselves.

THIS CHAPTER AT A GLANCE

Getting to Know the Story of Matthew

- Jesus Calls Matthew

Getting to Know Matthew

- True Happiness
- Be Special

Scripture Passages Related to Matthew

- Matthew 9:9–13, Mark 2:13–17, Luke 5:27–32 (Jesus calls Matthew)*
- Matthew 10:1–4, Mark 3:13–19, Luke 6:12–16 (Jesus chooses the twelve Apostles)*
- Acts 1:12–14 (Praying together)

Asterisk (*) signifies key passages to cover.

Break Through! Articles from *Breakthrough!* Related to Matthew

- *Breakthrough!* Interview with Matthew
- Introduction to the Gospel According to Matthew
- The Twelve (Matthew 10:1–4)

Matthew and Young Adolescents Today

- Although Matthew is scorned by many because of his occupation, he is still open to change. When Jesus takes hold of one's heart, nothing is impossible.
- Jesus calls Matthew to be a disciple. Jesus calls each of us to be faithful followers.
- Jesus is criticized for having dined with Matthew, a "public sinner." Young people may be unjustly labeled because of the friends they spend time with.
- Matthew is chosen to be one of the twelve Apostles and is given the directive to continue Christ's work in the world. Jesus calls all young people to respond to his call to be disciples. This is especially clear at the sacrament of Confirmation.

Highlighting God's Presence

Jesus left that place, and as he walked along, he saw a tax collector, named Matthew, sitting in his office. He said to him, "Follow me."

Matthew got up and followed him.

While Jesus was having a meal in Matthew's house, many tax collectors and other outcasts came and joined Jesus and his disciples at the table. Some Pharisees saw this and asked his disciples, "Why does your teacher eat with such people?"

Jesus heard them and answered, "People who are well do not need a doctor, but only those who are sick. Go and find out what is meant by the scripture that says: 'It is kindness that I want, not animal sacrifices.' I have not come to call respectable people but outcasts" (Matthew 9:9–13).

At that time Jesus went up a hill to pray and spent the whole night there praying to God. When day came, he called his disciples to him and chose twelve of them, whom he names apostles: Simon (whom he named Peter) and his brother Andrew; James and John, Philip and Bartholomew, Matthew and Thomas, James son of Alphaeus, and Simon (who was called the Patriot), Judas son of James, and Judas Iscariot, who became the traitor (Luke 6:12-16).

Then the apostles went back to Jerusalem from the Mount of Olives, which is about half a mile away from the city. They entered the city and went up to the room where they were staying: Peter, John, James and Andrew, Philip and Thomas, Bartholomew and Matthew, James son of Alphaeus, Simon the Patriot, and Judas son of James. They gathered frequently to pray as a group, together with the women and with Mary the mother of Jesus and with his brothers (Acts 1:12-14).

Getting to Know the Story of Matthew

Jesus Calls Matthew

In this activity, students explore the relationship between Jesus and Matthew by answering questions from the scriptural account of Jesus' call to Matthew.

Preparation

❑ Each young person will need a Bible.

❑ Make enough copies of handout Matthew-A, "Matthew's Call," for each person.

1. Have students read Matthew 9:9-13 and then individually answer the questions found on handout Matthew-A, "Matthew's Call."

2. When students have finished the handout, allow class time to review their answers. Conclude the lesson with the following questions:
- What was it about Jesus that made Matthew walk away from a high-paying position as tax collector to become a disciple of Jesus?
- Could Jesus have that effect on people today?
- Do you know of people who have had this transformation?

Getting to Know Matthew

True Happiness

In this activity, students use the Beatitudes to create a personal piece of artwork.

Preparation

❑ Each student will need a Bible.

❑ Provide a piece of white drawing paper and a set of colored writing implements (markers, crayons, or colored pencils) for each participant.

1. Divide the class into two groups and have each group alternately read aloud a verse from the following passage: Matthew 5:3-12.

2. Remind the students that the words they have just read are the Beatitudes. They are often seen as a summary of Christian life. Discuss the meaning of each verse and its relevancy for true happiness.

3. Have students rewrite the verses of the Beatitudes to include their own name. The object is to make the Beatitudes into a personal statement of their faith. Give the following example of the first verse:

"Happy is (name) who knows (he/she) is spiritually poor, the Kingdom of heaven belongs to (him/her)!" (Matthew 5:3).

Encourage the students to be creative with color, as this is to be displayed as artwork.

4. Conclude the activity by suggesting the students apply the lessons learned in the Beatitudes to their daily life.

Be Special

In this activity, students listen to a dramatic reading of Max Lucado's storybook *You Are Special.* This book is a fictional story about being cherished by God regardless of how others "label" you.

Preparation

❑ Obtain a copy of *You Are Special,* by Max Lucado (Wheaton, IL: Crossway Books, 1997).

1. Present a dramatic reading of *You Are Special* to the class.

2. After reading the story to the students, discuss the following questions:

- Can you personally relate to a particular group of Wemmicks?
- Is it easy to fall into the same mindset that Punchinello experienced because of what others felt and did toward him?
- What were your reactions to Lucia? (Neither stars nor dots stuck to her. Why not?)
- Why do you think Lucia didn't tell Punchinello her secret?
- Who do you really think Lucia is? Who is Eli?
- What was Eli's message to Punchinello?
- Does this message speak of God's love for us? How can a deep understanding of God's love for us help develop positive self-esteem?

3. Conclude with this observation and question:

- The Apostle Matthew went from outcast to Evangelist. How does this story about Punchinello relate to the story of Matthew as found in the Scriptures? (Matthew 9:9–13).

MATTHEW'S CALL

Read Matthew 9:9-13. Answer the questions below.

1. What are the words that Jesus uses when calling Matthew?

2. Matthew is known by another name. Read Luke 5:27-32 to discover what it is.

3. Matthew is a tax collector. Was this an admirable or undesirable occupation? What words found in the Scriptures indicate this?

4. How does Matthew respond to Jesus' invitation?

5. How does Jesus make Matthew feel?

6. Matthew invites Jesus to share a meal at his house? What is Matthew's reason for this?

7. Who else is at the house with Jesus and Matthew?

8. What group of people criticize Jesus for dining with Matthew?

9. What, do you think, is their reason for criticizing Jesus?

10. What is Jesus' response to his critics?

11. What is Jesus implying by stating, "People who are well do not need a doctor, but only those who are sick" (Matthew 9:12)?

JUDAS ISCARIOT

Preparing to Teach

Overview

Many people see the name Judas Iscariot as synonymous with traitor because Judas betrays Jesus to the Jewish leaders. It is likely that Judas is a very complicated person and that he made the decision to hand over Jesus for several reasons. We do see from his reaction to Mary's use of perfume to anoint Jesus that he struggles with greed, and because the betrayal involves money, it is likely that this is at least one motive.

Young people betray one another and feel regret on a smaller scale than Judas, but arc often as helpless as he is to know how to atone for their choices. As soon as Judas receives his money, he returns it out of guilt, and hangs himself because he believes he is beyond redemption because of this horrible act. A lesson from the Judas story and one important for young people is that no one is beyond redemption, no matter what they have done. Even if a juvenile court condemns and incarcerates them, young people always have a future with Jesus because his suffering, death, and Resurrection conquer all sin.

It may be important to show the students that although Judas is one of Jesus' closest companions, he is still tempted by greed and the awful crime of betraying his friend and mentor. Young people should know that choosing Jesus over money or possessions is a choice that needs to be chosen every day rather than assumed.

THIS CHAPTER AT A GLANCE

Getting to Know the Story of Judas Iscariot

- Jesus and Judas, a Story of Betrayal

Getting to Know Judas Iscariot

- A Mock Trial for Judas

Scripture Passages Related to Judas Iscariot

- Matthew 10:1-4, Mark 3:13-19, Luke 6:12-16 (Jesus chooses the twelve Apostles)*
- Matthew 26:14-16, Mark 14:10-11, Luke 22:3-6 (Judas arranges to betray Jesus)*
- John 6:68-71 (The words of eternal life)
- John 12:1-8 (Jesus is anointed at Bethany)
- John 13:1-11 (Jesus washes his disciples' feet)
- John 13:21-30 (Jesus predicts his betrayal)*
- Matthew 26:47-49 (Judas betrays Jesus)*
- Matthew 27:3-5 (The death of Judas)*

Asterisk (*) signifies key passages to cover.

Break/ Article from *Breakthrough!* Related to Judas _Through!_ Iscariot

- The Twelve (Matthew 10:1-4)

Judas Iscariot and Young Adolescents Today

- Jesus chooses Judas as an Apostle to do great things in his name. Judas chooses to betray Jesus. Jesus offers young adolescents the opportunity to be his followers, and they too have a choice about how to respond.
- Judas is disloyal to Jesus. Students are not always loyal to their friends.
- For Judas money is more important than God. Money tempts young adolescents and has the potential of replacing their love for God.
- Jesus gives Judas a position of trust by making him treasurer. Students have and will be given opportunities in life to display their trustworthiness.
- Judas allows Satan to influence his behavior. Satan tries to influence the behavior of young people as well.
- At the Last Supper, Jesus offers Judas an opportunity to change his plan of betrayal. Jesus offers young people numerous chances to begin again through forgiveness and grace.
- Remorse fills Judas after he betrays Jesus. Students need to know that there is no need to live in shame because of sin, because Jesus offers us mercy no matter how large the transgression.

Highlighting God's Presence

After Jesus had said this, he was deeply troubled and declared openly, "I am telling you the truth: one of you is going to betray me."

The disciples looked at one another, completely puzzled about whom he meant. One of the disciples, the one whom Jesus loved, was sitting next to Jesus. Simon Peter motioned to him and said, "Ask him whom he is talking about."

So that disciple move closer to Jesus' side and asked, "Who is it, Lord?"

Jesus answered, "I will dip some bread in the sauce and give it to him; he is the man." So he took a piece of bread, dipped it, and gave it to Judas, the son of Simon Iscariot. As soon as Judas took the bread, Satan entered in to him. Jesus said to him, "Hurry and do what you must!" (John 13:21-27).

Getting to Know the Story of Judas Iscariot

Jesus and Judas, a Story of Betrayal

In this activity, students read the Scripture account of Judas's betrayal of Jesus and then recall in sequence the events leading up to Jesus' arrest.

Preparation

❑ Make enough copies of handout Judas Iscariot-A, "The Story of Betrayal," for each student in the class.

❑ Each person needs to have a Bible.

1. Pass out handout Judas Iscariot-A, "The Story of Betrayal," to the young people. Allow the young people time to read the Scripture passages listed on the handout and to fill in the activity sheet on their own. Note to the students that there may be some slight differences between the account in Matthew and the one in John such as when Judas began to think of betraying Jesus.

2. Summarize the story of the betrayal by asking students to categorize the events into four headings: Jesus predicts his betrayal; Judas agrees to betray Jesus; the arrest of Jesus; and the death of Judas.

3. Conclude the activity by asking the following questions:

Judas Iscariot

285

- Could Jesus' betrayal have been prevented? If so, how?

- At what point in the sequence of events could the story have taken a different course? (At the Last Supper, when Jesus offered Judas the bread of life)

- What faith message can we take away from this story? (Among others, Jesus is merciful.)

- What can the story of Judas teach you about your everyday living?

Getting to Know Judas Iscariot

A Mock Trial for Judas

In this activity, students will either accuse or defend Judas as he is judged before the gates of heaven or hell.

Preparation

❑ Each student will need a Bible.

1. Have students decide whether they want to defend Judas as he is judged before the gates of heaven or become the devil's advocate in condemning him to hell.

2. Depending on the position they take, have the students write a deposition containing reasons why Judas should go to either heaven or hell. Students can use the readings that are found in "Scripture Passages Related to Judas Iscariot" to help them.

3. When the students have finished writing their defense, choose several volunteers from the class to share their writings, first from the devil's advocate and then from the defense attorney from heaven in a mock trial presentation. (If you would like to, you can assign a young person to be a judge and others to be part of the jury. Ask the whole class to vote on Judas's guilt or innocence after the arguments have been presented.)

4. Comment on their arguments and correct any misconceptions such as "anyone who commits suicide goes to hell." Conclude with a discussion of Christ's dying on the cross as an act of redemption for us all.

THE STORY OF BETRAYAL

Read the following Scripture accounts about Judas Iscariot: John 13:21–30, Matthew 26:14–16, 26:47–56, 27:3–10. Then number the sentences below in the order they take place in the Gospels.

_____ Judas threw down the coins he had been given and hung himself.

_____ The Jewish leaders gave Judas thirty silver coins.

_____ Jesus told his Apostles that one of them is going to betray him.

_____ Jesus and his disciples ate supper together. The Devil was in the heart of Judas and he was thinking of betraying Jesus.

_____ When Judas found out that Jesus had been condemned to death, he repented and took the thirty silver coins back to the chief priests and elders.

_____ Jesus said that the person to whom he gives a piece of bread is the one who will betray him.

_____ Judas told the crowd that he would kiss the person they should arrest in order to identify him.

_____ Judas recognized that he had sinned by betraying Jesus to death.

_____ Judas went to the chief priests and asked them what they would give him if he betrayed Jesus to them.

_____ Judas approached Jesus, gave him a greeting of peace, and kissed him.

PAUL

Preparing to Teach

Overview

Paul (known by his Jewish name Saul) was born in about AD 10 in Tarsus, now southern Turkey. Paul's Jewish family raises him in strict observance of the Law. Paul shows a familiarity with the Greek thinking of his day because he is an educated Roman citizen. Paul is small and of unimpressive stature, but he is passionate with strong convictions.

Young people who have been raised in households with mixed cultural or religious backgrounds can find a friend in Paul. Paul is able to use the diversity of his background to understand the people of his day and communicate with them. These young adolescents need to see that they also have special insights into more than one culture or religion, and like Paul, can become a bridge.

Paul becomes a fierce opponent of the fledging Christian movement, even to the point of playing a part in the martyrdom of Stephen. But, on the way to Damascus, he encounters the risen Jesus in a vision. Christ reveals to Paul that he is to be the Apostle to the nonbelievers. From then on he dedicates his life to serving Christ in proclaiming the Gospel of Jesus. Most young people do not expect to have the type of conversion experience that Paul has, but hopefully they continue to see that all "spiritual greats" become these people over time. Saint Paul and other converts do not always see the greatness in Christianity right away. In Paul's case, he needs to be knocked off his horse in order to take a closer look.

In becoming the "Apostle to the Gentiles," he, in a sense, provides the earliest "Gospel of Jesus" that is presented in the Church. His principal message is that all people, Jews and Gentiles, through faith in the Gospel can enter into new life with Christ. Many young adolescents want to be perceived as open-minded by their peers. They may want to look and see how "open-minded" Paul is on the subject of the Gentiles and their access to Christianity without becoming Jews. While Paul is not flexible on all subjects, he has an insightful heart about non-Jews during a crucial time in the early Church.

Paul is a tireless missionary who leads others in establishing vibrant faith communities throughout Greece and modern-day Turkey as well as suffering physically and emotionally for the Gospel even to the point of martyrdom. His theological letters to different faith communities are an essential component of our New Testament.

Saint Paul is likely a familiar name to many young people, but also a complete mystery. Through the stories about Paul in Acts and then from glimpses at his letters, they should come to see that Paul is a dynamic, take charge, and successful early Christian.

THIS CHAPTER AT A GLANCE

Getting to Know the Story of Paul

- Running the Race

Getting to Know Paul

- Conversion Experiences
- Letter Writing in the World of Paul
- Paul's Missionary Way

Scripture Passages Related to Paul

- Acts of the Apostles 9:3–19 (Paul's conversion)*
- Acts of the Apostles 14:8–20 (In Lystra, people mistake Paul and Barnabas as gods)
- Acts of the Apostles 16:16–40 (Paul and Silas are freed miraculously from prison)*
- Acts of the Apostles 20:17–38 (Paul gives a farewell speech in Ephesus)
- Acts of the Apostles 26:19–29 (Paul tells King Agrippa of his work)
- Romans 8:31–39 (God's love for us in Christ Jesus)*
- 1 Corinthians 12:12–30 (Christ is one body, many parts)*
- 1 Corinthians 13:1–13 (Paul writes about love)*
- 1 Corinthians 15:12–28 (Paul defends belief in human resurrection)
- 2 Corinthians 4:7–12 (Believers are like clay pots)
- Galatians 2:20 (Paul's life in Christ)*
- Philippians 2:5–11 (Christ is humble and great)*

Asterisk (*) signifies key passages to cover.

Articles from *Breakthrough!* Related to Paul

- *Breakthrough!* Interview with Paul
- Paul's Journeys (Acts, chapters 13–21)
- Jews and Christ (Acts 13:13–43)
- Risking Their Necks (Acts 14:1–20)
- Passing On the Faith (Acts, chapters 17–18)

Paul

- Welcome to the Stranger (Acts 18:1-3)
- Demons and Idols and Riots! (Acts 19:1-10)
- Blessing Paul (Acts 21:3-6)
- Turning to God (Acts 22:1-21)
- Longest Wait in a Holding Cell (Acts 24:22-27)
- Paul Put to the Test (Acts, chapters 25-26)
- Paul's Last Years (Acts 28:17-31)

There are many valuable articles within the Pauline letters. The ones below give some insight into the person of Paul.
- Introduction to the Letters of Paul
- Jew to Jew (Romans, chapter 4)
- Don't Get Too Comfortable (Romans 9:30—10:4)
- Side by Side (Romans 16:1-16)
- The Scoop on Corinth (1 Corinthians 1:4-9)
- Shape Up! (Galatians 4:8-21)
- Heart to Heart (Philippians 1:3-11)
- Stop Whining! (Philippians 2:12-18)
- Paul's a Working Man (1 Thessalonians 2:9-12)
- Long, Full Life (2 Timothy 4:6-8)
- Slaves Today (Philemon)

Paul and Young Adolescents Today

- Young adolescents likely recognize Paul's name but do not know much about him. Nevertheless, Paul's basic truths about living a life of faith are relevant to people in this age-group.
- Paul has his own style of communicating to faith communities through letters that are personal yet theological in style. Young people need to find ways to share the message of Jesus Christ in ways that suit their personalities. They can take Paul's spiritual themes and find relevant ways to share them today.
- Like a good marketing professional, Paul knows his audience and shapes his message to appeal to the minds and hearts of the communities to whom he is writing. Adolescents can see evangelization in ways that are not simply accidental but respond to the needs and questions of our times.
- Paul's experience of conversion is riveting and dramatic. Young people experience the process of conversion but may not recognize it because they associate conversion with experiences like Paul's.
- Paul's experience of faith in Christ is clearly tied to Christ's suffering, death, and Resurrection. Adolescents may struggle to grasp how suffering in faith can have value. Though this reality may remain a mystery of faith, they can look to God in difficulties and to see how they can be transformed by sharing their suffering with Jesus Christ.

Highlighting God's Presence

As Saul was coming near the city of Damascus, suddenly a light from the sky flashed around him. He fell to the ground and heard a voice saying to him, "Saul, Saul! Why do you persecute me?" (Acts 9:3-4).

About midnight Paul and Silas were praying and singing hymns to God, and the other prisoners were listening to them. Suddenly there was a violent earthquake, which shook the prison to its foundations. At once all the doors opened, and the chains fell off all the prisoners (Acts 16:25-26).

There is nothing in all creation that will ever be able to separate us from the love of God which is ours through Christ Jesus our Lord (Romans 8:39).

For we are partners working together for God, and you are God's field (1 Corinthians 3:9).

To show that you are his children, God sent the Spirit of his Son into our hearts, the Spirit who cries out, "Father, my Father" (Galatians 4:6).

And God's peace, which is far beyond human understanding, will keep your hearts and minds safe in union with Christ Jesus (Philippians 4:7).

Getting to Know the Story of Paul

Running the Race

Preparation

❑ Each student needs a Bible, paper, and a pen or pencil.

❑ Each team of participants needs to have three large sheets of butcher paper taped to a wall, markers, the readings listed in step 2, and masking tape. (One piece of butcher paper should read "Where?" the next, "Who?" and the third, "What happened?" Each group needs to have one of each type.) The room needs to be large enough to accommodate some running up to the butcher paper to write.

❑ Knowing the size of your group and the amount of time available, assign a number of events to small groups of three. Make sure that every group has to find the same number of events. (There is a suggested number of events corresponding to each set of readings.) It is okay if you assign the same events to more than one group. Assess how much time the students will need to read the passages and determine the basics of the story.

1. Introduce the activity to the students:

○ Paul describes his life like a race; he has been trained for this race and he wants to finish it strong in order to win the "crown of eternal life" (2 Timothy 4:8). To review Paul's life we too will have a race today. Only you will be racing from your seats up to the butcher paper in a relay race to fill in parts of Paul's life. The marker is the baton you will be passing.

2. Divide the group into even teams. Explain that each team will be responsible for reviewing the same number of readings about Paul's life. The readings are broken down into six units that each consist of two or three events.

- Acts of the Apostles 7:54-60, 22:1-5, 26:4-11 (Events in Paul's life prior to his conversion). Students should find two events.
- Acts of the Apostles 9:1-31, 11:19-30 (Paul's conversion and preaching). Students should find three events.
- Acts of the Apostles 13:1—14:28 (Paul's first missionary journey). Students should find three events.
- Acts of the Apostles 15:36—18:22 (Paul's second missionary journey). Students should find three events.
- Acts of the Apostles 18:23—21:16 (Paul's third missionary journey). Students should find three events.
- Acts of the Apostles 21:17—28:30 (Arrest in Jerusalem through imprisonment in Cesarea until imprisonment in Rome). Students should find two events.

3. Give the students an appropriate amount of time to read and discuss the passages they have been assigned. Participants should take notes that answer the three questions on the butcher paper: "Where?" "Who?" "What happens?"

4. Explain the safe parameters for this race. At a signal from you, have each group send one member to record their information on the "Where?" paper for their first event. When done, they run back to their team, pass the marker (baton) to the next group member, who fills in the "Who?" for the same event. The second and third group members exchange the baton to fill in the "What Happened?" column. The young people continue this process until their group has filled in all of their events under each heading. (You may want to have a prize for the quickest group.)

After all the young people have recorded their summaries, ask the groups to present them in the order they occur in Paul's life.

5. You may want to have maps of Paul's journeys available to review places and dates with the students so that the students can get a visual sense of Paul's travels. See *Breakthrough!* for a helpful map.

Getting to Know Paul

Conversion Experiences

Preparation

❑ Each student needs to have a Bible, paper, and a pen or pencil.

❑ Consider inviting an RCIA candidate or catechumen in the parish to come and talk with the class about coming into the Church. In advance, ask them to prepare a comparison between their own conversion experience and Paul's experience.

❑ Obtain a copy of the movie *Mother Teresa: Woman of Compassion* (AIM International Television, 50 minutes, NR) and a videocassette player. (See appendix 1, "Additional Resources," for more information about finding this film.)

1. To introduce the activity, ask these questions:

   ○ What do you think of when you hear someone talk about their "spiritual conversion"?

   ○ Does it bring to mind a sudden event or a more gradual experience? (Some people have dramatic encounters with God in the midst of some crisis that turn their lives around; for others it is a gradual changing of focus from themselves and their wants to a focus on God and what God wants.)

   2. Have a student read Acts 9:3–25 aloud. (You may want to have three students portray Paul, the Lord, and Ananias.) Then have another student read Acts 22:6–16. Ask students to discuss these questions:
   - How are the two accounts similar?
   - How are they different?
   - Is there a moral to this conversion story? If so, what is it? (God is at work in all our lives; and that through the conversion of one, others will also be challenged to grow in faith.)
   - What do you think was the scariest part of the conversion experience for Paul?
   - What was the most peaceful part of it for him?

3. Talk about conversion with the students:

○ *Conversion* is a word that has many different meanings. One of the most popular definitions is a move from one type of belief to another, as in one religion to another. This is one type of conversion, the type that Paul had on the road to Damascus. People can convert passes into touchdowns, currency from one country to another one, and chemical solutions.

○ Many people are born into one religion and remain within it throughout their lives. They too experience conversion. The *Catechism of the Catholic Church* defines the term as "a radical reorientation of the whole life away from sin and evil, and toward God" (p. 873). The *Catechism* also characterizes conversion as "a change of heart."

○ Conversion begins at Baptism and continues throughout life with God's grace. Sometimes people experience conversion as a gradual growth toward God. Other times, people have "aha" types of conversions more like Paul's.

○ Confusion can occur for young Catholics when the Catholic understanding of conversion meets with the understanding of conversion held by some Protestant groups. Instead of seeing infant Baptism as the beginning of life-long conversion, these groups believe that an older child or adult accepts Jesus Christ and that this acceptance leads to salvation. This model resembles Paul's powerful experience on the way to Damascus.

4. Ask the students these types of questions:
- Have you ever felt conversion, a change of heart that brings you closer to God? Was it more like a light suddenly turning on or more like the sun coming up?
- What signs would you see that could tell you that another person has had a conversion experience?
- Does every Christian need to have a conversion experience?

5. Show parts of the movie *Mother Teresa*. A moving part occurs where she describes her transition out of the Catholic girls' school when she taught to her eventual work in Calcutta, India. An event happened on a train ride that was key in her changing directions.

6. Close the lesson with a prayer to the Holy Spirit for conversion. Use Ephesians 3:15–19 and close with the Glory Be.

Letter Writing in the World of Paul

Preparation

❑ For each student have some pieces of thin parchment-type paper, bird feathers for quills, bottles of ink, masking tape, and ¾-inch diameter dowels a foot long. (In terms of obtaining historical writing supplies, local stationery stores often have ink and paper that will work. Local historical societies or museums can direct you to suppliers or Internet merchants who specialize in these items too.)

❑ Make copies of handout Paul–A, "Letters in Paul's Day," for each student.

1. Introduce the activity with these questions:

   ○ Letters have been an important part of human culture since the advent of writing. Why do people write letters?

   ○ Is an e-mail message the same as a letter?

   ○ Why does Paul write letters? (To teach, encourage, challenge, express thanks, ask a favor, share his feelings, correct a situation, explain, and so on)

2. Pass out handout Paul–A, "Letters in Paul's Day," to the students and go over it with them to answer the question, How did Paul write?

3. Instruct the students to take the tools for biblical "scribing" and begin either copying Paul's letter to Philemon, writing a letter to a friend or a family member, or composing a letter to a local representative about an issue of concern. Remind them to include all five parts in the letter. With a dowel, help the students make a scroll of it.

4. Discuss Paul's letter writing to close the activity. Use these points and questions:
   - Letter writing is important today, but it was much more so in Paul's time.
   - Does your family keep old letters? Why or why not?
   - Paul's letters contain inspiration from God that is so essential to our identity in Christ that the Church never wanted any believer to be without them.

Variations

   - To help students understand the feat that writing and illustrating the Bible is, show them some pictures from the Saint John's Bible, a modern-day illuminated and hand-written Bible. See the Saint Mary's Press Web site, *www.smp.org,* for links to this Bible or type "The Saint John's Bible" into an Internet search engine.

- Have students look at the Vatican Web site to see the various types of ways that the Church preserves and keeps its history alive. See the Saint Mary's Press Web site, *www.smp.org,* for links to this site or do a search for "Vatican" on the Internet.

Paul's Missionary Way

Preparation

❑ Each student needs to have a Bible, paper, and a pen or pencil.

❑ Make a copy of handout Paul-B, "What Would Paul Be Like Today?" for each young person.

1. Introduce this activity by reading 1 Corinthians 9:19–22 and then sharing this information with the students:

○ Because of Paul's diverse background, he is able to relate to many different kinds of people. Paul is determined to bring the Good News of Jesus to people in whatever way works best. He is convinced he could find a way to make the message of Jesus understandable to any person he met.

 2. Have the young people reflect on the adjustments Paul would need to make if he were to be an apostle today. Pass out handout Paul-B, "What Would Paul Be Like Today?" Go over the directions and have students fill in the handout individually.

3. Spend a fair amount of time going over the young people's answers and commenting on them in light of Paul's mission and message. Relate their comments about today back to his work in the first decades of the Church.

Paul

LETTERS IN PAUL'S DAY

Letters in Paul's day were quite different from what they are today.

A Different Format

Letters in Paul's day were formal and structured rather than "newsy" and free-flowing like our letters today. Paul's letters followed a consistent pattern.

1. A salutation in three parts—naming the sender (Paul), naming the persons addressed, and then offering a formal greeting

2. A thanksgiving to God for the blessings bestowed upon the receivers of the letter and upon Paul

3. The body of the letter, in which Paul took up various matters related to the Good News, the behavior of the people receiving the letter, and problems in the local church

4. Final instructions, at times regarding things unrelated to the body of the letter, such as preparations for an upcoming visit by Paul

5. A closing in two parts—final greetings to various people and a concluding word, often in the form of a prayer

Different Materials and Processes

In Paul's day, letters were ordinarily written on parchment (leather prepared for that purpose) or on papyrus (thin slices of the papyrus plant glued horizontally onto a backing formed by thin slices placed vertically). A pen was a split reed or a quill, and ink was a composite of materials like carbon and glue or gum. Creating a letter with these materials was such a tedious and lengthy process, and one requiring such skill, that it was normally done by professional scribes or writers.

In the case of his epistles, Paul would first think through what he wanted to convey to his intended audience. Just formulating his complex ideas may have taken weeks of work, especially in the case of a long letter like the one to the Romans. Then his ideas had to be dictated word by word to a scribe or, as was quite common, be expressed in more general terms, with the scribe acting as a kind of editor as well as a secretary.

A scribe could work no more than two or three hours at a stretch, normally crouched on the ground with a tablet in one hand and a quill in the other. It took the average scribe about one minute to write just three syllables, which comes to about seventy-two words per hour. (A skilled typist today can type about seventy-two words per minute.) The average sheet of papyrus could hold about 140 words. The First Letter of Paul to the Thessalonians, consisting of about 1,500 words, would have required about ten sheets of papyrus and more than twenty hours of work by a scribe. Paul's Epistle to the Romans, with over 7,000 words, would have required fifty sheets of papyrus and nearly one hundred hours of writing time!

Weeks, Not Hours

Any one epistle would have taken weeks, not hours, to complete. That may partly explain why some of the letters seem choppy, as if written in bits and pieces. The writing process was no doubt interrupted at times, when Paul would gain fresh ideas and insights. And to be sure, no scribe would have been inclined to go back to edit and polish a letter after it was completed! (Thomas Zanzig, *Jesus of History, Christ of Faith,* third edition [Winona, MN: Saint Mary's Press, 1999], pages 258–259. Copyright © 1999 by Saint Mary's Press. All rights reserved.)

WHAT WOULD PAUL BE LIKE TODAY?

Thinking about Paul's approach to bringing the Good News to different people in different ways (1 Corinthians 9:19–22), imagine Paul doing his ministry in today's world. Answer the following questions:

What CDs would Paul be listening to?

Given that Paul was a tentmaker in his own time, what job might he have today? Would his job today provide him with the same opportunities to share the message of Jesus Christ?

From the Acts of the Apostles and his letters, we know that Paul goes to the synagogue first when sharing the Good News. Today, where do you think he would go first?

What medium (for example, he uses letters in his own time) would Paul use to connect with people today?

If Paul had a Web site, what would his URL be? What would his e-mail address be?

To what kinds of people today would he want to bring the Gospel first? Why?

What questions would people bring to Paul today? How would he answer them?

What would be his favorite way to travel today?

Who might be his closest friends? Would they be part of his traveling mission?

How successful was Paul in being "all things to all people"? How successful would he be today?

BARNABAS

Preparing to Teach

Overview

Barnabas is one of the first people to bring the Good News to the Gentiles. A quiet companion to Paul, Barnabas often shows his faith in Jesus Christ through his compassion and his advocacy for the new converts among the Gentiles.

Barnabas is someone young people will recognize—a caring and generous friend, a good and faithful companion, and an advocate for what he believes in. Barnabas also sets a challenging example for young people. He is willing to do as Jesus commands—give everything he has and follow him.

THIS CHAPTER AT A GLANCE

Getting to Know the Story of Barnabas

- Pictures from the Road

Getting to Know Barnabas

- Generous to the Core
- Getting to Know You

Scripture Passages Related to Barnabas

- Act 4:36–37 (Barnabas sells his property and gives the money to the Apostles)*
- Acts 9:26-27 (Barnabas brings Saul to the Apostles)
- Acts 11:19-30 (Barnabas in Antioch)
- Acts 12:25 (Barnabas and Saul leave Jerusalem)
- Acts 13:1-52 (Barnabas and Saul's mission to Jews and Gentiles)*
- Acts 14:7-20 (People mistake Barnabas and Paul for gods and persecute them)
- Acts 15:1-21 (Paul and Barnabas attend the council of Jerusalem)*
- Acts 15:36-41 (Barnabas parts ways with Paul)

Asterisk (*) signifies key passages to cover.

Articles from *Breakthrough!* Related to Barnabas

- *Breakthrough!* Interview with Barnabas
- Risking Their Necks (Acts 14:1–20)

Barnabas and Young Adolescents Today

- Barnabas sells his property and gives the proceeds to the Apostles to help the poor in the community. Young people are often deeply and unexpectedly generous to those who are in need.
- Barnabas eagerly takes on Saul's cause by sharing his experience with the Apostles and bringing Saul to the Apostles to listen. Young people can be like both Barnabas and the Apostles. They are sometimes willing to stand up for others who are ignored and sometimes unwilling to welcome those who want to spend time with them.
- In Acts, Barnabas travels and preaches with a companion, for the most part, Paul. Young people go through their day often surrounded by a group of friends.
- At Lystra, Barnabas and Saul are disturbed that the people there mistake them for and call them "gods." Young people can become easily frustrated with adults who make assumptions about who they are.

Highlighting God's Presence

While they were serving the Lord and fasting, the Holy Spirit said to them, "Set apart for me Barnabas and Saul, to do the work to which I have called them" (Acts 13:2).

The believers were filled with joy and the Holy Spirit (Acts 13:52).

The whole group was silent as they heard Barnabas and Paul report all the miracles and wonders that God had performed through them among the Gentiles (Acts 15:12).

Getting to Know the Story of Barnabas

Pictures from the Road

Preparation

❑ Provide a total of six to twelve bibles, or two bibles per small group.

❑ Cut out six "city papers" or square sheets of butcher paper and label each sheet with the following city names and citation from Acts.
  • Cyprus (Acts, chapter 13)
  • Antioch (Acts, chapters 13-15)
  • Iconium (Acts, chapter 14)
  • Lystra (Acts, chapter 14)
  • Derbe, Pamphylia (Acts, chapter 14)
  • Jerusalem (Acts, chapter 15)

❑ Provide enough markers, colored pencils, or crayons so that there are four to five for each small group.

Break **Through!**

❑ Using butcher paper, draw a map of the region at the center of the paper, noting where the six cities were located. (You can use the map of Paul's journeys in the back of *Breakthrough!*) Leave room so that the young people can either tape, glue, or pin the city papers on the map at the end of the activity.

1. Divide the class into six small groups and distribute one city paper and the materials to each group. Give the young people the following instructions:

○ You are photographers who are following Barnabas during his ministry. You have been asked to take pictures of Barnabas while he is in your city.

○ Read aloud the chapters from Acts that cover your city assignment. Discuss what pictures you want to take that will tell the story of Barnabas's trip to your city.

○ As a group, decide which pictures you want to "take" (at least four) and who will take them. Draw the photographs that you would take on your city paper.

Barnabas

2. When the young people are finished, invite them to present the story of Barnabas's trip to the city using the "photographs." Begin with Cyprus and work through the cities in order. After each presentation, highlight the key points about Barnabas that the group related. Tape, glue, or pin each group's pictures near the name of the city on the map.

Getting to Know Barnabas

Generous to the Core

Preparation

❑ Have a Bible opened to Acts 4:36–37.

1. Have the young people stand, and ask them, "What would you be willing to do to stay up later on a school night?" After thinking about it individually, have them find two other people and give them a minute or two to share their answers with one another. When time is up, ask some of the young people to share their responses and explain why they made that choice.

2. Continue the activity in the same way as above, using the following questions and dividing the young people into differently sized groups—pairs, groups of four, and so on:
- What would you be willing to do to . . . ?
    + help your best friend out of a bad situation?
    + make your mother happy?
    + provide a home for a homeless person?
    + show people that you love God?

3. Read the passage you have identified from Acts. Highlight what Barnabas is willing to do to help the poor. Ask the young people why they think Barnabas makes that choice. Ask, "Would you be able to make that choice if you were in his shoes?"

Getting to Know You

In this activity, young people enter into the experience that Paul and Barnabas have of being misunderstood. They then strategize about ways they might correct a misperception held by another.

Barnabas

Preparation

❑ Have enough markers, colored pencils, or crayons so that each young person can draw and color pictures.

❑ Each student needs to have a Bible.

❑ Give each person a blank sheet of white paper and an envelope.

1. Ask the young people to find a private place in the room. Distribute one sheet of paper to each young person. Place a handful of markers, colored pencils, or crayons near every three to four people. Remind the young people that they will share the markers, colored pencils, or crayons but without talking.

2. Read Acts 14:8-20 to the young people. Highlight Barnabas and Saul's experience of not being recognized for who they are. Have a brief discussion about who in their lives misunderstands them and why. Then have them quietly pick one person in their individual lives who does not see them for who they are or misunderstands them.

3. Using the paper, have the young people draw a picture of this individual's face on the paper. Ask them to think of one thing that person does not understand about them. Have students decorate the picture of their face with pictures, symbols, and colors that would help that person better understand that one thing about the student. Ask them not to use words.

4. When the young people finish, have them fold the pictures into thirds and have them put the paper in the envelope, seal it, and put the name of the person on the outside. Ask them to think about what they could do or say that might help that person better understand them. Invite them to do or say whatever it is to the person sometime in the next week. If they feel comfortable and want to, encourage them to give the person the picture and explain what it means.

TIMOTHY

Preparing to Teach

Overview

Timothy was born in Lystra in about the year AD 30. His father was a Greek nonbeliever while his grandmother, Lois, and mother, Eunice, were devout Jewish Christians. As a teenager, Timothy commits himself to his faith life. Paul's talk of the new life in Christ attracts him. Young people may be interested to know that while Timothy was younger than other Christian missionaries of the time, he was ready at an early age to take on the responsibility. It is important to note that many saints were very young either at the time of their death or when others began to recognize their saintliness.

With the support of Timothy's mother and the blessing of other Christians, Timothy accepts Paul's invitation to travel with him to Greece. From then on, Timothy becomes one of Paul's most faithful companions and trusted workers. Timothy represents Paul regularly to different Christian communities. When Timothy is in his thirties, Paul appoints him bishop of the Christian community in Ephesus. Paul writes several letters to Timothy in Ephesus in order to offer advice on the pastoral care of the believers and to provide support and encouragement.

Timothy is apparently meek in his demeanor but spiritually gifted enough to take on the leadership responsibility of the missionary church. He is sensitive and loyal and Paul expresses a deep fatherly pride for this young man's role in the early Church.

THIS CHAPTER AT A GLANCE

Getting to Know the Story of Timothy

- Where in the World Is Timothy Now?

Getting to Know Timothy

- Dear Paul: Letters from Timothy

Scripture Passages Related to Timothy

- Acts 16:1-4 (Paul recruits Timothy for his ministry)*
- Acts 19:22 (Paul sends Timothy on to Macedonia while he stays in Ephesus)*
- 1 Corinthians 4:17, 16:11 (Paul sends Timothy to Corinth)
- Philippians 1:1, 1 Thessalonians 1:1, 2 Thessalonians 1:1, and Colossians 1:1 (Timothy is listed as a coauthor for these letters)
- Philippians 2:19-24 (Paul's relationship with Timothy)*
- 1 Thessalonians 3:1-10 (Timothy reports back on the faith of the Thessalonians)
- 1 Timothy 1:3-7 (Paul tells Timothy to stay in Ephesus)
- 1 Timothy 4:6-16 (Paul instructs Timothy about being God's servant)*
- 1 Timothy 5:23 (Paul advises him about his health)
- 2 Timothy 1:3-14 (Paul encourages Timothy)*
- 2 Timothy 2:1-13 (Paul encourages Timothy to be strong despite suffering)*
- 2 Timothy 3:14-17 (Paul reminds Timothy of his training from his youth)

Asterisk (*) signifies key passages to cover.

Articles from *Breakthrough!* Related to Timothy

- *Breakthrough!* Interview with Timothy
- "It's PPRT-y Easy to Pray" (1 Timothy 2:1)
- Never Too Young (1 Timothy 4:11-16)
- Strive (1 Timothy 6:11-14)
- God's Revealed Truth (2 Timothy 3:14-17)

Timothy and Young Adolescents Today

- Though Timothy's mixed faith household could be seen as a detriment to his growth in Christian faith, it prepares him for work as a missionary. Students also have aspects of their family life that both encourage and discourage their growth in faith.
- Timothy's family supports him in his new venture with Paul. Young adolescents receive their parents' and teachers' support to different degrees as they step out in faith and service ventures.

Highlighting God's Presence

Run your best in the race of faith, and win eternal life for yourself; for it was to this life that God called you when you firmly professed your faith before many witnesses (1 Timothy 6:12).

For this reason I remind you to keep alive the gift that God gave you when I laid my hands on you. For the Spirit that God has given us does not make us timid; instead, his Spirit fills us with power, love, and self-control (2 Timothy 1:6–7).

Getting to Know the Story of Timothy

Where in the World Is Timothy Now?

Students become familiar with the story of Timothy and some of the main passages from Paul's letter to him. They then map where the stories occur.

Preparation

❑ Each student needs to have a Bible, a pen, and a list of the readings from and about Timothy (see "Scripture Passages Related to Timothy").

❑ Each group of students needs to have photocopied 11-by-17-inch paper maps of the Mediterranean area with the regions and cities that Paul visited on his three missionary journeys noted. (Each map on handout Timothy–A, "The Travels of Paul," could be enlarged 235% to fit 11-by-17-inch paper.)

❑ Provide each group of students with a dozen index cards.

❑ Do this exercise yourself ahead of time.

1. Divide the class into groups. Give each group a dozen index cards and the photocopied maps. Have the group read the sections about Timothy and then write what is happening in each biblical section on a separate card.

2. Have each group place their cards on the maps at the correct city or area that corresponds to the passage about Timothy, using arrows as needed, depending on space. Go over the maps as a class and look up the answers in the Bible if there is disagreement about the correct places.

3. As you discuss Timothy's story, talk about the importance of the traveling and distances on his ministry. Ask: "Do you think Timothy would have been as effective if he had stayed in his own hometown? What kind of insights does traveling and moving from place to place give a person?"

Getting to Know Timothy

Dear Paul: Letters from Timothy

In this activity, students write letters back to Paul with thoughts that Timothy might have wanted to share with him.

Preparation

❑ Make sure each student has a copy of the Bible, paper, an envelope, and a pen or pencil.

1. To introduce this activity, draw students into a discussion about the Pauline letters and our styles of communication today.
- What is the difference between receiving a letter in the mail compared to e-mail? What are the similarities and differences?
- In Timothy's time, letters were critical means to communicate with others. Paul writes many types of letters, but his letters to Timothy are more personal than his other ones.

2. Have the students briefly review Paul's First and Second Letters to Timothy, using the scriptural citations from "Scripture Passages Related to Timothy."

3. After the students review Paul's letters to Timothy, have each student imagine that she or he is Timothy receiving these letters from Paul. Remind the young people that Paul is in prison and will not see Timothy again. Give these instructions to the students (You may want to refer to handout Paul-A, "Letters in Paul's Day," page 297, to explain the parts of a Pauline letter.):

  ○ Write a letter back to Paul in Rome describing how grateful you are for his kind advice and support. Include whatever else you think that the younger Timothy would express to Paul after reading the letters. After you write the letter, put it into a sealed envelope and then "mail it" to Paul by giving it to me.

4. You may want to bring the activity to a close by writing an open letter back to the class expressing your thanks for their letters in the Pauline style.

THE TRAVELS OF PAUL

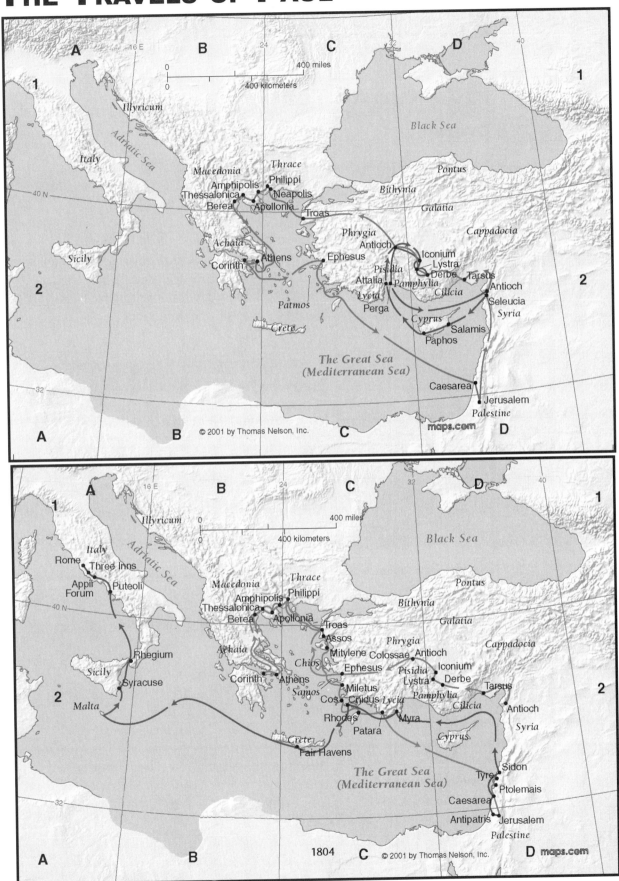

PRISCILLA AND AQUILA

Preparing to Teach

Overview

Priscilla and Aquila are faithful followers of Paul. Wherever they live—in Rome, Ephesus, or Corinth—they try to spread the Good News about Jesus Christ. This couple reminds us that hospitality is an important aspect of being a Christian.

It is good for young people to see a married couple active in ministry because often the early Christians are not married or their marriage is not discussed. Priscilla and Aquila are living examples of how Jesus welcomed and treated people during his ministry. They also show us what it means to be a good Christian friend.

THIS CHAPTER AT A GLANCE

Getting to Know the Story of Priscilla and Aquila

- Greetings To and From

Getting to Know Priscilla and Aquila

- The Welcome Mat
- Inside and Outside: A Reflection

Scripture Passages Related to Priscilla and Aquila

- Acts 18:2-3 (Paul meets Priscilla and Aquila in Corinth)*
- Acts 18:18-20 (Priscilla and Aquila travel to Ephesus with Paul)*
- Acts 18:24-26 (Priscilla and Aquila teach Apollos)*
- Romans 16:3-5 (Paul greets Priscilla and Aquila and their community)*
- 1 Corinthians 16:19 (Paul sends Priscilla and Aquila's greetings to the community in Corinth)*
- 2 Timothy 4:19 (Paul asks Timothy to greet Priscilla and Aquila)*

Asterisk (*) signifies key passages to cover.

Articles from *Breakthrough!* Related to Priscilla and Aquila

- *Breakthrough!* Interview with Priscilla and Aquila
- Welcome the Stranger (Acts 18:1–3)
- Side by Side (Romans 16:1–16)

Priscilla and Aquila and Young Adolescents Today

- Priscilla and Aquila are forced to leave their home in Rome because they are Jews. Many young people have been excluded because they are different from their peers.
- Exiled from Rome, Priscilla and Aquila are initially outsiders in their new home of Corinth. Young people sometimes feel like outsiders in school, with their teammates, or at home.
- Priscilla and Aquila share a common skill with Paul—they are tent makers. Young people seek out friends with whom they share common interests, experiences, and skills.
- Priscilla and Aquila are so influenced by Paul's preaching and teaching that they move from Corinth to Ephesus with him. Young people recognize and listen to peers and adults around them who are leaders. They sometimes follow them into certain activities or imitate them.
- Priscilla and Aquila open their home to be a church for the followers of Jesus. Young people generously welcome their friends, peers, and teammates to their homes for various fun and important activities.
- Priscilla and Aquila believe in Jesus so much that they are willing to take risks, even the risk of death, for him, for their faith, and for their community. Young people have strong loyalties to their friends and to what they believe in.

Highlighting God's Presence

He had been instructed in the Way of the Lord, and with great enthusiasm he proclaimed and taught correctly the facts about Jesus. However, he knew only the baptism of John. He began to speak boldly in the synagogue. When Priscilla and Aquila heard him, they took him home with them and explained to him more correctly the Way of God (Acts 18:25–26).

I send greetings to Priscilla and Aquila, my fellow servers in the service of Christ Jesus. . . . (Romans 16:3).

Getting to Know the Story of Priscilla and Aquila

Greetings To and From

In this activity, participants create greeting cards based on Bible passages about Priscilla and Aquila.

Preparation

❑ Each group needs to have a Bible.

❑ Fold six pieces of newsprint in half like a card.

❑ Using a black marker, write one of the following phrases on the front side of each "card." At the bottom of the front side, list the Scripture passages noted in parentheses in small but legible print.
  • Greetings from Rome (Acts, chapter 18)
  • Greetings from Corinth (Acts, chapter 18, 1 Corinthians, chapter 16, Romans, chapter 16, 2 Timothy, chapter 4)
  • Greetings from Ephesus (Acts, chapter 18)
  • Greetings to Apollos (Acts, chapter 18)
  • Greetings to Timothy (2 Timothy, chapter 4)
  • Greetings to Paul (Acts, chapter 18, 1 Corinthians, chapter 16, Romans, chapter 16, 2 Timothy, chapter 4)

❑ Provide markers, crayons, or colored pencils in many colors for use by the small groups.

1. Divide the young people into six small groups. Distribute the bibles, one per group, and one of the large cards to each small group. Provide the following instructions:

  ○ Your task is to create a greeting card based on the title that is written on the cover of your card. To do this, pretend to be Priscilla and Aquila. You will know what to write on the inside of the card when you read the Bible passages. Note that the places and people are all mentioned in the assigned Scriptures.

  ○ Read the passages on the front of the card out loud and then discuss what you learn about Priscilla and Aquila and about either the place from which they are writing or the person to whom they are writing. Your group should write three to five sentences on the inside of the card that describe what you discussed. The statements should sound like they were written on a card and directed to someone. Create a design for the card and color it appropriately.

2. When the students are done, invite each small group to present what they learned to the large group by sharing their card.

3. Ask the students, based on what they have learned, to reflect on what it must have been like to be a follower of Jesus at that time like Priscilla and Aquila.

Getting to Know Priscilla and Aquila
The Welcome Mat

Preparations

❑ Gather sheets of newsprint and a marker.

❑ Make a time line on one sheet of newsprint that starts with "When visitors arrive" and ends with "When visitors leave."

1. Review with the students that Priscilla and Aquila welcomed many people into their home to pray. Have the students brainstorm ways in which they do and could welcome strangers into their homes (as permitted by their parents or guardians). List their ideas on newsprint. Remind them that welcoming happens not only when they arrive, but throughout a person's visit. Encourage them to come up with ideas for the entire visit.

2. Divide the group into small groups of two or three people. Ask them to select one of the ideas on the newsprint. Once each group has its idea, ask them to put their ideas on the time line you have created on the second sheet of newsprint.

3. Instruct the groups to create a role-play in which they will be the welcomers and the rest of the groups are the visitors. For example, one way to welcome might be to have food. The group might create a role-play about serving food to the visitors. Have students notice where their role-play falls on the welcoming time line so that they will know when to do their activity.

4. When the groups are prepared, invite the group with the first idea on the time line to come forward and present its role-play. Ask each group to come forward in order and present its role-play.

5. Ask the group these types of questions:
- Why is welcoming strangers into your home important?
- Fill in the blank: "I feel welcomed when _____ "

Inside and Outside: A Reflection

Preparation

❑ Make copies of Priscilla and Aquila handout-A, "Inside and Outside," one for each person.

❑ Gather pens or pencils for each person.

 1. Distribute handout Priscilla and Aquila-A, "Inside and Outside," to each of the young people as well as pens or pencils. Ask the students to spread out around the room for privacy.

2. Read the first sentence on the handout with the group. Share the first and second bullet points under "Priscilla and Aquila and Young Adolescents Today" about being on the inside and outside of a group of people.

3. Invite the students to complete the first two statements on the handout. When they are done, ask them to write a prayer to Jesus asking him to help them when they feel like they are on the inside and the outside of a group. End in a group prayer by asking some of the students to share their prayer.

INSIDE AND OUTSIDE

Everyone knows what it feels like to be on the inside and the outside of
a group of people. Fill in the statements below and then write a prayer to
Jesus asking for his help when you are an outsider or an insider.

I feel like I am on the inside when . . .

I feel like I am on the outside when . . .

Dear Jesus,

Appendix 1

Additional Resources

This appendix is divided into several sections. The first section contains books that can provide you with more information about the Scriptures. The second section contains books related to the Scriptures that you can use directly with young adolescents. The third section lists books about the Bible that young adolescents can use on their own. The fourth section lists resources about ministry with young adolescents in general. The books are followed by sections that list music, films, and organizations.

Background Reading and Reference About the Scriptures for You

Achtemeier, Paul J., ed. *The HarperCollins Bible Dictionary.* San Francisco: HarperSanFrancisco, 1996.

Alter, Robert. *The Art of Biblical Narrative.* New York: Basic Books, 1981.

Bergant, Dianne, ed. *The Collegeville Bible Commentary Based on the New American Bible: Old Testament and New Testament.* Collegeville, MN: Liturgical Press, 1992.

Buechner, Frederick. *The Son of Laughter.* New York: HarperCollins, 1993.

Brown, Raymond E. *An Introduction to the New Testament (Anchor Bible Reference Library).* New York: Doubleday, 1997.

———. *Responses to 101 Questions on the Bible.* New York: Paulist Press, 1990.

Brown, Raymond E., Joseph A. Fitzmyer, and Roland E. Murphy, eds. *The New Jerome Biblical Commentary* (paperback reprint). Third edition. Englewood Cliffs, NJ: Prentice-Hall, 2000.

———. *The New Jerome Biblical Handbook.* Collegeville, MN: Liturgical Press, 1992.

Brown, Robert McAfee. *Unexpected News: Reading the Bible with Third World Eyes.* Philadelphia: Westminster Press, 1984.

Brueggemann, Walter. *The Bible Makes Sense.* Rev. ed. Louisville, KY: Westminster/John Knox Press, 2002.

Charpentier, Etienne. *How to Read the Old Testament.* New York: Crossroad, 1982.

Frank, Harry Thomas, ed. *Atlas of the Bible Lands.* Maplewood, NJ: Hammond, 1977.

Gardner, Joseph L., ed. *Reader's Digest Atlas of the Bible: An Illustrated Guide to the Holy Land.* Pleasantville, NY: Reader's Digest Association, 1981.

Gilles, Anthony E. *The People of the Book: The Story Behind the Old Testament.* Eugene, OR: Wipf and Stock Publishers, 2001.

———. *The People of the Way: The Story Behind the New Testament.* Cincinnati: St. Anthony Messenger Press, 1984.

Girard, Robert C., edited by Larry Richards. *Life of Christ*, volumes 1 and 2 from the "God's Word for the Biblically Inept™ series." Lancaster, PA: Starburst Publishers, 2000.

Hiesberger, Jean Marie, ed. *The Catholic Bible: Personal Study Edition.* New York: Oxford University Press, 1995. Includes five hundred pages of excellent, easy-to-understand background on each book of the Bible; New American Bible translation.

Holladay, William Lee. *Long Ago, God Spoke: How Christians May Hear the Old Testament Today.* Minneapolis: Fortress Press, 1995.

Hollyday, Joyce. *Clothed with the Sun: Biblical Women, Social Justice, and Us.* Louisville, KY: Westminster/John Knox Press, 1994.

Kohlenberger, John R., III, ed. *The Concise Concordance to the New Revised Standard Version.* New York: Oxford University Press, 1993.

Libreria Editrice Vaticana. *Catechism of the Catholic Church.* Trans. United States Catholic Conference (USCC). Washington, DC: USCC, 1997.

McKenna, Megan, and Tony Cowan. *Keepers of the Story: Oral Traditions in Religion.* Maryknoll, NY: Orbis Books, 1997.

McKenzie, John L. *Dictionary of the Bible.* Reprint edition. New York: Touchstone Books, 1995.

Newland, Mary Reed. *A Popular Guide Through the Old Testament.* Winona, MN: Saint Mary's Press, 1999.

———. *Written on Our Hearts: The Old Testament Story of God's Love.* Rev. ed. Barbara Allaire. Winona, MN: Saint Mary's Press, 1999.

Perkins, Pheme. *Reading the New Testament: An Introduction.* Rev. ed. New York: Paulist Press, 1988.

Ralph, Margaret Nutting. *"And God Said What?" An Introduction to Biblical Literary Forms for Bible Lovers.* New York: Paulist Press, 1986.

———. *The Bible and the End of the World: Should We Be Afraid?* New York: Paulist Press, 1997.

———. *Discovering the Gospels: Four Accounts of the Good News.* New York: Paulist Press, 1990.

———. *Discovering Old Testament Origins: The Books of Genesis, Exodus, and Samuel.* New York: Paulist Press, 1992.

Rohr, Richard, and Joseph Martos. *The Great Themes of Scripture: New Testament.* Cincinnati: St. Anthony Messenger Press, 1988.

———. *The Great Themes of Scripture: Old Testament.* Cincinnati: St. Anthony Messenger Press, 1987.

2003 Scripture from Scratch Sourcebook. Cincinnati: St. Anthony Messenger Press, 2003.

Senior, Donald, ed. *The Catholic Study Bible.* New York: Oxford University Press, 1990.

Vatican Council II. *Dogmatic Constitution on Divine Revelation (Dei Verbum).* Council document, November 18, 1965.

Whalen, W. Terry. *Alpha Teach Yourself the Bible in 24 Hours.* Indianapolis: Alpha Books, 2003.

Witherup, Ronald D. *The Bible Companion: A Handbook for Beginners.* New York: Crossroad, 1998.

Zanzig, Thomas. *Jesus of History, Christ of Faith.* Winona, MN: Saint Mary's Press, 1999.

Scripture Resources to Use with Young Adolescents

Benson, Susan C. *My Catholic Identity: Marks of the Church (and More).* Dayton, OH: Hi-Time*Pflaum, 2001. This book has some nice worksheets about Mary of Nazareth.

Calderone-Stewart, Lisa-Marie. *Faith Works for Junior High: Scripture- and Tradition-Based Sessions for Faith Formation.* Winona, MN: Saint Mary's Press, 1993.

Catucci, Thomas F. *Time with Jesus: Twenty Guided Meditations for Youth.* Notre Dame, IN: Ave Maria Press, 1993.

Claussen, Janet. *Biblical Women: Exploring Their Stories with Girls.* Winona, MN: Saint Mary's Press, 2002.

Crocetti, Enzo and Mario Giordano. Illus. by Sergio Toppi. *A Crowd of Witnesses: Interviews with Famous New Testament Men and Women.* Boston: St. Paul Books and Media, 1990.

Furey, Richard G. *Mary's Way of the Cross.* Mystic, CT: Twenty-Third Publications, 1984.

Haas, David. *Prayers Before an Awesome God: The Psalms for Teenagers.* Winona, MN: Saint Mary's Press, 1998.

Hakowski, Maryann. *Sharing the Sunday Scriptures with Youth.* Winona, MN: Saint Mary's Press. Published in three separate volumes with the subtitles *Cycle A* (1998), *Cycle B* (1996), and *Cycle C* (1997).

Introductions to the Books of the Bible. Boston: Daughters of Saint Paul, 1983.

Koch, Carl, ed. *You Give Me the Sun: Biblical Prayers by Teens.* Winona, MN: Saint Mary's Press, 2000.

Lucado, Max. *You Are Special.* Illus. Sergio Martinez. Wheaton, IL: Crossway Books, 1997.

Marmouget, C. Rosemary. *Scripture Alive: Role-Plays for Youth.* Winona, MN: Saint Mary's Press, 1997.

O'Connell-Roussell, Sheila. *Saint Mary's Press Essential Bible Dictionary.* Winona, MN: Saint Mary's Press, 2005.

O'Connell-Roussell, Sheila, and Terri Vorndran Nichols. Illus. by Vicki Shuck. *Lectionary-Based Gospel Dramas for Lent and the Easter Triduum.* Winona, MN: Saint mary's Press, 1999.

The ScriptureWalk series contains two books for young adolescents: *ScriptureWalk Junior High: Bible Themes* (Maryann Hakowski, 1999), and *ScriptureWalk Junior High: People of Promise* (Joseph Grant, 2002). Winona, MN: Saint Mary's Press.

Singer-Towns, Brian, ed. *Bringing Catholic Youth and the Bible Together: Strategies and Activities for Parishes and Schools.* Winona, MN: Saint Mary's Press, 2000.

Theisen, Michael. *Ready-to-Go Scripture Skits (That Teach Serious Stuff).* Winona, MN: Saint Mary's Press, 2004. This resource features skits about Abraham and Isaac, Samson, and those disciples present at Pentecost.

Scripture Resources for Young Adolescents Themselves

Brost, Corey. *Gospel Connections for Teens: Reflections for Sunday Mass, Cycle B.* Winona, MN: Saint Mary's Press, 2005.

Haas, David. *Prayers Before an Awesome God: The Psalms for Teenagers.* Winona, MN: Saint Mary's Press, 1998.

Heisberger, Jean Marie, and Maureen Gallagher. *Take Ten: Daily Bible Reflections for Teens.* Winona, MN: Saint Mary's Press, 2004.

O'Connell-Roussell, Sheila. *Saint Mary's Press Essential Bible Dictionary.* Winona, MN: Saint Mary's Press, 2005.

Background Reading, Resources, and Reference for Ministry with Young Adolescents

Braden-Whartenby, Geri, and Joan Finn Connelly. *One-Day Retreats for Junior High Youth.* Winona, MN: Saint Mary's Press, 2000.

Delgatto, Laurie, ed. *Catholic Youth Ministry: The Essential Documents.* Winona, MN: Saint Mary's Press, 2005.

East, Thomas, and others. *Effective Practices for Dynamic Youth Ministry.* Winona, MN: Saint Mary's Press, 2004.

The HELP series. This seven-book series is for adults working with young teens. Each book covers a different topic. The topics are community building, family ideas, hands-on ideas, holiday and seasonal ideas, justice and service ideas, prayer ideas, and retreat ideas.

The Journey of Faith series. This series serves the developmental needs of younger teens and helps them see the relevance of their faith.

Shrader, Mary, with Therese Brown and Tony Tamberino. *Journey of Faith for Advent and Christmas: Creating a Sense of Belonging Between Young People and the Church.* Winona, MN: Saint Mary's Press, 2005 (student book and leader's guide).

Shrader, Mary. *Journey of Faith for Lent: Creating a Sense of Belonging Between Young People and the Church.* Winona, MN: Saint Mary's Press, 2005 (student book and leader's guide).

Kehrwald, Leif. *Youth Ministry and Parents: Secrets to a Successful Partnership.* Winona, MN: Saint Mary's Press, 2004.

Lindle, Jane Clark. *Affirming Their Faith, Dispelling Old Myths: Ministry with Young Adolescents.* Winona, MN: Saint Mary's Press, 2005.

McCarty, Robert J. *The Vision of Catholic Youth Ministry: Fundamentals, Theory, and Practice.* Winona, MN: Saint Mary's Press, 2005.

———. *Thriving in Youth Ministry.* Winona, MN: Saint Mary's Press, 2005.

Music

Jump5. "Spinnin' Around." *The Very Best of Jump5.* Sparrow/Emd, 2005.

Pomanowski, Jeannie. *Faith with an Attitude.* Chesapeake Music Works, 2001.

Pomanowski, Jeannie. *Prayer Warrior.* Chesapeake Music Works, 2004.

Spirit and Song 1. Oregon Catholic Press, 1999. This music book has over 200 songs by different musicians and a nine-CD set to accompany it. The music is upbeat and attractive for young people.

Spirit and Song 2. Oregon Catholic Press, 2005. This music book has over 200 songs by different musicians and a ten CD set to accompany it.

Webber, Andrew Lloyd. *Joseph and the Amazing Technicolor Dreamcoat.* Universal Studios, 2000.

Films

Jesus of Nazareth (1977): 6hours, 11minutes VHS or DVD.

This is a classic feature-length film directed by Franco Zeffirelli, packaged in a three-video set.

Available for rental at video stores or for purchase from Gateway Films/Vision Video.

Joseph, King of Dreams (2000): 74 minutes. VHS or DVD.

This movie from Dreamworks is an engaging presentation of the story of Joseph and his brothers. The film does a good job of capturing Joseph's internal journey as well.

Available for rental at video stores or for purchase online.

Josh and the Big Wall (1997): 30 minutes. DVD.

In this movie, the Veggie Tale characters star in the story of Joshua. If your students like Veggie Tales, you might look into some of the other videos and DVDs.

Available for rental at video stores or for purchase online.

Mother Teresa, Woman of Compassion (2002): 56 minutes. VHS and DVD.

This film is the fourth in a series called "Great Souls." This movie talks about Mother Teresa from the views of many people whose lives were touched by her.

Available from Gateway Films/Vision Video.

The Prince of Egypt (1999): 99 minutes. VHS or DVD.

This movie from Dreamworks presents the story of Moses. Interestingly, the movie does not stay as close to the biblical story as the film about Joseph, but this actually provides an opportunity to discuss with young people why a feature-length film might make certain changes in the story.

Available for rental at video stores or for purchase online.

Social Justice Organizations

The author suggests the organizations below for an activity about the prophet Amos. Basic contact information is provided for the organizations listed. See the Saint Mary's Press Web site, *www.smp.org,* for information about finding these groups on the Web.

Amnesty International USA 5 Penn Plaza, New York, NY, 10001; phone 212-807-8400; fax 212-627-1451.

Bread for the World 50 F Street NW, Suite 500, Washington, DC 20001; phone 202-639-9400 or 800-82-BREAD; fax 202-639-9401.

Casa Juan Diego Catholic Worker House PO Box 70113, Houston, TX 77270; phone 713-869-7376.

Catholic Relief Services 209 West Fayette Street, Baltimore, MD 21201-3443; phone 410-625-2220 or 800-736-3467.

Habitat for Humanity International 121 Habitat Street., Americus, GA 31709-3498; phone 229-924-6935.

Heifer Project International PO Box 8058, Little Rock, AR, 72203; phone 800-422-0474. Heifer International has a very good curriculum guide for grades 6–8 called *Get It: Global Education to Improve Tomorrow.*

Maryknoll PO Box 308, Maryknoll, NY, 10545-0308; phone 800-227-8523; fax 914-762-6567. This contact information is for finding out about videos, DVDs, and posters.

National Right to Life Committee 512 10th Street NW, Washington, DC 20004; phone 202-626-8800

Distributors

Gateway Films/Vision Video PO Box 540, Worcester, PA 19490; phone 800-523-0226.

Oregon Catholic Press (OCP) 5536 NE Hassalo, Portland, OR, 97213-3638; phone 800-LITURGY (548-8749).

Saint Mary's Press 702 Terrace Heights, Winona, MN 55987; phone 800-533-8095.

Appendix 2

Tools for Teaching

Introducing the Story of Biblical Characters to Young People

Every chapter in this book has an initial activity that enables the young people to get to know the story of the biblical character. Some of the activities submitted by the authors of this book were so creative that it seemed like a good idea to put them together in case you never found one of them buried in Hezekiah or Timothy. These approaches will work well with numerous biblical figures. Several of the activities use modern media to portray the story.

A Newspaper Account

In this activity, Rick Keller-Scholz asks his students to create part of a newspaper based on the scripture passages related to the biblical figure.

Preparation

- Each student needs to have a Bible, a pen, and paper.
- Prior to class, write the list of readings about the biblical character in a visible place. Base the size of the groups on the number of readings, because all the passages will be read by a group member.
- If you have completed this or a similar activity in the past, you may want to provide students with examples to jump-start their thinking.
- If you have computer access, you can invite the students to use Word Publishing to access a newsletter template that would be useful for this exercise.

1. Divide the class into small groups. Ask the members of the groups to divide the Bible passages from "Scripture Passages Related to the Biblical Character" among themselves and read them.

2. Propose the following scenario to the students:
- Imagine that as a group, you are publishing a front page report on the life of this biblical figure. Each of you within your groups should prepare one column (headline and then article) based on your section of the reading.

3. Have the students first write their column on paper so that they can discuss how they would like to present their passage with the others in the group. One might want to do a "here on the scene" report while another may want to do a letter to the editor or a spotlight on biblical character, and so on. Then have the students transfer their columns to a front page of a newspaper layout complete with the name of the paper and assorted other newspaper items. At this point, students can further their creativity by posting a list of events at the Temple, creating an advertisement for "wisdom," announcing a support group for prophets, and so on.

4. After each group has completed their newspaper, make copies and distribute them to each group to read.

Pictures from the Road

Therese Brown provides an excellent activity for biblical figures who do quite a bit of traveling.

Preparation

- Provide enough bibles for every small group to have at least two.
- Cut out "city papers" or square sheets of butcher paper and label each sheet with city names (and citations) that appear in the biblical character's story.
- Provide enough markers, colored pencils, or crayons so that there are four to five for each small group.
- Using butcher paper, draw a map of the region at the center of the paper, noting where the cities were located. Leave room so that the young people can tape, glue, or pin the city papers on the map at the end of the activity.

1. Divide the class into several small groups and distribute one city paper and the art materials to each group. Give the young people the following instructions:

  - You are photographers who are following a biblical character during his or her ministry. You have been asked to take pictures of this biblical figure while he or she is in your city.

  - In your small group, read aloud the chapters from the city paper (butcher paper) that cover your city assignment. Discuss what pictures you want to take that will tell the story of the character's trip to your city.

  - As a group, decide which pictures you want to "take" (at least four) and who will "take" them. Draw all the photographs that you would take on your city paper.

2. When the young people are finished, invite them to present the story of the biblical character's trip to the city using the "photographs." Begin with the early part of the story and work through the cities in order. After each presentation, highlight the key points about the biblical figure that the group related. Tape, glue, or pin each group's pictures near the name of the city on the map.

The Comic Book Approach

In this process, described by Rick, students create comic strips of the assigned biblical story.

Preparation

- Make copies of handout Tools-A, "The Comics," for the students. The number of copies you make will be determined by the number of frames that you would like your students to use.
- Students need to have markers or colored pencils.
- Students need to have a Bible.
- Provide different comic strips as models for the students.

1. Assign the relevant passages of the narrative about the biblical character to the students.

2. Explain that each student needs to read the assigned passages and then create a comic strip of between x and y number of frames. (Four frames are often enough.) Encourage the students to be careful in their work but let them know that stick figures *can* tell the story. Remind them that the figures need to be big enough and dark enough for other students to see. Have the students write the biblical citation below the drawing. (Decide ahead of time how much writing you want the students to have in the comics. Should the students summarize the story below their drawings or include dialogue in little balloons?)

3. Have the students present their comic strips to the rest of the class in the order that their passages appear in the Bible. Consider taping all the comic strips together in a line so as to retain a visual version of the story.

4. After all various sections have been completed, consider photocopying the pages and stapling them together to create a comic book version of the biblical character story for each student to read.

Character Book Covers

In this activity, Rick has students work as graphic designers who create and illustrate a mock book series that follows the story of the biblical character.

Preparation

- Provide art supplies such as 11-by-17-inch copy paper, markers, colored pencils, and straightedges.
- Divide the readings about this character in a way that works well for the size of the class and the number of readings available and relevant. Each group needs to have one person responsible for each of the readings because each group will produce a complete series of book covers.
- Each student needs to have a Bible and a hardcover book that can be covered with the 11-by-17-inch paper.
- Bring in copies of several book series in hardcover, like the Harry Potter books or the Chronicles of Narnia.

1. Begin the activity by showing the series of books you have brought in. Point out that for a sense of continuity, a book publisher will use a similar motif on the covers of the books for an entire series or may use similar sounding titles. Explain to the students that they will create a series of book covers that represent the major events in a biblical character's life, resulting in a collection.

2. Divide the class into the predetermined number of groups and assign each student within the group their particular reading.

3. Give each student a piece of 11-by-17-inch copy paper, some markers, a straightedge, and a hardcover book that they can use to make a book cover with the piece of copy paper. (Students can share a single book for the sake of measuring their piece of paper for the spine, two covers, and flaps with folds.)

4. Have the students individually read their assigned passages and then talk together as a group. They may want to talk about some common design elements for their series even though the students will design a book jacket based on their own reading selection of the biblical character. Each jacket must have the following elements:

- The volume number in the Saga of [biblical character's name] both on the cover and on the spine of the book.
- The title of the "book" in the Saga of [biblical character's name] on the cover and the spine of the book. The Scripture citation should also be on the spine and cover.
- Drawings and images that summarize the readings on both the front and back covers.
- On the inside cover of the book jacket, a brief synopsis of the individually assigned reading, and on the back inside cover, a brief "bio" of the book cover's designer.

5. After the group has finished their series, have them explain their part of the story and their book cover from the series to the others in their group. Have the books "shelved" together for others to examine, or pass them around for other groups to peruse.

The Chronology of a Bible Character's Life

For the chapter about Moses, Jeannie Pomanowski creates a handout on page 75 that lists major events in Moses's life. The students then need to look through the Book of Exodus and not only put the events in the proper order but also list the biblical citation that corresponds to the event. After the students have finished the handout, they break into groups to read the Scripture events more thoroughly. The activity culminates when each group gives an in-depth retelling of the story, in chronological order, of course.

This approach works especially well when a character has a long story.

THE COMICS

Appendix 3

Answer Key for *Breakthrough!* Workbook Puzzles

Bible Books

Hidden Books of the Bible Names

1. Hosea
2. Job
3. Sirach
4. Daniel
5. Matthew
6. John
7. Romans
8. Numbers
9. Amos
10. James

Introduction to the Old Testament

Answers to Old Testament Questions 1–10

1. 46
2. Genesis
3. Malachi
4. Obadiah
5. Psalms
6. Pentateuch, History, Wisdom, Prophets
7. Genesis, Exodus, Leviticus, Numbers, Deuteronomy
8. Proverbs
9. History, Prophets
   Wisdom, Prophets

Completed Sentence

The Old Testament is the story of the **Israelites** (10), God's **chosen** (11) **people** (12).

Introduction to the New Testament

Answers to New Testament Questions 1–8

1. 27
2. Matthew
3. Revelation
4. Acts of the Apostles
5. 2 John has the fewest number of verses of any book in the Bible, and 3 John has the fewest number of words of any book in the Bible.
6. Matthew, Mark, Luke, John
7. (Varies)
8. Acts of the Apostles

Completed Sentence

The New Testament tells us about **Jesus** (9) **Christ** (10) and the **first** (11) **Christians** (12).

Connections

OLD TESTAMENT PASSAGES		
Isaiah 61:1–2 Luke 4:16–19 **2**	Malachi 3:1–3 John 2:13–17 **9**	Isaiah 9:1–2 Matthew 4:12–16 **4**
Micah 5:2 Luke 2:4–7 **7**	Isaiah 35:5–6 Matthew 11:3–6 **5**	Genesis 12:1–3 Matthew 1:1 **3**
Jeremiah 31:31–34 Luke 22:20 **6**	Isaiah 7:14 Matthew 1:23 **1**	Zechariah 9:9 Matthew 21:1–11 **8**

All numbers add to 15

SALVATION HISTORY

After the students have reviewed the time line provided in this book, ask the students to be creative and draw a picture representing an event or two from the time line. If the students are stumped, you might suggest some of the following:

- Primeval History—Creation to 2000 BC
  + tower; boat and rain
- Patriarchs—2000 BC to 1700 BC
  + handshake; map
- Egypt and the Exodus—1700 BC to 1250 BC
  + broken chains; law tablets; mountain
- Settling the Promised Land—1250 BC to 1050 BC
  + judge's gavel; flag on land

- Kingdoms of Judah and Israel—1050 BC to 587 BC
  + temple; cityscape; crown; prophet's sign
- Exile and Return—587 BC to AD 1
  + chains; countdown numbers 50–1
- Life of Jesus Christ— AD 1 to AD 33
  + heart; cross; tomb with an open door
- Early Christian Church— AD 33 to AD 100
  + *Good News* paper; pulpit; map of Italy with Rome marked; dove

ADAM AND EVE

WORDS HIDDEN IN WORD SEARCH

1. RAIN
2. GROUND
3. EDEN
4. LIFE
5. FOUR
6. MAN
7. GOOD
8. ANIMALS
9. RIBS
10. FRUIT
11. FIG LEAVES
12. TREES
13. MOTHER
14. LORD GOD
15. SWORD

FILL-IN ANSWER: ADAM AND EVE DISOBEYED GOD.

ABRAHAM

EVENT ORDER WITH LETTERS TO BE INSERTED IN BLANK SPACES AT BOTTOM

(1) 7 **b** and **e**	(4) 8 **s**	(7) 1 **b**	(10) 4 **e**	(13) 5 **d** and **h**
(2) 10 **e**	(5) 9 **i** and **d**	(8) 14 **h**	(11) 12 **A**	(14) 11 **s**
(3) 3 **r** and **i**	(6) 13 **r** and **a**	(9) 6 **i** and **m**	(12) 2 **u**	

FILL-IN ANSWER: BURIED HIM BESIDE SARAH

SARAH

SCRAMBLED WORDS UNSCRAMBLED WITH LETTERS TO BE TRANSFERRED TO BLANK SPACES

1. RAIAS	= SARAI	**S** (11) and **R** (6)	6. NOTECNVA	= COVENANT	**O** (5) and **E** (13)
2. RNAHA	= HARAN	**H** (19) and **R** (17)	7. SIACA	= ISAAC	**S** (12) and **A** (16)
3. EFMNIA	= FAMINE	**A** (18) and **E** (3)	8. EMHASLI	= ISHMAEL	**S** (15) **H** (2) and **L** (4)
4. YETABU	= BEAUTY	**B** (8) and **T** (1)	9. LIDEF	= FIELD	**E** (10) and **D** (7)
5. HULAGDE	= LAUGHED	**L** (9) and **D** (14)			

FILL-IN ANSWER: THE LORD BLESSED SARAH.

ISAAC

STATEMENTS
1. God promised to keep his Covenant with Isaac just as he had kept it with Abraham.
2. Isaac had twin sons named Esau and Jacob.
3. Isaac was tricked by his wife and son.

JACOB

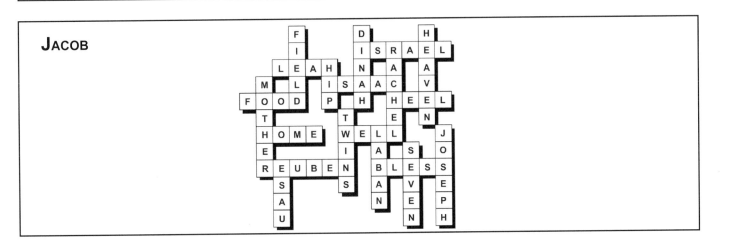

LEAH AND RACHEL

"IF" - "THEN" STATEMENTS WITH LETTERS TO BE USED IN BLANK SPACES AT BOTTOM

1 = I	4 = E	7 = L	10 = E
2 = N	5 = T	8 = E	11 = M
3 = B	6 = H	9 = H	

FILL-IN ANSWER: IN BETHLEHEM

JOSEPH

PROBLEM REFERENCE

GENESIS 37:2	17 YEARS OLD	GENESIS 41:25	2 DREAMS
GENESIS 37:5–11	11 STARS	GENESIS 41:45	30 YEARS OLD
GENESIS 37:28	20 SILVER PIECES	GENESIS 41:50	2 SONS
GENESIS 40:5–8	2 PRISONERS' DREAMS	GENESIS 42:17	3 DAYS IN PRISON
GENESIS 40:16–19	3 DAYS	GENESIS 43:34	5 TIMES AS MUCH
GENESIS 41:17–19	7 COWS	GENESIS 46:27	70 OF JACOB'S FAMILY
		GENESIS 47:1	5 BROTHERS

FILL-IN ANSWER: 110

MOSES

EVENT ORDER WITH LETTERS TO BE INSERTED IN BLANK SPACES AT BOTTOM

(1)	9	**a and f**	(4)	10	**r**	(7)	2	**a**	(10)	6	**f and a**	(13)	3	**c and e**
(2)	12	**e**	(5)	7	**c and e**	(8)	4	**t**	(11)	11	**i**	(14)	5	**o**
(3)	13	**n**	(6)	1	**f**	(9)	14	**d**	(12)	8	**a and s**			

FILL-IN ANSWER: FACE TO FACE AS A FRIEND

AARON AND MIRIAM

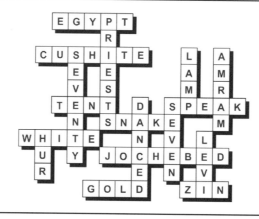

JOSHUA

WORDS HIDDEN IN WORD SEARCH

1. EPHRAIM
2. ISRAEL
3. JERICHO
4. JORDAN
5. KINGS
6. LAW
7. LORD
8. MOUNTAIN
9. SEVEN
10. STANDSTILL
11. WISDOM

FILL-IN ANSWER: MOSES APPOINTED JOSHUA HIS SUCCESSOR.

DEBORAH

STATEMENTS

1. Deborah was a prophet and a judge of Israel.
2. She and Barak defeated the army of Sisera.
3. Deborah sang a song of praise to the Lord.

GIDEON

ANSWERS TO CLUES (KEY LETTERS IN BOLD)
1. **J**oash
2. Ang**e**l
3. Ja**r**s
4. Three H**u**ndred
5. A**b**imilech
6. Ore**b** or Zee**b**
7. Midi**a**nites
8. Ophr**a**h
9. A**l**tar

HIDDEN NAME: JERUBBAAL

WHAT DOES THIS NAME HAVE TO DO WITH GIDEON? Gideon was called Jerubbaal because he destroyed the altars to Baal.

SAMSON

THE MOTHER OF SAMSON WAS NOT TO DRINK WINE

| THE | MOTH | ER | OF | SA | MSON | WAS |
| NOT | TO | DRIN | K | WI | NE |

SAMSON TORE APART A LION WITH HIS BARE HANDS

| SAMS | ON | TORE | APAR | T | A | LION |
| WIT | H | HI | S | BA | RE | H | ANDS |

THE LORD MADE SAMSON STRONG ENOUGH TO BREAK THE ROPES THAT HELD HIM

THE	LOR	D	MA	DE	S	AMSO	N	ST
RONG	EN	O	UGH	TO	B	REAK	THE
ROP	ES	T	HAT	HELD	HIM

SAMSON KNOCKED DOWN A BUILDING AND KILLED THE PHILISTINES

SAMS	ON	K	NOCK	ED	D	OWN	A	BU
ILD	ING	AND	K	ILLE	D	THE	PH
ILIS	TINE	S

RUTH

"IF" - "THEN" STATEMENTS WITH LETTERS TO BE USED IN BLANK SPACES AT BOTTOM

1 = G	5 = T	9 = N	13 = T
2 = R	6 = G	10 = D	14 = H
3 = E	7 = R	11 = M	15 = E
4 = A	8 = A	12 = O	16 = R

FILL-IN ANSWER: Great-Grandmother

SAMUEL

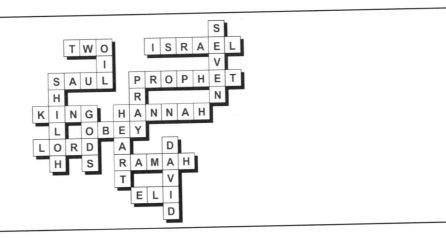

Saul

David

ANALOGIES

1. Jonathan is to Saul as Amnon is to **DAVID**. (son to father)
2. Kish is to Saul as **JESSE** is to David. (father to son)
3. Samuel is to Saul as **SAMUEL** is to David. (one who anoints)
4. Jonathan is to Michal as Absalom is to **TAMAR**. (brother to sister)
5. Nabal is to Abigail as Uriah is to **BATHSHEBA**. (first husband to wife of David)
6. Saul is to the Ammonites as David is to the **PHILISTINES**. (conqueror to conquered)
7. Jerusalem is to Solomon as **BETHLEHEM** is to David. (hometown to person)
8. Nathan is to a prophet as Joab is to a **GENERAL/ARMY COMMANDER**. (person to vocation)

Solomon

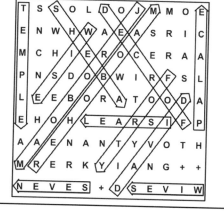

WORDS HIDDEN IN WORD SEARCH

1. DAVID
2. WISE
3. TEMPLE
4. ISRAEL
5. SEVEN
6. PALACE
7. FORCED
8. SHEBA
9. WIVES
10. JEROBOAM
11. FORTY
12. REHOBOAM

FILL-IN ANSWER: SOLOMON WAS RICHER AND WISER THAN ANY OTHER KING.

Elijah

SCRAMBLED WORDS UNSCRAMBLED (KEY LETTERS IN BOLD)

V S A R E N = **RAVE**N**S**	T H E R P O P =	PROP**HET**
DIWWO = **WI**DOW	VELWET =	**TW**ELVE
BAHA = A**HAB**	CIVOE =	**V**OICE
MERCAL = **CARMEL**	DVRIANYE =	VINE**YARD**

FILL-IN ANSWER: A FIERY CHARIOT CAME BETWEEN ELIJAH AND ELISHA, AND ELIJAH WENT TO HEAVEN IN A WHIRLWIND.

334

ELISHA

ELISHA'S MIRACLES		
Elisha causes an ax head to float. **6**	Elisha purifies bad water. **1**	Elisha causes one jar, or jug, of oil to fill many jars, or vessels. **8**
Elisha revives someone who has died. **7**	Elisha cures a man of leprosy. **5**	Elisha makes poisoned stew good to eat. **3**
Elisha blesses a childless woman so that she may have a son. **2**	Elisha multiplies loaves and grain. **9**	Elisha divides the Jordan River. **4**

All numbers add to 15.

HEZEKIAH

KEY LETTERS ARE IN BOLD (numbers, left to right, correspond to numbers in the fill-in answer)

(1) **A** ha**z** (37 & 3)
(2) **Ki**ng (5, 20 & 29)
(3) **Ne**hushta**n** (14 & 4)
(4) **P**hilis**t**ines (9 & 15)
(5) **Ju**dah (10, 31 & 23)
(6) **Re**l**y** (16, 38 & 39)

(7) **Isai**ah (6, 18, 13 & 1)
(8) **Or**der (26, 28 & 2)
(9) **Nothi**ng (21, 32, 11, 12 & 34)
(10) **Four**teen**th** (33, 30, 17, 36, 22, 24, 19 & 8)
(11) Jer**usal**em (27, 35, 7 & 25)

FILL-IN ANSWER: HEZEKIAH PUT HIS TRUST IN THE LORD GOD OF ISRAEL.

JOSIAH

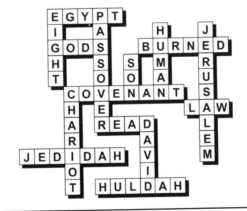

EZRA AND NEHEMIAH

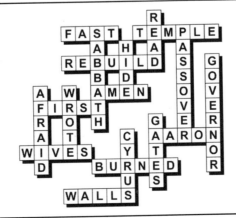

JUDITH

EVENT ORDER, WITH LETTERS TO BE INSERTED IN BLANK SPACES AT BOTTOM

(1)	9	i	(5)	14	s and J	(9)	13	a and n	(13)	2	h	(16)	5	a and m

(1) 9   i
(2) 7   J and u
(3) 8   d
(4) 6   e

(5) 14   s and J
(6) 10   t
(7) 3   e
(8) 15   e

(9) 13   a and n
(10) 12   m and e
(11) 16   w
(12) 18   s and s

(13) 2   h
(14) 17   e
(15) 4   n

(16) 5   a and m
(17) 11   h
(18) 1   t

FILL-IN ANSWER: The name Judith means Jewess.

ESTHER

EVENT ORDER, WITH LETTERS TO BE INSERTED IN BLANK SPACES AT BOTTOM

(1) 8   t
(2) 9   o
(3) 3   e

(4) 7   s
(5) 10   f
(6) 11   l

(7) 4   f
(8) 6   a
(9) 1   t

(10) 14   s
(11) 13   t
(12) 12   o

(13) 5   e
(14) 2   h

FILL-IN ANSWER: The feast of Purim is also called . . . the feast of Lots.

THE MACCABEES

ANSWERS TO STATEMENTS

1. Mattathias
2. Judas
3. Antiochus

4. Rededicated
5. Eleazar
6. Burn

7. Rome
8. Galilee
9. Simon

In what year did the Jews win their battle for freedom?   170

What year is that in the current calendar?   142 BC

JOB

SCRAMBLED WORDS UNSCRAMBLED (KEY LETTERS IN BOLD)

N A S T A	= SA**TAN**	N I E N S D	= S I **NNED**
MASNILA	= ANIMALS	ERTAH	= HEART
NELHIRCD	= CHIL**DR**EN	CONNEMD	= CONDEMN
DGO	= **GOD**	WIDKEC	= **WICKE**D
ROTSEUBL	= **T**ROUBLES	SJTU	= JUST

FILL-IN ANSWER: human and cannot understand God.

LADY WISDOM

WISDOM BEGINS WHEN WE SINCERELY WANT TO LEARN

| WIS | DOM | BE | GIN | S | WHEN | WE | SI |

| NCE | REL | Y | W | ANT | TO | LE | ARN |

WISDOM IS SO PURE THAT SHE PENETRATES EVERYTHING

| WIS | DOM | IS | SO | PU | RE | THAT | S |

| HE | PEN | ET | R | ATE | S | EVER | YTH | ING |

WHAT YOU GET FROM WISDOM IS BETTER THAN GOLD OR SILVER

| WHAT | YOU | GET | FR | OM | WIS | DOM |

| IS | BE | TTE | R | THAN | GO | LD | OR |

| SIL | VER |

WISDOM RESCUES US FROM DANGER

| WIS | DOM | RE | SCU | ES | US | FROM | D |

| ANG | ER |

ISAIAH

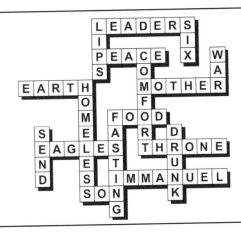

JEREMIAH

WORDS HIDDEN IN WORD SEARCH

1. YOUNG
2. DEATH
3. ONE
4. BREAK
5. PRIEST
6. FIRE
7. LETTER
8. COVENANT
9. PROPHET
10. IMPRISONED

FILL-IN ANSWER: Jeremiah was forced to flee to Egypt.

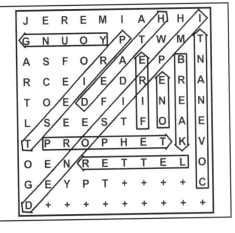

EZEKIEL

WORDS HIDDEN IN WORD SEARCH

1. EXILES
2. WHEELS
3. SCROLL
4. SIDE
5. HAIR
6. HOLE
7. GLORY
8. COVENANT
9. EVIL
10. JERUSALEM
11. SHEPHERD
12. DRYBONES
13. TEMPLE

FILL-IN ANSWER: Ezekiel was a prophet to Judah and was taken into exile in Babylon.

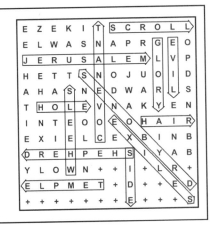

HOSEA

ISRAEL WAS UNFAITHFUL TO GOD AS GOMER WAS UNFAITHFUL TO HOSEA

ISRAEL WAS UNFAITH FUL TO
GOD AS GOMER WAS UNF AIT
HFUL TO HOSEA

HOSEA MARRIED A WOMAN NAMED GOMER WHO WAS UNFAITHFUL TO HIM

HOS EA MAR RIE D A WO MAN NA
MED GO MER WHO W AS UNF AIT
HFU L T O HIM

THE LOVE OF HOSEA FOR HIS WIFE WAS AS CONSTANT AS THE LOVE OF GOD FOR ISRAEL

THE LO VE OF HOSEA FOR HI
S W IFE WA S A S C ONS TAN T A
S THE LOVE OF G OD FOR IS
RAE L

AMOS

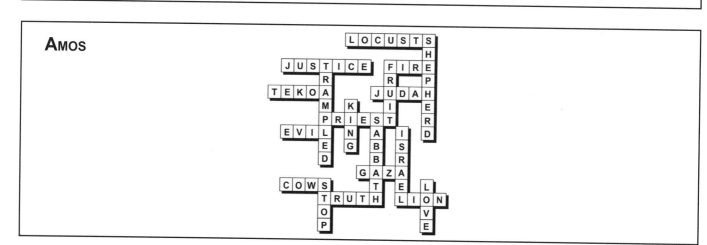

MARY OF NAZARETH

ANSWERS TO STATEMENTS

1. Simeon
2. Joseph
3. Water
4. Bethlehem
5. Elizabeth
6. Nazareth
7. Gabriel
8. Holy Spirit
9. Blessed

JOHN THE BAPTIST

WORDS HIDDEN IN WORD SEARCH

(1) ZECHARIAH
(2) ELIZABETH
(3) JORDAN
(4) HEAD
(5) HEROD
(6) GOOD NEWS
(7) PRISON
(8) DESERT
(9) SINS
(10) LAMB OF GOD
(11) DISCIPLES
(12) CAMELS HAIR

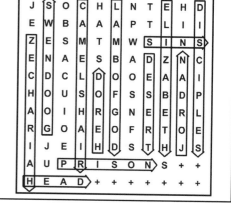

FILL-IN ANSWER: JOHN THE BAPTIST WAS A COUSIN OF JESUS.

PETER

MARY MAGDALENE

ANSWERS TO STATEMENTS

1. Mother
2. Appeared
3. Gardener
4. Lord
5. Apostles
6. Angels
7. Spices
8. Stone
9. Seven

MARY AND MARTHA

"IF" - "THEN" STATEMENTS WITH LETTERS TO BE USED IN BLANK SPACES AT BOTTOM
First number represents statement order—number in parentheses is letter assignment.

1 = S (7)	5 = E (11)	9 = U (13)	13 = J (10)
2 = R (2)	6 = N (5)	10 = F (1)	14 = E (4)
3 = O (8)	7 = F (9)	11 = I (3)	
4 = D (6)	8 = S (12)	12 = S (14)	

Mary and Martha were . . . friends of Jesus.

JAMES

WORDS HIDDEN IN WORD SEARCH

(1) ZEBEDEE
(2) JOHN
(3) NETS
(4) PEOPLE
(5) SIMON
(6) FISHERMAN
(7) THUNDER
(8) JAIRUS
(9) TRANSFIGURATION
(10) PRAYED
(11) SLEPT

FILL-IN ANSWER: JAMES ASKED JESUS FOR A SPECIAL PLACE IN HIS KINGDOM

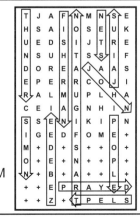

JOHN

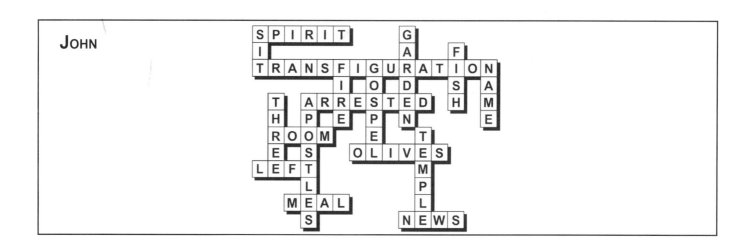

(Crossword grid answers: SPIRIT, SIT, TRANSFIGURATION, GARDEN, FISH, NAME, THREE, ARRESTED, PREPARE, ROOM, MEALS, OLIVES, TEMPLE, LEFT, MEAL, NEWS)

THOMAS

THE FIRST TIME THAT JESUS APPEARED AFTER HIS RESURRECTION

THE	FIRST	TIME	THAT	JESU
S	APPE	ARE	D	AFTER	HIS	RES
URR	ECT	ION

HE WAS WILLING TO DIE WITH JESUS

| HE | WAS | WI | LL | I | NG | TO | DIE | WI |
| TH | JES | US |

HE SAW THE SCARS AND PUT HIS HAND IN THE SIDE OF JESUS

HE	SAW	THE	SCARS	AND	PUT
HIS	HAND	IN	THE	SIDE	OF
JE	SUS

THOMAS WAS PRESENT AT THE LAST SUPPER

| THO | MAS | WAS | P | RES | ENT | AT | TH |
| E | L | AST | SUP | PE | R |

MY LORD AND MY GOD

| MY | LOR | D | AN | D | MY | GOD |

MATTHEW

	SOME		PEOPLE	
CRITICIZED		JESUS	
	FOR	HAVING	A	
	MEAL	AT	THE	
HOUSE	OF	MATTHEW

MATTHEW	THE	TAX
	COLLECTOR	WAS
CALLED	BY	JESUS
	TO	BE	HIS
	FOLLOWER

JUDAS ISCARIOT

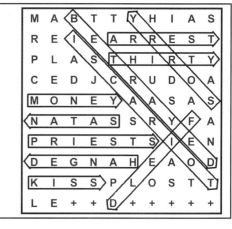

WORDS HIDDEN IN WORD SEARCH

(1) ISCARIOT   (5) THIRTY   (9) SORRY
(2) MONEY   (6) ARREST   (10) HANGED
(3) PRIESTS   (7) BETRAYED   (11) FIELD
(4) SATAN   (8) KISS

FILL-IN ANSWER: MATTHIAS REPLACED JUDAS AS AN APOSTLE.

PAUL

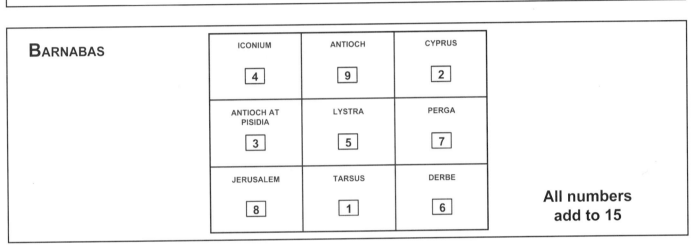

BARNABAS

ICONIUM	ANTIOCH	CYPRUS
4	9	2
ANTIOCH AT PISIDIA	LYSTRA	PERGA
3	5	7
JERUSALEM	TARSUS	DERBE
8	1	6

All numbers add to 15

TIMOTHY

PRESENT AND THE FUTURE

PRE SEN T A ND THE FUT URE

HIS SPEECH CONDUCT LOVE FAITH AND PURITY

HIS SP EEC H C OND UCT LO VE
FAI TH AND PU RIT Y

TREAT THEM WITH RESPECT

TRE AT THE M WITH RE SPE CT

BE ASHAMED OF HIS FAITH

BE ASH AME D OF H IS FAI TH

SALVATION THROUGH FAITH IN CHRIST JESUS

SAL VAT ION THR OUG H FAI TH
IN CHR IST JE SUS

PRISCILLA AND AQUILA

WORDS HIDDEN IN WORD SEARCH

(1) ITALY
(2) CLAUDIUS
(3) CORINTH
(4) PAUL
(5) TENTMAKERS
(6) SYRIA
(7) EPHESUS
(8) APOLLOS
(9) WAY OF GOD
(10) LIVES
(11) HOUSE

FILL-IN ANSWER: PRISCILLA AND AQUILA WERE WORKERS IN THE SERVICE OF JESUS.

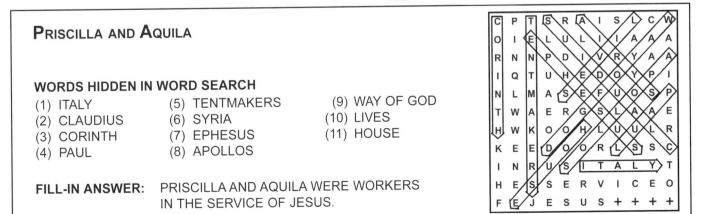

APPENDIX 4

INDEX OF ACTIVITIES BY TOPIC

Appendix 4

ACKNOWLEDGMENTS

The scriptural quotations contained herein are from the *Good News Bible with Deuterocanonicals/Apocrypha,* second edition. Copyright © 1992 by the American Bible Society. All rights reserved. Used with permission.

The map on handout Abraham-A was revised by maps.com.

The prayer on page 37 is from the *Sacramentary,* English translation prepared by the International Commission on English in the Liturgy (ICEL) (New York: Catholic Book Publishing Company, 1985), page 483. Excerpts from the English translation of the *Roman Missal* © 1973 by the ICEL. All rights reserved. Illustrations and arrangement copyright © 1985-1974 by Catholic Book Publishing Company, New York. Used with permission.

The activity on pages 34-36 and the images on resources Sarah-A, Sarah-B, and Sarah-C are adapted from and taken from *The Seven Habits of Highly Effective People: Restoring the Character Ethic,* by Stephen Covey (New York: Free Press, 1989), pages 45, 25, and 26, respectively. Copyright © 1989 by Stephen R. Covey. Used with permission.

Handout Jacob-A, "The Patriarch Family Tree," is adapted from the handout "My Own Genesis," in *Faith Works for Junior High: Scripture- and Tradition-Based Sessions for Faith Formation,* by Lisa-Marie Calderone-Stewart (Winona, MN: Saint Mary's Press, 1993), page 25. Copyright © 1993 by Saint Mary's Press. All rights reserved.

The story on page 66 and the reflection on pages 221-222 are from *Sadhana: A Way to God, Christian Exercises in Eastern Form,* by Anthony de Mello (New York: Image Books, Doubleday, 1984), pages 85-86. Copyright © 1978 by Anthony de Mello. Used with permission of Doubleday, a division of Random House.

The activity "Moses: A Calling" on pages 71-72 is adapted from "What If They Won't Believe Me?" in *Old Testament: Seminary Student Study Guide,* by the Church Education System (Salt Lake City: Church of Jesus Christ of Latter-day Saints, 1998), page 43. Copyright © 1998, 2002 by Intellectual Reserve.

The song lyrics on handout David-B are from the song "Prayer Warrior," by Jeannie Pomanowski (Chesapeake Music Works, 2004, Be Attitude Music, BMI).

The excerpt on page 190 is from the Franciscans' Web site, *www.franciscans.ie/8.0.html,* accessed September 22, 2005.

The quotation on page 193 is found at *www.brainyquote.com/quotes/quotes/t/tseliot121647.html,* accessed September 22, 2005.

The material in "The Annunciation" on pages 230-232 is adapted from *Biblical Women: Exploring Their Stories with Girls,* by Janet Claussen (Winona, MN: Saint Mary's Press, 2002), pages 89-90. Copyright © 2002 by Saint Mary's Press. All rights reserved.

The material in resource Mary-A is from *Mary Remembers: Cherished Memories of Jesus,* by Velma McDonough (Mystic, CT: Twenty-Third Publications, 1987), pages 13-15, 39-41, and 55-56, respectively. Copyright © 1987 by Velma McDonough. Used with permission.

The quotations on page 255 and handout Mary Magdalene-B and on page 294 are from the English translation of the *Catechism of the Catholic Church* for use in the United States of America, pages 866 and 873. Copyright © 1994 by the United States Catholic Conference, Inc.—Libreria Editrice Vaticana. Used with permission.

The material on handout Paul-A is from *Jesus of History, Christ of Faith,* third edition, by Thomas Zanzig (Winona, MN: Saint Mary's Press, 1999), pages 258-259. Copyright © 1999 by Saint Mary's Press. All rights reserved.

To view copyright terms and conditions for Internet materials cited here, log on to the home pages for the referenced Web sites.

During this book's preparation, all citations, facts, figures, names, addresses, telephone numbers, Internet URLs, and other pieces of information cited within were verified for accuracy. The authors and Saint Mary's Press staff have made every attempt to reference current and valid sources, but we cannot guarantee the content of any source, and we are not responsible for any changes that may have occurred since our verification. If you find an error in, or have a question or concern about, any of the information or sources listed within, please contact Saint Mary's Press.